FOR THE
TIME BEING

Also by
Sydney J. Harris

Strictly Personal
Majority of One
Last Things First
On the Contrary
Leaving the Surface

FOR THE
TIME BEING

Sydney J. Harris

HOUGHTON MIFFLIN COMPANY
BOSTON

To Milton Mayer

who taught me that asking
the right questions
can be more important than
having the right answers

Once, when Rabbi Pinhas entered the House of Study, he saw that his disciples, who had been talking busily, suddenly fell silent.

He asked them: "What were you talking about?"

"Rabbi," they said, "we were saying how afraid we are that the Evil Urge will pursue us."

"Don't worry," he replied. "You have not gotten high enough for it to pursue you. For the time being, you are still pursuing it."

— Martin Buber
Tales of the Hasidim

CONTENTS

1	OF THE LIFE OF THE SPIRIT	1
2	OF MEN, WOMEN AND CHILDREN	47
3	OF THE SOCIAL ANIMAL	99
4	OF WAR AND PEACE	175
5	OF THE MIND AND PASSIONS	217
6	OF WORDS AND PHRASES	309

FOR THE
TIME BEING

I

OF THE LIFE
OF THE SPIRIT

How Facts Differ from Whole Truth

WHAT IS a "lie"? What does "telling the truth" consist of? These are seemingly simple questions, but there are no simple answers to them. This is why parents, and educators generally, have such a hard time explaining lies and truth to children.

In the introduction to her autobiography, *Journey from the North*, Storm Jameson, the novelist, writes: "I am an accomplished professional novelist and nothing would have been easier for me than to draw a self-portrait which, without telling a single lie, would be dishonest from beginning to end, intelligent, charming, interesting — and a lie."

On the surface, a "lie" is a statement that does not correspond to fact, or to what we believe to be a fact. But "facts" and "truth" are by no means the same thing; as Miss Jameson reminds us, a book of memoirs can be absolutely truthful in its facts and yet be a total lie.

Truth is the *inner spirit* of a statement, not just its outer shell of facts. Of course, if the facts are falsified, the inner spirit is injured; but the opposite does not hold — a report consisting of nothing but facts can be totally dishonest in its intent and effect.

In one of Bonhoeffer's last unfinished essays (written in prison), he takes up the subject of the "always truthful" man, and reminds us that there are evil truths as well as necessary and healing truths. The man who always says what he thinks, under the guise of "candor," is not living in the spirit of truth, but in the spirit of hate.

He tells of a teacher who asked a young pupil in front of the class whether his father usually came home drunk in the evening. The father did, but the boy was within his rights in lying about it, since the teacher was absolutely without his rights in asking the question — and the boy was not mature enough to give an answer that rebuked the teacher for his impertinence without either admitting the truth or lying.

The hardest metaphysical thing to grasp about the truth is that it is both *absolute* and *relative* at the same time: in one sense, the truth is always the same for all men everywhere; in another sense, it is relative to the person, the time, the place, the situation. Wisdom consists in being able to distinguish between these two, and to know when the spirit of universal truth is being served, and when not.

Both the absolutists and the relativists are dishonest in this — the absolutists when they insist that circumstances do *not* alter cases; the relativists when they insist that truth is wholly subjective. No wonder our children are confused, conflicted and cynical about it.

Any creed whose basic doctrines do not include respect for the creeds of others, is simply power politics masquerading as philosophy.

Organized Merriment — Humbug!

I WAS WALKING AROUND with kind of a glum face during the recent holidays and somebody asked me if anything was wrong. "No," I said, "it's just that determined cheerfulness always makes me a little sour."

There is a perverse streak in my nature that reacts against the extremes of jollity and gloom. The relentless merriment of Christmas often gives me a sense of sadness, while the unrelieved melancholy of funerals makes me want to be flip or frivolous.

If this were just a personal neurosis, I wouldn't even mention it — but I suspect a great many people feel the way I do, only they manage to conceal it more successfully.

Any "organized" sentiment strikes me as factitious and a little sterile. Funeral services are the worst, and if I had my way, the whole business would be abandoned — the casket, the pallbearers, the oleaginous lies about the deceased, the conventional trappings of grief. Mourning should be private, not a public competition or a display.

And the "merriment" of Christmas, certainly, is just as contrived in most cases, providing a temporary exchange of hearty sentiments so that people can feel good about going back to be their mean old selves as soon as the official "spirit" has been declared dead.

The regulation of emotions reminds me of those "spontaneous demonstrations" that are held in places like Russia, where the people are prodded and stimulated to scream and applaud and march for some despotic hooligan's birthday; only in the United States the regulation of emotions is commercially rather than politically exploited.

The funeral racket is certainly among the worst here, and

I have not been to two funerals out of a hundred that showed a modicum of dignity, taste, honesty, or a truly pious appreciation of the equilibrium between the precious gift of life and the inexorable demand of death. Even when one sincerely cared for the deceased, there is an uneasy air of hypocrisy about such proceedings.

In my view, the best way to be memorialized is to donate one's body for medical research and transplant use; in this way, one is being of some value to society, present and future, and even achieves a kind of immortality by providing the organs for someone else to enjoy God's gift of life longer than he otherwise might.

It is mere vanity that prompts our current funeral and burial practices, and a barbaric kind of vanity at that. Just as it is mostly vanity that propels us into the fierce exchange of Christmas gifts as a substitute for the year-round caring that Jesus stood for.

Confidence, once lost or betrayed, can never be restored again to the same measure; and we learn too late in life that our acts of deception are irrevocable — they may be forgiven, but they cannot be forgotten by their victims.

*

We all know about people who live on the installment plan, but we still lack comprehension of the many who die on the installment plan, who commit suicide little by little, day by day, who, in Albee's words, "want to die, and take a lifetime doing it." (The alcoholic and narcotics addicts are only the most dramatic examples, but by no means the most numerous.)

Men Can Fear and Love God

IF THERE IS someone you respect enormously, and whose good opinion you value highly, what is it that makes you act well in this person's presence? It is the fear that otherwise he might withdraw his favor from you, might lose his good opinion of you.

There is nothing wrong with such fear; it is perfectly logical and legitimate. All love relationships are controlled by an element of fear — that of acting, or becoming, unworthy of the loved one's approbation.

When modern people, however, deplore the Bible's emphasis on "fear of the Lord," they fail to understand what it properly means. Worship of the Lord, they insist, should be based on "love," not on "fear" — but there is no love unless it is accompanied by the kind of fear that helps us to live up to the loved one's conception of us.

The reason for this widespread confusion is that we equate all "fear" with fear of punishment. This, indeed, would be the worst reason for doing honor to God — that we are afraid of being eternally punished. Fire-and-brimstone religion has fallen into a deserved disrepute because it stressed such punishment, which would be unworthy of any God we would care to worship.

But not all fear is of this punitive kind, which is a childish conception of God's power. Fear of losing respect, of the loved one's withdrawal, of the severing of the bond, is what is psychologically true in our relationships. All moral authority is based on this legitimate form of fear, not on power or punishment or retaliation.

Hell is to be loveless. To be abandoned. To have forfeited one's interdependence. To live only for oneself. No fire and brimstone can equal this desolation. God has no need to "do anything" to us; we are our own punishers, we create our own Hell, we either become what we were meant to be, or go to our death without ever having known what it was to live.

All this has nothing to do, incidentally, with "believing" in God. Avowed atheists can be closer to Him than devout churchgoers. God is not "religious" in any petty human sense of the word; this is why there can be no "right" religion — only right people, many of whom profess no religion at all.

Those who respect the cosmos, who treat all men as brothers, who know there is a law higher than that of self-aggrandizement and self-preservation, "who walk humbly and act mercifully," live in constant fear of the Lord, whether they know it or not. They fear becoming unworthy of the humanhood they were created with, and for.

We prefer our saints dead, cold and remote; a living saint among us would be as perpetually irksome as a pebble in the collective shoe of society.

*

The concept of a personal, physical immortality seems to be more of an impious than a religious thought, a way by which we can put ourselves on a footing with God if we but obey what we believe to be divine laws; it's hard for me to conceive that the universe is arranged in such a cozy fashion, much as I might like to.

Buber Epitomized Beauty of Age

I'VE BEEN READING, and enjoying, a biography of Martin Buber, one of my great guides through the wilderness of thought. The book jacket bears a photograph of Buber which I would like to have for my own.

Here is a face of a man in his eighties, and beautiful — beautiful with character, with spirit, with humor, with understanding and compassion. And with a kind of "youthfulness" one rarely sees in the faces of young people today.

While I was reading the book, Picasso celebrated his ninetieth birthday, while Pablo Casals conducted an orchestra at the UN in his ninety-fifth year. Their faces, too, while not as radiant as the saintly Buber, were likewise alive with vitality and strength and sensitivity.

What I resent most about the "young" movement today — while sharing most of its criticism of the elder generation — is its equation of temporal youth with spiritual youth. Plus the implication that nobody except the young is really attractive, or worth looking at.

This implicit (and often explicit) contempt for age as such is an ugly barbarism as falsely based as it is insensitive. Its prevalence and intensity has made older people understand something about the force of discrimination (and this is all to the good), but it has also put a false premium on youthful looks as a virtue in themselves.

But growing older does have, and should have, a beauty of its own, if the spirit remains vibrant and the mind resilient. The unlined, characterless features of youth may have a bland and innocent attractiveness of their own, but no less does the weathered face of age, when it has learned from experience and not merely become the captive of it.

Older people should try to keep young in a basic sense —
in the sense that Buber was still sublimely childlike when he
died — but not in a cosmetic sense; not in racing frantically
to keep up with the whirligig of fashion, or denying the en-
croachments of age with artifices and devices that divest them
of inner dignity.

Many, if not most, older people may have forfeited the
right to respect from youth, but this does not mean that age
itself, and the aging process, is to be demeaned or despised.
The loveliest tree on our property is an ancient, gnarled oak
whose splendor is unrivaled by any of the straight young
birches still untouched by time.

Rejection of the past has almost turned into a pandemic
disease; and, of course, it is as absurd and self-defeating an attitude as repression of the future. The old and young need
each other as much as any polarity needs both opposites to
maintain a fruitful tension. When we cease to see the beauty
that is possible in age, we wither the very roots of our own
existence.

*The fact that we are so preoccupied with the idea of "con-
forming" is the best evidence that we are not conforming too
much — for a genuinely conforming culture is unaware of
what it is doing, and assumes that the conventional is the
natural.*

*

*We are rarely satisfied with our portraits, for each of us
carries around inside himself a self-image that is quite im-
pervious to reality.*

The "Devil" Made Us Do It . . . All

WITHOUT WHAT WE CALL the "evil" in man, nothing would get done. It is the so-called "evil impulse" that accounts for our activity — and this is the dilemma in man's nature.

Two letters arrived this morning which prompted this reflection. One, from a reader in North Carolina, asks about the "ego trip" we get from being altruistic. He is afraid that too much ego involvement is harmful to the creative effort.

The second, from a professor of economics at a state university, thanks me for mentioning his recent book, and for giving him credit for "honesty" in his conclusions. But, he adds, the "honesty" was also "motivated by the less-pretty desire to deflate and injure" some writers he despised for puffing up the importance of their researches.

Both these men, like most people, are suffering from a "dualism" in thought. They imagine that "good" and "evil" are opposite extremes, and that we must somehow "get rid" of the evil in order to realize the good. And they are realistic enough to recognize the ineradicable nature of evil in man.

Martin Buber, in my view, is the best philosophical guide to this perplexity, when he denies that good and evil are "opposites" like wet and dry or hot and cold.

It is the "evil" that is the active principle within us — the part that makes us strive and compete, that gives us pride of accomplishment and self-satisfaction. To repress, or try to extirpate, this part of ourselves is deadeningly "spiritual" in the worst sense of the word.

The "good" is the reflective principle within us — the part that we feel is closest to our "real self," to what we would like to be and know we should be. It is not the "conscience" society imposes upon us, but a deeper ontic level of self-awareness, of knowing our responsibility to creation and our proper response to it.

The task of the human, according to Buber, is to put the evil principle under the service of the good one, as we tame a horse to the service of its rider, without breaking its spirit or crushing its source of energy. Evil is raw power; goodness is control.

There is no pure goodness any more than there is pure evil; it is the alloy that matters. Becoming more fully human means employing the evil impulse for an end beyond its own gratification, thus at the same time gratifying and transcending itself.

If we fail to gratify the evil within us, we wither into impotence. If we fail to transcend it, we fall into corruption and eventual self-disgust. Goodness will remain weak, and badness sterile, until we start thinking of them synergistically, and not as opposites.

Of all old proverbs, the most stupid is the one warning that "the road to hell is paved with good intentions" — for what it is really paved with are rationalizations *for not carrying out our good intentions.*

*

It's astonishing how quickly we come to accept a blessing as a natural event, yet how long it takes us to recover from a blow of fate that we continue to resent as "unfair."

*

There is only one real tragedy for a human being — all the rest is mere accident, misfortune or catastrophe — and that is dying still a stranger to himself.

What "Love Your Enemies" Implies

MOST PEOPLE look upon the Biblical injunction "Love your enemies" as either impossibly utopian or impossibly sentimental. This is because they fail to understand the meaning of *agape*, or love, as Jesus meant it.

To love your enemies does not mean that you have to like them. It does not mean that they are no longer enemies. Nobody can command us to like what we do not like, for emotions cannot be directed by moral laws.

And enemies remain enemies if their ultimate goals conflict with ours, no matter whether we love them or not. So that "Love your enemies" does not order us to something either utopian or sentimental.

What it means, properly understood, is that no matter what we "feel" about another person, or how we oppose his beliefs, there must be an acknowledgment that what binds us together is greater than what divides us.

It is the "personhood" of the other that unites us in something that is above, and greater than, both of us; and our respect for this common ground of being must take precedence over our likes and our beliefs. This is the hardest lesson for any people (and any church) to learn.

We mistakenly imagine that if we could "love" our enemies, then we might become friends or allies; but this is not necessary, nor even possible in many cases. We would still be enemies — but we would treat our enmity as athletes do in a contest, not as soldiers in a war.

It may sound odd, but true athletes "love" their adversaries. That is, they respect them as other persons striving toward an opposite goal. And they oppose them only within rules that both obey, so that the winner wins on merit, not on fouls.

This is the kind of spirit Jesus was urging upon us, not a sticky sentimentality that tries to blink away human conflict or pretend that people can like each other better than they do. He was saying that it doesn't matter if you like someone or not, it doesn't matter if you agree or not — the only thing that matters is treating the other as fairly and cleanly as athletes do in a championship game.

This is a union that goes beyond sympathy or friendship, for there is no merit in behaving nicely toward the people we like; the only merit is acting decently toward people we don't like or disagree with — for this kind of "love" is an act of the will, not an emotion or an intellectual conviction. What a tragedy that we honor it only in our games, which we take so seriously, but not in our lives, which we play away with such perilous flippancy.

A religion devoid of theology soon loses its structure and collapses into mere sentimentality; whereas a religion dominated by theology soon loses its content and rigidifies into mere ritualism; in sacred matters, no less than in secular ones, balance is all.

*

It is possible to do good with all one's soul, but not to do bad with all one's soul; in the latter case, a part of oneself is always hanging back, subliminally aware of the transgression and unconsciously seeking to frustrate it — thus, more criminals are caught because of their own lapses than by the superb detection of others.

Thou Shalt Not Kill — But When?

EVERY SO OFTEN, I receive a letter from a reader who suggests that most of our troubles on earth would be solved "if only we followed the Ten Commandments." How easy it would be if life were that simple.

These unthinking persons have never actually submitted the Ten Commandments to a careful scrutiny. If they did, they would come to the same conclusion as Paul Tillich, perhaps the finest theological mind of our time.

In his last book, *My Search for Absolutes*, Tillich admits that such sacred laws as the Ten Commandments "are, on the one hand, too abstract to cover any concrete situation and, on the other, not abstract enough to become general principles, but depend on the culture that produced them."

Take the most crucial law in the Decalogue — "Thou shalt not kill." Even if one translates the Hebrew word *katla* as "murder," Tillich points out, how is murder to be defined as distinct from killing in general? What about military killing? Juridical killing? Killing in self-defense? If the Commandment were taken literally, every nation would be pacifistic, and there would be no capital punishment.

Even the First Commandment is most difficult to interpret, much less put into practice. "Thou shalt have no other gods before me." Which God are we commanded to worship? And even if the two-and-seventy disputing sects could agree upon this, what about all the modern idolatries that substitute for God — such as the nation, the race, the class, the worship of money and success and position and respectability?

What about the Commandment to honor one's parents? As Tillich says, "This law presupposes something like the fetal situation of complete dependence. How can we apply it to our liberal democratic institutions and to our need to free ourselves from the authority of our parents?"

The Decalogue, indeed, is in much the same position as the Hippocratic Oath for physicians — which tells doctors little or nothing about a host of modern medico-social problems, such as contraception and abortion, euthanasia, sex changes, organ transplants and the many other perplexities of modern medical science.

In turbulent times such as ours, people like to cling to simplistic answers; but neither the Golden Rule nor the Ten Commandments can take the place of hard thinking and right feeling in a concrete situation. Religion can provide the *motivation* for decent acts and attitudes toward others; it cannot supply a specific answer.

No religion has any right to missionaries until it could send out any of its communicants as an example to the heathens.

*

Those who look for "inspiration" before they begin to work fail in recognizing the basic creative truth that work can engender inspiration.

*

The worst harm to human nature comes from the futile attempt to "repress" the evil within us, rather than learning how to mobilize this demonic force in the service of a higher good; for repressed evil instincts always strike back with redoubled fury in a crisis. (It is no accident that the pre-Nazi German people were the most lawful, clean, industrious, obedient and repressed in all of modern Europe.)

Our Scientists Discover Life

ONE OF THE QUIET REVOLUTIONS taking place today — and possibly more significant than many of the noisy ones — is the change in attitude of modern scientists. They have begun to think, and feel, and act, more like total human beings.

Science is traditionally a "descriptive" discipline, not a "normative" one — that is, it tells, or explains, or shows; it does not make value judgments. It scrupulously keeps its own prejudices and feelings out of the scientific equation.

But, now, scientists are beginning to recognize that they cannot separate the social consequences of their activities from the "pure" research in the laboratory. They are worried, they are concerned, they feel they can no longer ignore the ethical implications of their work.

In an unusual display of candor, a few months ago, three young Harvard Medical School scientists announced an historic breakthrough in molecular biology — the isolation of a single gene — with the word "frightening!" They also warned that their work "may have bad consequences over which we have no control."

This was an extraordinary departure from "proper" scientific announcements, which simply state facts and make no judgments.

In this case, the "frightening" aspect of their discovery is that mankind may shortly have the ability to manipulate the mechanisms of heredity. While this can prove enormously beneficial in avoiding or controlling diseases and deficiencies, it also now makes possible a new kind of "genetic warfare" among peoples.

The more knowledge advances, the more it seems to be used for destructive purposes. Since the discovery of atomic energy, only a minuscular part of our efforts has gone to developing atomic energy for constructive ends; the overwhelming share has gone for weaponry that can blow up the world in an instant of paranoid, irresponsibility.

Scientists in all fields are increasingly aware that they have little control over the consequences of their work; that their knowledge is transmuted more into raw power than into social benevolence; and that society does not have the moral integrity or emotional stability to utilize such discoveries for the greatest good of all.

Thus, scientists are quietly but determinedly repudiating their traditional attitude of neutrality. They are refusing to work on projects whose potential for evil is at least equivalent to their potential for good. And they are warning the public about possible perversions of their disciplines. If this revolution prospers — and it shows every sign of doing so — life may begin to be served more than death.

The tragic irony of our century was our belief that we could eliminate "fanaticism" by disavowing religion, and produce reasonableness by preaching the gospel of science; we succeeded only in reaching new heights of fanaticism through the political religions of fascism and communism.

❋

The person who says "All moral laws are absolute" fails to understand the human predicament; but the person who says "All moral laws are relative" fails to understand the responsibility placed upon us by the human predicament.

Puritanism Crimps War on Crime

IF WE WEREN'T such an absurdly moralistic nation, our "war against crime" might be twice as effective and half as expensive. As it is now, enormous wastes of money, men and energy are diverted from "intrinsic" crime-fighting to shadowboxing with morality.

"Intrinsic" crime is a law violation with a victim — somebody's person or property is injured or stolen. Murder, rape, burglary, robbery are instances of "intrinsic" crime, which every community must protect its citizens against.

But most American communities — hypocritically and ineffectually — divert a large and unnecessary part of their law-enforcement machinery to "crimes without victims." These include gambling, prostitution, drug addiction, abortion and sexually deviant behavior.

And these latter are, precisely, the areas where enforcement is bound to be least successful, and where politicians and police have traditionally been able to extort graft for offering "protection." Ninety per cent of the corruption of public officials comes from trying to legislate private morality.

I am not arguing here whether gambling or prostitution should be "legalized" or not. There is no good and decisive answer to that vexing question. But certainly both these activities should be treated on the civil side of the law, not the criminal side, which would take a crushing (and corrupting) burden off the police.

Gambling is a human problem. Prostitution is a social problem. Drug addiction is a medical and psychiatric problem. Abortion, in my view, is a purely private decision. And sexual behavior of any kind is nobody else's business, so long as it involves consenting adults.

But our puritanical culture has channeled all these problems into the law, with disastrous results. Gambling has not been reduced; it has merely been driven into the protective arms of the Syndicate. Prostitution has not been lessened; it has simply gone underground, where it festers in more ugly form. Illegal abortions make women dead, doctors hypocritical and policemen rich. Nothing more.

If we are genuinely concerned about the alarming rise of crime against persons and property, then we should stop our futile moralizing and set up agencies to study and deal with these problems in their appropriate areas. Instead, we perpetuate the costly illusion that these "crimes" can be reduced while crimes with victims continue to mount in every hallway and highway in the land.

True greatness in a man consists in saying what he means and doing what he says — which must be based on knowing who he is; as a friend said of Martin Buber, one of the few great men of our time: "He stands at the bottom of his personality, looking up."

*

Most people would not "believe in God" at all if they were not allowed to re-create Him in the image of their own race, nation, dogmas and prejudices.

*

If you can understand a play the first time you see it, it wasn't worth seeing; the purpose of dramatic art is not to illuminate a situation but to provide us with an Ariadne's thread to guide us through the dark labyrinth of our own unconscious.

Who Perils Our Survival? We Do

ON DARK DAYS, when all the news is bleak, there seem to me only three avenues left open to the human race — mass psychoanalysis, mass conversion or mass extinction.

Everybody complains about "conditions" or "situations" or "sorry states of affairs," but virtually all these conditions and situations and states are created by human beings and not by the objective world we live in.

In one of his great sermons, John Donne concluded, "I am mine own executioner," and he was speaking for all of us, not just for himself. We are the enemies of our own survival and welfare.

Salvation is not to be found outside ourselves — in our institutions, our laws, our education, our social or political or economic systems. We can make *improvements* in all these — but no changes in the mechanisms alone can keep us from plunging off the cliff.

In truth, we are half mad. One part of us is reasonable and decent and mature; another part is irrational and prejudiced and infantile. In any deep or prolonged crisis, the lunatic half takes possession of us.

Mass psychoanalysis — if it were possible, as it is not — might give our rational selves more control over the childish part of our nature. We might then begin to see our bigotries and fears and rages for what they truly are, instead of projecting them outward to others.

Mass conversion — not to a particular church or creed, but to a simple acceptance of the basic religious truth that it is better to suffer an injury than to do one — might permit us to pull back from the brink of the precipice and save our species from extinction.

I see little hope outside these two highly improbable courses. There is more hatred and divisiveness in the world today than in any time since I was born. More struggle, more conflict, more anger, more hate, more closed minds and deaf ears and distorted vision.

Everybody thinks that "the answer" rests largely upon someone else's doing the right thing, and nobody is willing to move first. Nobody will turn the other cheek, walk the extra mile, return good for evil. We do not really believe — if believing means acting upon — any of the things we profess. (And we persecute the few who do.)

We have turned religion into a consolation, nationalism into an idol, science into a juggernaut, community into a jungle, education into a treadmill, law into a bludgeon and politics into a bloody farce. Our moral insanity is the agent of our doom.

All institutions tend toward serving their own ends rather than the human ends of the persons who compose them. This is as much true of religious institutions as of any others, and explains why church organizations eventually debase or dehumanize the spiritual aims of their founders, and must be perpetually renewed by creative reform.

*

If you tell me what you find funny, and what you don't, I can make a far better estimate of your character than if you told me what you "believe."

*

Every spiritual and ideological leader should make a special prayer each morning, not to be relieved of his enemies, but to be saved from his disciples.

We Want a Messiah, Not a Leader

PEOPLE KEEP SAYING, "We need a leader" or "We need better leadership," but that is not what they really mean. What most of them are looking for is not a leader, but a Messiah.

They want someone who will give them the Word. And the Word would be one that is agreeable to them, that appeals to their preferences and prejudices, so that they can follow it wholeheartedly.

But this is not what a true leader does — a leader tells people hard truths, gives them a difficult path to follow, calls upon their highest qualities, not their basest instincts. A true leader does not tell us what we *want* to hear, but what we *ought* to hear.

Indeed, this is the difference between a false Messiah and a true one. A false Messiah — such as a Hitler, in our time — caters to and inflames the fears, hates, angers and resentments of his people, and drives them to destruction rather than to salvation or self-realization.

A true Messiah — such as Jesus, even taken on the worldly plane — rebukes his people, shows them their errors, makes them want to be better, not stronger or richer, and asks them to make sacrifices for the common good and for the good of their own souls. He is never followed by very many, usually killed by the majority, and venerated only when he is safely dead and need not be taken seriously.

What we are looking for, I am afraid, is neither a true leader nor a true Messiah, but a false Messiah — a man who will give us oversimplified answers, who will justify our ways, who will castigate our enemies, who will vindicate our selfishness as a way of life, and make us comfortable within our prejudices and preconceptions.

We are seeking for leadership that will reconcile the irreconcilable, moralize the immoral, rationalize the unreasonable and promise us a society where we can continue to be as narrow and envious and shortsighted as we would like to be without suffering the consequences. In short, we are invoking magic, we are praying for the coming of the Wizard.

But there is no Wizard. There are only false prophets — and they come equally from left, right, center and below. Wherever they come from, no matter how they differ, they can all be distinguished by the same sign: those we like make us feel better, instead of making us feel worse. We want to follow them because they "understand" us.

But all the true prophets, from the Old Testament through Jesus, made us feel worse. They knew, and said, that the trouble wasn't with our enemies, but with ourselves. They demanded that we shed our old skin and become New Men. And this is the last thing we want to do. What we are looking for is a leader who will show us how to be the same old men (or women) only more successfully — and his ancient name is Satan.

"Conscience" is a much abused word in our society, for we commonly use it to worry over personal trifles instead of training it to be troubled about big things; and this dissipates our moral energy and permits us at the same time to develop an insensitiveness to the monstrous inequities of our time.

*

Some women go through life in such a state of chronic complaint that if in the next life the doors of heaven were flung open to them, they would immediately demand to see the Manager.

Unity or Cowardice?

ATTENDING THE PREMIÈRE of Aleksandr Solzhenitzyn's first play, a few days after he had won the Nobel Prize for Literature, I wondered if the people who pride themselves on being the "silent majority" have any idea what it costs to speak up and speak out in a hostile environment.

It nearly cost Solzhenitzyn his life, and may still. For his criticisms of the stupid brutalities, repressions and injustices of the long Stalin regime in Russia, he spent eleven years in prison, work camp and exile from his beloved country.

He has been expelled from the National Russian Writers' Union, and officially declared to be an "unperson." There is doubt that the communist authorities will permit him to receive the award. And none of his work has been published in Russia.

How many of us would have the courage to speak and write as he has, when the punishment is so swift, severe and certain? I am not at all sure I would; perhaps I would find some way to compromise with the tyranny of the state, to rationalize it as somehow "the lesser evil."

This is what the "silent majority" has done in Russia; what it did in Nazi Germany; what it has always done when faced with state power. It is what the majority of American colonists did before our Revolution.

It is worth keeping in mind that throughout history it has not been the ordinary man who took a militant position against despotism; it has always been the intellectual, the creative person, the academician, the person who values the works of the mind and spirit.

If we look at contemporary Russia, we see it is the poets and the students, the professors and the intellectuals who are the only voices raised against the repression of thought, speech and action in the Soviet Union. Everybody else is just "doing his job."

In Germany, it was the great middle classes who went along with Hitler, who felt it was "patriotic" to support Germany's expansionist policies, who refused to believe the atrocities on every side. They supported their government, and thought they were being good citizens when they were being bad men.

What worries me about Vice-President Agnew's intemperate attacks on dissenters is not that he disagrees with them, but that he apparently thinks they have no right to disagree with him. It is not that he opposes their view of the state — he has a right and a duty to oppose it — but that he seems to think we would all be better off if they, too, were silent. But a silent majority must be balanced by a clamorous minority, or the whole democratic process is doomed. What Mr. Agnew thinks of as "unity" is what Mr. Solzhenitzyn knows as moral cowardice.

I don't believe that people, even juveniles, are "led astray" by others; when they follow, it is because something in their nature has been conditioned to respond to the tune of these Pied Pipers; at one level of our being, we always know what we are doing, even though we may not know why we are doing it.

*

Sometimes scientists can have better prayers than theologians; witness Thomas Huxley's: "God give me the strength to face a fact though it slay me."

Spirit Key to Man's Personality

LET ME ASK a simple, even a dumb, question of all my scientific friends — my friends in neurology and physiology and chemistry and biological physics.

If it is true, and it is, that the cells in the human body are constantly changing, so that about every seven years we are composed of utterly new cells — then what accounts for the "continuity" in a personality? How can we call him the "same" person he was seven years ago?

We could say that the continuity persists in the "brain," but the brain changes along with the rest of the body, sloughing off old cells and taking on new ones. How does the new brain know who it is, and how does the cortex "remember" its identity under these conditions?

Take a coat. Suppose each week it tore and we replaced it with a patch, until finally it was a coat entirely made up of these patches. Would it still be the "same" coat? And at what time, at what particular patching, would it change from the "old" coat to a new and different one?

It is plain to see that a garment undergoing these constant changes, so that every seven years it was made up entirely of new material, could not be called the same garment you originally bought — so in what way is the person the same person he was seven years ago?

Yet we know he is. Except for certain differences that experience and aging make in him, he looks the same, talks the same, thinks the same, feels the same, identifies himself as the same entity. Obviously, there is something "in" him that retains its identity regardless of the molecular and chemical changes in every part of the tissue and nerves, and all the synapses of the neurons.

Now, we know that the cells somehow "replicate" themselves. That is, if the liver is damaged, and there is no treatment of it, a new cell coming into that region of the liver will be damaged in exactly the same way as its predecessor. But we don't know why, or exactly how. And we are aware that some of these pathologies will spontaneously remit themselves — including cancerous growths.

But if every cell is constantly changing, and eventually dying, in the body, how can one believe that what we call the "identity" of a creature is a material, physical thing consisting merely of biological and chemical processes? To me, this old-fashioned mechanistic view is as superstitious and obsolete as the medieval belief in the "four humours."

Thus, the "personality" or the "psyche" or the "mind," call it what you will, of a person, is something quite other, and different, from the mere arrangement and chromosomes of the body — something beyond these, a unifying and identifying element we should not hesitate to call "spirit."

The worst injury that so-called religious people have done to Christian theology is to promote a false conception of a Heaven that no sensible person would be willing to inhabit for an eternity; this stained-glass religiosity is a greater enemy of faith than atheism is.

*

People who are militantly "anti-superstitious" are as foolishly dogmatic as their opposites who are blindly enslaved to superstitions; for many so-called superstitions are rooted in biological and psychological truths that we have not yet rationally apprehended.

How Does One Judge "Obscenity"?

It's INTERESTING how people are "relativist" about things it suits them to be relativist about, and "absolutist" about other things it suits them to be absolutist about.

A man called me on the phone this morning to ask about a play I recently reviewed. He wanted to know if it is "morally offensive." All I could reply was that it didn't offend me, but I couldn't speak for him or his friends.

Now, this man would never call me up to ask whether a certain piece of music is "beautiful." He no doubt believes that beauty is in the eye (and the ear) of the beholder. If I recommended a certain poem he didn't like, he would shrug it off with a phrase about "a matter of taste."

People tend to be relativistic about their aesthetic standards, but absolutist about matters of "sex" and "decency" and "obscenity." They want the right to judge for themselves whether a painting or a piece of music is beautiful and appealing, but ask for an objective judgment on whether a play or a novel is "immoral" or "offensive."

But if "beauty" is in the eye of the beholder, so is "obscenity." I personally happen to find the collected works of Mickey Spillane "obscene" in their crude combining of indiscriminate violence and mindless sex — but the public bought such books in the millions, while at the same time regarding D. H. Lawrence as "obscene."

In my own view, aesthetic judgments are much more absolutist than sexual ones. There is not a trained musician in the Western world who would not agree that Beethoven wrote greater music than Grieg, or that Schnabel was a finer pianist than Liberace — no matter what the uninstructed in such matters might believe.

But the very people who would bellow with outrage if we tried to impose such aesthetic standards upon them ("I may not know music, but I know what I like") are the same ones who demand absolute conformity in sexual matters, and who think that "dirtiness" can be defined by counting noses and accepting the majority opinion.

There *are* certain absolutes for the human race — in that the nature of our being cannot be violated with impunity — but sexual customs and practices and attitudes are not among them. It's odd that the people who worry whether certain plays are "morally offensive" so rarely worry about the moral offensiveness of war, poverty and bigotry.

The Biblical injunction ought to be modified to read — love of other people's money is the root of evil.

*

Why does the Bible present us with the creation of one man, Adam, which we know is not historically or biologically true, instead of the creation of our species? Is it not to underline the most important metaphor for the human race — that we all come from one man, and from one Maker? Thus, if we fail to grasp the meaning of the Book of Genesis, the whole rest of the Bible is simply a collection of fables.

*

Some people actually pervert the words of Jesus, "The poor ye always have with you," to justify their indifference to the problem of poverty; which is as wickedly absurd as saying that because "the sick ye shall always have with you," therefore nothing or little should be done to find a cure for cancer or heart disease.

Charity Doesn't Start at Home

NOT LONG AGO in the column I mentioned the Biblical phrase, "an eye for an eye, and a tooth for a tooth," observing that it is invariably misunderstood by people who use it as an excuse for retaliation, when it originated as a plea for justice.

There is another common phrase that is damaged even more in popular usage, and that is, "charity begins at home." Whenever this saying is trotted out, it is to justify taking care of one's own before concerning one's self with the needs of others.

Yet this is not at all what the phrase originally meant. As first published, in 1642, in Sir Thomas Browne's *Religio Medici*, it meant "charity" in the Pauline sense of "loving-kindness," not almsgiving or philanthropy.

And it did not mean that we should first "take care" of our own, but that if we do not display loving-kindness to our family and our friends, then whatever alms or philanthropy we engage in is done out of pride or vanity or ostentation, not out of deep human compassion.

I have known more than a few celebrated philanthropists who gave away huge sums to worthy causes of all sorts, but whose personal relationships were devoid of loving-kindness, and who used public magnanimity as a cloak for private skullduggery.

This common subterfuge, of course, is the reason for another widely misunderstood saying — Jesus' injunction that your left hand should not know what your right hand is doing.

If anyone troubled to read the whole verse, he would learn that Jesus is addressing himself to the philanthropists of his time, who would stand up in public and make known their large donations to charity. He is telling them to give so quietly and anonymously with one hand that not even the other hand is aware of it, much less the community.

Charity, of course, does *not* begin at home; it must begin where it is *most needed*, whether this be at home or in some remote Indian village. What must begin at home are love and respect and tender treatment of those closest to us — for unless we radiate such feelings in our daily, intimate relationships, the money we give away to others is simply a bribe, allowing us to maintain our self-esteem while we continue to injure the fabric of social life.

The poor know it and resent it when they are the objects of help without the commensurate feelings of respect; when they are aided to make the giver feel better, not because they are worthy of aid. In a psychological sense, the philanthropist needs the poor more than they need him — charity brings him honors, but leaves them only scraps.

Young people searching for their "real self" must learn that the real self is not something one finds as much as it is something one makes; and it is one's daily actions that shape the inner personality far more permanently than any amount of introspection or intellection.

*

Superstitions persist long after the legends that gave birth to them have been utterly forgotten; not one person in ten thousand could explain why horseshoes are supposed to be "lucky," or even recall the name of the saint associated with the myth.

We Are Dr. Jekyll and Mr. Hyde

IF SOMEONE WERE TO ASK flatly, "What is the prevailing characteristic of the human race?" the only honest answer would be "schizophrenia." We are a schizophrenic race of beings, and the left hemisphere of the brain doesn't want to know what the right hemisphere is doing.

Two distinctly different minds inhabit the body of mankind. One mind can fly us to the moon, and the other plunges us into hell. One mind makes the most magnificent contributions to science and medicine and technology, and the other is still slithering in the muck of the Dark Ages.

We are willing and eager to benefit from every development devised by theoreticians and scientists and intellectuals and inventors; but at the same time we wallow in obsolete prejudices, we engage in wildly irrational behavior, we exhibit the same parochialism and rigidity and hostility that have always perverted new human tools to the use of old inhuman hates.

We are now approaching a technology that can, if not interfered with, provide all of mankind with enough physical power, enough food, enough material goods, to assure stability and comity among all the nations — but most of this technology is the servant of our passions.

We are both Dr. Jekyll and Mr. Hyde — but the faster Dr. Jekyll discovers better ways for us to live, the faster Mr. Hyde turns these devices into more devastating ways to die. Even our schizophrenia is out of balance, for the wicked hemisphere of the brain corrupts whatever the wise hemisphere creates.

What we cannot see is that it is too late to be anything but a man, a whole man, operating as an integrated unit. Whatever divides us will kill us; whatever separates us will eventually fracture this delicate spaceship we are traveling on; whatever does not bring our social system up to the level of our technical system will compel us to turn the technical system against ourselves in global suicide.

Provincialism is a luxury we can no longer afford; even nationalism, only a few hundred years old, is dangerously obsolescent. The rule of force, which has been the only universal law of mankind, is now our greatest common enemy — for it is now unlimited in its potential to eradicate everybody, everywhere, for all time.

One part of us knows this; the other part prefers to ignore it, living in a fantasy-world, hoping to cling to the past while surviving in the future. But there can be no future unless we repudiate that part of the past that lures us in demonic fervor to our doom.

No computer in existence, or practicable for the discernible future, has a capacity that is more than a small fraction of man's brain — and we must understand, in order to prevent a mass inferiority complex, that the computer's forte is speed, not sensibility.

*

When you fail to get something you deserve, the best way to curb resentment is to recall the times you got things you didn't deserve.

*

The chief charge against the God of the Puritans is that He has absolutely no sense of humor, which is surely a defect in an all-perfect Being.

How to Be a Selfish Druid

AFTER A COLUMN of mine about Jesus appeared in the paper around Christmas, a woman called and asked me what religion I professed. I told her I was a Reform Evangelical Druid. She didn't seem to know what that was.

We Druids — small in number, but ardent in faith — have a most peculiar theology, but it seems to work for us. Most of the time.

We don't think it's important if you "believe" in God — as long as God believes in you.

And there is only one way to make Him believe in you — to be as selfish as possible at all times. This means to want whatever is best for you, and you alone, in every situation.

If you are truly, deeply, unremittingly and wholly selfish, you are saved. We don't know what you are saved *for*, but that is none of our business. That is God's business, and we don't interfere in it.

Now, the art of being selfish seems to most people to be the easiest thing in the world, but that delusion is just a trap of Satan. Pure unadulterated selfishness is about the hardest thing in the world to accomplish, and it often takes a lifetime of unceasing effort.

In order to be genuinely selfish, you have to *want* what is best for the self, and to *do* what is best for the self. This implies *knowing* what is best for the self — and this is what makes Druidism so hard.

To be a Druid in good standing (even a non-Reform un-Evangelical one), you first of all have to understand the *nature of man*. You have to know that he was designed for something, just as an acorn is designed to be an oak tree.

If you properly understand the nature of man, even in part,

then you know that the basic need, and the basic aim, of your true self is *to become as human* as it is possible to be. The only way your self can ever be satisfied is by turning its *potentiality* for humanhood into *act*.

Next, you have to understand what it means to become as human as possible: how the reason and the will and the appetites work together, how man can *live* and *control* his humanhood without falling into the error of angelism on the one hand or bestiality on the other.

When you have mastered this knowledge — which involves retraining the emotions as much as the mind — then you are ready to become the most selfish person in the world, doing only those things which are of benefit to your true self. This is why we are such a small sect.

Learning only from experience is one of the dumbest ways to learn, for experience can condition us to limit our field of learning too drastically; as Mark Twain vividly put the same thing: "A cat who has jumped on a hot stove once will never jump on a hot stove again — but it will never jump on a cold stove, either."

*

I read a motto the other day that went: "Shallow men believe in luck; strong men believe in cause and effect." It should have added that wise men know that luck often intervenes between cause and effect.

*

If we could accept ourselves, half our battles would be over; as Camus said, "Man is the only creature that refuses to be what he is."

How Would You Label This Man?

THE CENSUS TAKER from Rome was sent to Galilee around A.D. 28. As he entered the region, he came across a man sitting on a donkey. The man had long hair and a flowing beard; he wore an old tattered cloak, sandals and beads.

"Pardon me," the census taker said, "but I'm taking the census. Do you mind answering a few questions?"

"Not at all," said the man on the donkey. "I believe in rendering unto Caesar the things that are Caesar's."

"What is your job?" asked the census taker.

"I have no job," replied the man. "Consider the lilies of the field — they toil not, neither do they spin."

"What is your family?"

"I have no family," the man answered. "I have left my parents and my brothers and sisters, and I live alone."

"What is your address?"

The man sighed. "The foxes have holes, and the birds of the air have nests; but I have not anywhere to lay my head."

"Humph," muttered the census taker to himself. "No job and no fixed abode. Now, do you belong to any clubs or social affiliations?"

"None," said the man. "For no man can serve two masters."

"Do you go to school?"

"Nay," replied the man, "for which of us by taking thought can add one cubit to his stature?"

"Do you have any money or visible means of support?"

The man shook his head. "Lay not up for yourselves treasures upon earth, where moth and rust doth corrupt," he chanted.

"Have you registered for military service?"

"I resist not evil, but return good for evil," replied the man. "And whosoever shall smite me on the right cheek, I shall turn to him the other also."

"Who are your friends?"

"I go among publicans and sinners."

"What political party do you belong to?"

The man shrugged. "Only this — a new commandment I give unto you: That ye love one another."

The census taker scribbled on his sheet: "Hippie character, school dropout, no permanent address, no job, probable draft-dodger and pacifist, alienated from family, no wife or children, no church attendance, dubious associates among lowest elements in town."

"One more thing," he asked. "What is your name?"

The bearded one smiled sadly. "Some call me the Son of Man."

The true aim of religion — which too few religionists understand — is to abolish itself, that is, to get rid of itself as a separate institution and approach to life, and become inextricably interwoven in the personal and social life of the community; otherwise, it hardens into ritual, idolatry and superstition.

*

The second-rate is to be despised only when it pretends to be more or better than it is; an honest craftsmanlike work, that respects its own limitations (the way a good mystery book does) is preferable to a pretentious "serious" novel that is inflated with self-importance.

Opposing Threats to Civilization

WHAT I WISH I HAD KNOWN AT EIGHTEEN:

— That every day marks a fork in the road, in some little way; and that by the time the big fork comes along we have already made so many little decisions that we have no real choice left in the crucial turning.

— That it is easier to feel than to think, and easier to feel hate than to feel love, and easier to act on hate than to act on love — and we must resist the easier path every inch of the way every day of our lives.

— That we should be firmly resistant toward ideas we believe to be wrong, but immensely tolerant toward the people who hold such ideas, never for a moment confusing the person with the idea, which is the besetting sin of bigotry in all of its manifold forms.

— That every time we use a person for our own purpose, ignoring his needs, we diminish ourselves more than we diminish him, for his is a wound that can heal, while ours is an amputation that cannot grow back.

— That our differences are superficial, and our similarities are profound; and those who are afraid to acknowledge the similarities are forced to live — and die — by the differences.

— That most of what we call "love" is a form of vanity, and that the genuine thing (far from being as common as grass) is as rare as holiness or courage or wisdom, which have a million counterfeits for every one real manifestation.

— That we learn only what becomes a part of us; abstract knowledge is not only useless but dangerous until we have assimilated it to the core of the personality.

— That human society is confined in a lifeboat, not dispersed on an ocean liner; and unless each one is permitted the same rights, he will not assume the same responsibilities, and the craft has no chance to survive.

— That "education" is not a formal discipline, but an attitude, an approach, an appetite, even a *tone*, that must begin in the home atmosphere if it is to be successfully translated to the outer world.

— That the two greatest threats to the security of civilization come from the "absolutists" who think they know precisely what is right and wrong, and from the "relativists" who insist there is no right and wrong — for each doctrine, pushed to its ultimate, leads to death by suffocation or by disjection.

"It is more blessed to give than to receive" is a religious statement some may doubt; but *"It is more* gratifying *to give than to receive"* is a psychological truth no mature person can deny.

*

What fanatics fail to understand was succinctly expressed by Gracian, when he warned: "Push rightness to the extreme and it becomes wrong; press all the juice from an orange and it becomes bitter."

*

It is hard to know which horrifies the average person most — to hear religion bitterly maligned, or to see it seriously practiced.

*

It is tiresome to keep hearing that the Bible is "the best-selling book" of all time, as though the fact that many people buy it indicates that they read it, understand it or follow it.

The Great Failure of Capitalism

IN ALL THE SCATHING CRITICISMS that the communists make against capitalist society, they have never put their finger on the one just accusation that can be leveled against us.

For the big failure of capitalist society is neither economic nor political, as the communists wrongly insist. It is social, cultural and educational. We have failed to raise the *quality* of life nearly as much as we have increased the mere *quantity* of goods and opportunities.

The general quality of life in our society is low and brutish. The violence we are lately so concerned about is merely an extension of our incivility, our bad manners, our coarseness of values and crudeness of sensibility.

The original idea of the American Revolution was to raise the level of all citizens, to educate them, civilize them, make them responsive to the grand ideas and broad sentiments expressed by Jefferson and his colleagues. Americans were to become a different breed of people.

But something went wrong. In the process of exercising our economic and political freedom, we somehow forgot that these are just *means*, not ends. The ends must include a citizenry ruled by *reason* and *compassion*.

We have failed dreadfully, thus far, in this crucial area. Just walk along a crowded downtown street in any American city and you will see what I mean. Or visit a beach on a hot day. Or drive along a congested expressway at rush hour. The spirit is sour and cheap, the very quality of life is disputatious, uncivil, mean and petty.

Our massive educational system has not educated. Our imposing religious establishment has not Christianized the tribalism of our people. And our affluence has merely convinced us that *possession*, rather than decency or merit, should be our prime and ultimate goal.

We do not understand the meaning of law, the workings of democracy, the relevance of religion, the roots of civilization — we do not even comprehend the virtues and limitations of capitalism in a way that will permit us to benefit from the former while escaping the dangerous consequences of the latter.

Most Marxist criticism of us is a mad mixture of malice and ignorance, half-truths and utter distortions. The kind of "capitalism" they fulminate against disappeared a long time ago. But if our enemies are too dumb to disclose our true defects, we should be smart enough to see them and to take prompt steps to rectify them. For if the quality of American life keeps degenerating, there will be no need for a revolution. We will disintegrate from within, for we are our own worst enemies.

There is always one sin waiting for us at the bottom of the stairs: the person who can resist all temptations usually cannot resist the temptation to feel smug about this — and thus succumbs to the deadliest of sins, which is pride, and lurks in wait for all "virtuous" folk.

*

Most of us take it as a compliment when an old friend tells us our looks haven't changed much in twenty years; but I would construe it as an insult, for I want my face and bearing to show some signs of the struggle for self-mastery over the years.

"If Only the Reds Would Disappear"

IF EVERY COMMUNIST government were wiped off the face of the earth in a single stroke — the remaining capitalist governments would sooner or later come to blows among themselves.

If every white person were wiped off the face of the earth in a single stroke — the remaining black people and their nations would sooner or later come to blows among themselves.

If the state of Israel were wiped off the face of the earth in a single stroke — the Arab countries would sooner or later come to blows among themselves.

If any living, breathing "enemy" were to disappear tomorrow morning, a new enemy would make its appearance the day after, or the week after, or the year after.

It is hard for contending groups to see this, but it must be seen. Otherwise, by destroying the enemy, we only create within ourselves the precondition for a new enemy.

The living, breathing enemy can only be absorbed, not conquered or destroyed. Taken in, not struck down. Changed, as we ourselves change. Otherwise, the vicious circle of history will be unending — or will end when we all perish in the ultimate confrontation.

A few years ago, in a Baptist church in Atlanta, the late Peter Howard said to the Negroes what must be said to all contending groups everywhere in the world:

"Be passionate for something bigger than color. Be passionate for an answer big enough to include everybody, powerful enough to change everybody, fundamental enough to satisfy the longings for bread, work and the hope of a new world that lie in the heart of the teeming millions of the earth."

Most of all, we must begin to learn the ancient lesson that the only true enemy is within, not without. *The enemy is that part within us which makes our differences seem more important than our similarities.* This is the human trap almost all of us fall into — the trap that makes us act so inhumanly.

If we can mature as a species, and learn to avoid this trap, then we can unite against our real and common enemies — injustice and inequality, disease and decay, flood and famine and pestilence and all the ills that flesh is heir to.

We expend our passion on objects too small, on enemies too temporary, on goals too trivial. We must learn — as our children are beginning to recognize — to become passionate for something bigger than color or creed or geography or ideology or any other partial loyalty that has always seduced man away from largeness of soul. If we can diminish the enemy within us, the enemy outside us will begin to look more like a friend, a neighbor, a brother.

It is worth remembering that Jesus was sent to His death by the Roman officials not at all for any religious reason, but because He was considered a "troublemaker," an "anarchist," and, no doubt, an "outside agitator."

*

One of the chief sins of old-fashioned theology is the preachment that God "sends" some people to hell, when the true spiritual (and psychological) fact is that hell is a place reserved only for those who insist on going there. As C. S. Lewis wisely and wittily put it, "Hell is locked only from the inside."

The Way to Persuade Someone

WHAT I WISH I HAD KNOWN AT EIGHTEEN:

— That the weakness in ourself we recognize as a weakness can be made either endearing or compensated for; but the weakness in ourself that we regard as a *strength* is what will ultimately betray and defeat us.

— That we do not grow up *uniformly*, but in spots and streaks; so that we may be mentally mature but *still* emotionally underdeveloped, or have a good practical grasp but *still* lack spiritual depth; and we must not make the mistake of confusing our categories of grown-upness.

— That candor in order to cure is very different from candor in order to hurt, and putting someone *right* is quite a different thing from putting someone *down*.

— That the way to persuade someone is not to beckon him to come and look at things from where *you* stand, but to move over to where *he* stands and then try to walk hand in hand to where you would like both of you to stand.

— That the best (and, ultimately, the only) way to make a "good impression" is by *becoming who you are*, not by trying to conform to anyone else's standard of what you ought to be.

— That wanting to be liked and admired by persons whose opinions or characters you do not really respect is the most common, and pernicious, form of emotional prostitution in the world.

— That if you do not find pleasure in solitude, you will not develop enough resources within yourself to find genuine pleasure in company; and, conversely, if you do not find pleasure in company, your solitude will be barren and involuted rather than creative and expansive.

— That while it is true in the world of arithmetic that two and two make four, it is not true in the world of real things that two apples and two lamps make four of anything; and thus, we cannot add up disparities and expect to come out with a neat sum, but must accept the fact that the real world is composed of "irrational numbers."

— That, in the deepest Platonic sense of the word, you do not truly "know" something until you act upon it; and that "know thyself" is a meaningless injunction unless and until such knowledge compels you to put it into action, in immediate and practical terms.

— That the world of experience is divided, roughly, into those things which are matters of *taste* and those which are matters of *judgment;* and the rigid relativist who turns matters of judgment into mere matters of taste is as foolish as the rigid absolutist who turns matters of taste into matters of judgment.

Every idea — no matter how good — that exists in isolation is a dangerous error.

*

We are not punished for what we do; we are punished by what we do.

*

The most overvalued trait in the arts is "sincerity," considered as a good thing in itself; the worst singers I have ever heard were suffused with sincerity — so much so that they could scarcely hear their lack of talent.

Be a Now Person? No, Thanks

"Don't you want to be one of the Now people?" asks an ad for a new soft drink, going on to urge, "Become one of the Now generation!"

The only thing I can think of that is worse than being one of the Now people is being one of the Then people. As a member of civilization in good standing, I reject both the *nowness* and the *thenness* of the generations. I opt for the *alwaysness*.

To be a Now person means to be wholly concerned with the present and the immediate future; to be involved in fads, sensations and the whole pulsating ephemera of what's-going-on; to be perpetually on the *qui vive* for the newest, the latest, the coolest, the in.

It also means to be insensitive to the past, to cut oneself off from the roots of tradition, to favor the sensory and the subjective over the rational and the real, to become a new kind of technological barbarian, which is more frightening than the old kind of preliterate barbarian.

To be a Then person means to cling to the past for its own sake, to apply lessons that are not relevant today, to engage in a mixture of nostalgia, envy, rage and fear toward "modern youth," and to imagine that twentieth-century problems can be solved by sixteenth-century moralism or eighteenth-century politics.

These are false alternatives, for they are not exclusive alternatives. There is a better way than either: and that is to be in Always person, transcending both the frantic cult of the new and the feeble cult of the old.

This means selecting from both what is valuable, and discarding what is useless or harmful — which, of course, implies the ability to make such judgments. It means, further, learning to discriminate between values that are permanent and universal and mere matters of convention or taste or the times.

The Always person does not throw out the baby with the bath water as the Now person does — who thinks that because we have had a false and hypocritical morality in the past that therefore *all* morality is merely a matter of taste or preference. Nor does he, like the Then person, operate on the basis that *everything* that was true for previous generations is equally true and relevant today.

Life is primarily the art of selecting and combining, not accepting or rejecting any philosophy in toto. The Now generation rejects the past too categorically, just as the Then generation embraces it too hysterically. To be an authentic person, in any age, means in some way to surmount the age and stand for the kind of order that permits and encourages graceful change.

If mankind collapses, it will be for sins of omission, rather than of commission; as Voltaire put it long ago, "Every man is guilty of all the good he didn't do."

*

When a clergyman has been imported to say the invocation before a banquet, the chances are dismally great that he will talk to God far longer than God cares to hear him.

*

The best way to start a grim day is to think of people starting it in hospital beds, on battlefields and in prisons — to get a necessary perspective on our own life situation.

2

OF MEN, WOMEN
AND CHILDREN

Our Society Could Stand Feminizing

ONE REASON I am in favor of the Women's Lib movement goes beyond the fact that simple justice demands full and equal rights for women. It is because I believe that the future of the human race may depend upon a wider and deeper acceptance of "feministic" qualities in our civilization.

To say that men and women are, and should be treated as, *equal* is not to say that the two sexes are *identical*. There are profound differences between them, not only in terms of biology but in terms of the *affective mode* of living.

Not all characteristics are "culture-bound." Some, I believe, are inherent in the maleness or femaleness of every species. The woman's endocrine glands seem to work differently from the man's; her central nervous system may organically respond in a different way. What we call "masculine" or "feminine" traits may be exaggerated or diminished by the culture, but I believe they are there from birth.

Given this difference, what the "liberation" of woman would mean is not simply allowing her equal rights and opportunities with men, but also incorporating more of the "feministic" traits into the dominant fabric of our culture.

In all male-dominated cultures of the past, the "masculine"

qualities have been the most prized and sought for — aggressiveness, acquisitiveness and independence. In primitive, pre-industrial societies, these were indeed the traits most required to keep alive and combat nature and defend oneself against enemies, personally and tribally.

In our modern technical, almost postindustrial society, these same traits are more dangerous than useful, unless tempered and modified by the "feminine" traits of sympathy and sensitivity and the need to nurture rather than to conquer. The goals of women have always been more personalistic and humanistic than those of men.

Woman's added status in the coming world could be a tremendous instrument for peace, for more humane treatment of one another, for the understanding that preservation of life is more important than the pursuit of trophies. So long as we continue to undervalue these goals, women will simply strive to become "more like men," which would defeat the whole purpose of a meaningful "liberation" movement.

Woman must enter the mainstream of culture not as a man *manqué* but as herself, with her own unique endowment and the special contribution she brings to the solution of our problems in living together. To become "equal" with men means not to do everything they do, but to become fully herself and fully contributing to mankind's goals.

The chief difference between the sexes is that a woman wants to be loved for herself, and a man wants to be loved in spite of himself.

*

There's something splendid about a woman who, when advised by the bank that she is overdrawn, simply writes out a check to cover it.

The He-Man and the Homosexual

A READER in Massachusetts wants to know if, in my opinion, the United States is seeing a rise in the number of homosexuals, and if the same rise is discernible in Europe and the rest of the world.

Nobody has the statistical answer to such a question. For one thing, since our laws and mores are now more permissive than in the past, a larger number of homosexuals feel free to disclose themselves; and this, of course, makes it seem as if the number has increased.

My own feeling is that there is a smaller percentage of homosexuals in Europe than in the United States, principally because the American ethos is aimed at turning out one particular kind of boy.

We are still very much a frontier country in our ideal of the "masculine image." The kind of man we most needed in conquering the wilderness and settling the West is still much the pattern for defining "masculinity" in American society. Europe has had time for other, and differing, masculine "types" to compete with that primitive image.

In the United States, it is still considered suspect for a young man to be interested in aesthetic matters; to like poetry, or enjoy opera, or appreciate the ballet. Indeed, these activities have been institutionalized mostly by females in our society.

In Europe, the concept of masculinity does not exclude such interests — the Italian males enjoy opera as much as the women do, the French consider a poet no less virile than a stockbroker, the Russian male dancers in the Bolshoi ballet are as masculine as any prizefighter.

Americans have always insisted on pushing their boys to one extreme or the other; there is little room for the balanced personality. If a boy at an early age exhibits interest in aesthetic matters, this is often considered "unmanly." And so, because he cannot or will not adjust to the prevailing frontier ethos, he moves toward those who "sympathize" with his bent — which already includes a large homosexual community.

No doubt, the Freudians are right that the early family pattern and the roles played by both parents are tremendously important in shaping the psychosexual life of a boy; on the other hand, the cultural pressures cannot be ignored, either, and a wavering and sensitive boy is more likely to turn away from the mainstream in the United States than in Europe, where he can find plenty of heteros who share his interests.

It is significant that even confirmed homosexuals do not behave so flagrantly in Europe as they do here, for they are accepted casually as an ordinary fact of life. Our frontier mentality not only produces more such men; it also keeps them alienated, anxious and aggressively defensive about their place in our society.

It is often easier to be just to those we care little about than to those we love.

*

I've never yet held a door open for a man behind me without getting a "Thank you"; but dozens of times I've held a door open for a woman behind me without even getting a nod of appreciation as she sails through in a mist of self-approval. Wasn't it Gertrude Atherton, a long time ago, who wrote a scathing article called "Ladies Are Not Gentlemen"?

Wise Parent Loves Child as He Is

LISTENING to my favorite FM station the other night, I heard an old recording of Leslie Chabay, the former Metropolitan tenor, and recalled a dinner I had with him and his wife in Aspen many years ago.

His little boy of five had wandered in to kiss his parents good night, and when the lad had left, Chabay told us how he had decided that the boy was not going to be a musician.

For several weeks Chabay had sung the boy to sleep with a lovely old German lullaby. One night, instead of singing the words, he merely hummed the tune, and asked his son, "What is this I'm humming?"

The boy promptly replied, "Jingle Bells."

More fathers should make such simple little tests before trying to squeeze their sons into a mold of the father's choosing. I shudder to think how many inept doctors and lawyers (and musicians) we have just because fathers refuse to admit that their sons might not have the same capacities, tendencies and temperaments as they.

They think this is love, but it is the exact opposite — pride of possession. Love accepts a person for what he or she is; the proud parent is not content to have the child grow up in conformity with his natural bent, but projects his own desire for glory into the child.

The classic case in English biography is that of Lord Chesterfield, the polished man of affairs, who utterly ruined his son's life, by trying to make him a carbon copy.

Those who have read Chesterfield's letters to his son — which seem such a model of worldly instruction — ought to know that the boy was emotionally crippled for life by his father's efforts to make his son as much like him as possible.

"Be not too much a parent," was Emerson's terse advice, which has never been improved upon. This does not imply that the child should grow up without direction or discipline, but that the discipline should encourage the child to *become who he is* — to develop in the way most natural to his talent and personality.

A child's need for *acceptance* is as deep and basic as his need for security and affection. Such acceptance is more often found in poor or non-achieving families than in affluent and goal-oriented ones, and it is hardly remarkable that most rebellious adolescents today spring from the latter type of family.

Our modern mania for sending children to college to fit them for vocations that may be far beyond their capacities is not kindness, but cruelty, like forcing a kitten to crawl up a barbed-wire fence. It's a wise parent that knows, and accepts, a child's limitations.

For the modern youth, home is where you hang your posters.

*

Being a good parent is so difficult because it calls for two opposite qualities in balance: giving up just enough childishness so that we are mature, and retaining just enough childishness so that we can empathize with youngsters — an equilibrium as admirable as it is rare.

*

A marital argument is usually one in which two half-truths are joined to make a perfect falsehood which libels both parties.

Parents Have Their Limitations

THE COMMON PHRASE, "a good parent," can be a misleading one, because it tries to take in too much ground. There is practically no such thing as a good parent for all of a child's various ages and stages of life.

Some parents are at their best when the child is an infant; others operate most effectively in the toddler and preschool range; still others make their finest contribution to older children, or teen-agers.

Temperamentally, all of us are more or less sympathetic to one age or another, and can identify better or worse with any particular stage of growing up. It is the rare person who possesses the same capabilities along the whole spectrum of growing up, from infancy through adolescence.

A mother might be "a good parent" from the time a baby is born until it is three, while it needs her protection and loving care; but the start of a child's independence might upset and alarm her, and she might then become ineffectual for a few years.

A father might be awkward and uncomfortable with a small child, but could turn into a superb parent when the child is old enough to be taught skills or taken on trips. Some parents feel easier with boys, and others with girls — and then only at certain ages or stages.

It is important, I think, for parents to understand and accept their own limitations in this regard, just as they must accept the child's limitations of temperament and talent. Otherwise, they will feel guilty and blame themselves for inadequacies that are not their fault.

If we know we are not particularly congenial to a certain age or stage of growing up, we will not try to force ourselves or pretend to ourselves (or to the child, who has an uncanny faculty for detecting emotional fraudulence). We will simply do the best we can and wait for a period in the child's life when we can genuinely be more helpful. (Hoping, meanwhile, that the other parent can take up the slack at present.)

Much of the guilt of the modern parents comes from the misplaced feeling that he or she ought to be all things at all times to the child, which is manifestly absurd. In past ages, grandparents and uncles and aunts lived with the family, and provided different kinds of impetus or support; in our present "nuclear" family, too many roles are demanded of the two parents, which they cannot possibly fulfill.

Just as a child operates better at some stages than at others, so do parents. Recognizing and accepting one's natural abilities and antipathies is surely the first step to sensible and realistic parenthood.

How beautifully and imaginatively and gracefully most children draw and paint — until they enter the average art class.

*

A skeptic isn't merely one who doubts — any child growing out of Santa Claus does that — but one who examines his doubts as rigorously as he has examined his earlier beliefs.

*

Failure to respect a child's privacy — of spirit, as well as of material existence — is responsible for more estrangement between parents and children than any other single cause.

Children Think, If We Let Them

IT IS ABSURD and condescending to suggest, as so many adults do, that young children are incapable of dealing with "abstract" ideas. Abstract ideas fascinate children almost from the time they are able to think — but most formal education buries this interest deep under the debris of "hard facts."

Not long ago, the smartest nine-year-old girl I know (who is conceited enough without getting her name in print) said to me, "Daddy, there's something peculiar about that whole story of God and the Devil and Hell — it just doesn't hold together."

"Oh," I said, in that tone of false brightness a parent puts on when he thinks a child is out of its intellectual depth. "And why doesn't it hold together?"

"Well," she pondered aloud, "God is supposed to love good people, and the Devil is supposed to favor bad people, right? The good people go to God, but the bad people go to Hell, where the Devil punishes them forever. Isn't that the story?"

"Pretty much," I replied. "What's wrong with it?"

"It doesn't make sense," she continued. "In that case, the Devil couldn't be the enemy of God."

"How do you mean?" I asked.

"I mean if the Devil really was on the side of the bad people, he wouldn't punish them in Hell, would he? He'd treat them nicely and be kind to them for coming over to his side. He'd give them candy and presents and not burn them up."

"You've got a point," I admitted. "So how do you work it out?"

"It seems to me," she reflected, "that if the whole story is true, then the Devil is secretly on the side of God, and is just pretending to be wicked. He works for God as a kind of —

secret agent, testing people to find out who's good or bad, but not really fighting against God."

"That's a remarkable theological insight," I said. "Do you think there's any proof?"

"Well," she said, "here's another thing. If God is really all-powerful, no Devil would have a chance against Him. So if a Devil really exists, it must be because he's secretly in cahoots with God."

Here is a child who is busy learning the multiplication table, the capitals of states and the proper use of punctuation marks. All of them necessary, of course — but how long will it be before such metaphysical speculations are stifled out of mind under the pressure of a pedagogical system that imagines young children can't think?

If we genuinely want to decrease population growth, birth control alone won't do it; what is also needed is a reshuffling of our social values and forms so that marriage won't seem so "normal" and imperative for millions of people who wouldn't — and shouldn't — marry at all, if our society didn't make the state of singleness seem so abnormal.

*

The relativity of standards is neatly expressed by the actress I heard about who visited a marriage counselor and was asked if she had been faithful to her husband. "Oh, yes." She nodded gravely. "I've been faithful lots of times."

*

"Certainly, two can live as cheaply as one," said the man at lunch. "My wife and I get along on what it takes my daughter to go to college!"

Nothing Like Them Ever Was?

WHAT ARE THEY COMING TO, these children of ours? They just seem to get worse all the time.

A couple of days after Halloween, I picked up the small-town Wisconsin newspaper I subscribe to, and read the following item:

"The usual pranks were perpetrated on the public Halloween eve, consisting of tearing up sidewalks, knocking over small houses, tearing down fences, etc. Time was when only harmless jokes were indulged in, but of late years it appears that the juvenile population are not content unless they can inflict damages that entail a monetary loss on the victims."

Before your middle-aged hackles of indignation begin to rise, let me hasten to add that this item was in a column called "Traveling Back." It was a reprint of 60 years ago, from the Door County *Advocate* of November 2, 1911.

And the good burghers of 1911 looked back upon that golden era of 1850, when kids were still kids, and indulged in only "harmless jokes." But "of late years" things are indubitably getting worse. No doubt, if we could find a paper of 1850, we would learn that juvenile conduct has shockingly degenerated from the golden era of 1790.

Now, in the year of 1972, let us go back even further — to the era of Shakespeare, more than 400 years ago. His plays are replete with fathers complaining that children aren't what they used to be, that the old rules of behavior have gone by the boards, that elders are no longer respected — "the baby strikes the nurse and quite athwart goes all decorum."

(Amusingly enough, the same complaints are made about servants throughout the ages; in *As You Like It* (c. 1600), one of the old family retainers is praised as the last of the vanishing "true servants" of the kind they used to have in antiquity but can hardly be found "now.")

If children are "worse" today than they were in the past, it is only because society has given them more things to be worse about; not because their natures are any more corrupt. As we multiply our material benefits, children have more access to more implements, and children have always used whatever implements were at hand to strike back at the irrational repressiveness of adults.

Comparing the post-Halloween paper of 1911 with the same issue of 1971, it appears as if there were less vandalism now than then, despite the growth in population. But the illusion of "time was" dies hard among the old; it may be one of the things that keeps them alive — and kicking.

What many parents still don't understand is that negative rules tend to stimulate the very behavior they prohibit; flatly forbidding an action is one of the most effective ways of generating a motive for it.

*

Despite our pious injunctions, children quickly learn not to tell the truth, because they soon realize that we want to hear from them what pleases us, not necessarily what is true.

*

The supreme irony of our time is our zealous effort to keep old people alive longer, combined with our acute embarrassment at what to do with them when they have outlived their productivity.

The All-American Girlie Show

THE CHILDREN wanted to watch the "Miss America" finals on TV this fall, because they find it funnier than "Laugh-In," which speaks well for their sense of values.

They are not quite old enough, however, to find it pathetic, which it also is. Despite superficial efforts to award points for "talents" and "personality" as well as mere pulchritude, it is basically a horseflesh auction of the most crass and commercial sort.

I recall a candid interview given many years ago by James Montgomery Flagg, the man who did magazine illustrations of more "beautiful" women than anyone else in the world.

"The beauty contest," Flagg said, "is one of the most glaringly absurd phenomena of our life today. I have consented to judge many of these venal and tawdry carnivals, chiefly for the sardonic laughs I got out of them. I have seen prize winners chosen for many reasons, none of which ever included beauty."

With few exceptions, he continued, the professional contestants in these grim charades are "shallow, thin-souled creatures, emotionally anemic and intellectually underdone."

Our national idea of "beauty" has changed little since Flagg's magnificent tirade against it as "juvenile, characterless, skin-deep, and as two-dimensional as the movie screen on which so much of it is projected."

The reason that beautiful girls are not selected as contest winners (and rarely become even contest entrants) was succinctly underscored by the painter: "Obviously, truly beautiful girls would not enter such contests, for a truly beautiful woman could not be so unutterably vulgar."

The children remarked, indeed, that they knew a half-dozen young women far more attractive than the ones parading across the TV screen, and certainly this is true. But the beauties they know would no more put themselves on the auction block than jump into Niagara Falls.

If Women's Lib is looking for a legitimate issue, they should rally against the "beauty contest" in all its ugly aspects. If men were to be subjected to the same animal-trainer routine, they would be humiliated beyond endurance or ridiculed out of existence. I'd just love to see Bert Parks prancing around in a bathing suit.

"There he goes . . ."

All the fuss about "artificial insemination" puzzles me; for unless passion and affection and a desire for procreation are present, all insemination is artificial.

*

The same person often demands constancy in love, but variety in sex; yet not even the most agile of emotional contortionists can bring off this trick successfully.

*

A marriage vow is a blank check, written in a fit of hysteria, filled in for an impossible sum, and when subsequently presented for cashing, returned for "insufficient funds."

*

Most parents make the dual mistake of trying to reason with a child before it has reached the age of reason, and then becoming so fatigued in the process that the technique is abandoned by the time the child has reached the age of reason.

Producing Large Family No Big Deal

IF WE ARE going to cut down seriously on our population growth — and I think it is an absolute necessity — then we will first have to change our simple-minded attitude toward the parents of large families.

Most people who meet me for the first time ask about my family, and when they find I have five children they emit little murmurs of admiration and respect, as if I had done something notable.

Now I am pleased and proud to have these children, but there was nothing especially meritorious about their conception. Their existence does not testify to my virility, or even to any exceptional fertility, and certainly is no evidence that I am suited for parenthood.

Anybody with the nominal equipment can have children; it is no great achievement. Indeed, in most cases it happens during a fit of absent-mindedness. No child should ever be called a "mistake," but some are certainly miscalculations.

Parents with four children are not twice as good or twice as loving or twice as intelligent as parents with only two children. True, they have more experience, but as Bismarck said of his donkey, "He has been through nine campaigns with me, and knows no more than he did after the first."

Apart from our population problem, I am convinced that an immense number of people who have children should not have them, and do not particularly want them, except as "symbols" of family life. What they want are ideal children, not real ones; and as soon as the real ones show no intention of conforming to the ideal in the parent's mind, they are treated as burdens, shipped away to school, or otherwise neglected.

Somebody once said that if many people had not read about romantic love and seen it on the screen, they would never look for it themselves. I believe this, and along with it I believe that if many people were not ashamed to be thought deficient in "family feeling" they would never have children.

Nor have I noticed that the parents of large families exhibit any more proficiency in bringing them up, except in terms of establishing a barracks-room regimen which is necessary for simple survival. Some studies have indicated, in fact, that children coming from large families suffer from a loss of sharply defined personality and lack a sense of individual identity.

At any rate, we have to begin to recognize that it is the *quality* of parenthood that is more essential than the quantity. Rousseau, be it remembered, wrote a masterly book on education — and then sent his five children to a foundling home. He was more honest than most.

A "honeymoon" these days is apt to last two years — and then culminate in marriage.

*

The man who accuses his wife of having poor judgment rarely reflects on the fact that she picked him.

*

A woman rarely finds shoes that fit both the occasion and her feet; and so she invariably opts for the former and complains about the latter.

Can't Tell a Hippie by His Cover

In one of G. K. Chesterton's delightful Father Brown stories, a crime is successfully committed by a waiter in an exclusive private club — because the guests and the waiters are both dressed in tuxedos, and cannot be told apart except by their actions and attitudes.

Chesterton is making the point that people who dress the same are looked upon the same, until they begin to function. I thought of this story in relation to the hippie costume that is so popular among the young today.

The hippie costume has been a blessing to a whole generation of misfits, losers and rotten eggs. For the first time, they are now able to disguise themselves as hippies, permitting the hippie movement to take the blame (in the public eye) for all their neurotic misconduct.

Until the adoption of this regulation uniform a few years ago, the losers had nothing to identify with and no place to hide. They were forced to take individual responsibility for their behavior, and were not condemned as part of a youth bloc.

Now, by the simple subterfuge of adorning themselves with a few beads or a belt, they can be their old noxious selves and pass the onus along to the movement they pretend to belong to.

The ranks of the true flower children have become so infiltrated by these "plastic hippies" that I doubt if more than 50 per cent of the youth wearing these costumes have even the remotest conception of the original principles that animated the movement. Or care at all.

Simply by masquerading as hippies, they feel they can get away with the most outrageous conduct, in violation of all genuine hippie beliefs — knowing that the straight public cannot discriminate between them and the real thing and always mistakes mere form for substance.

This is why the movement has to die before very long. In a year or two, only sub teen-agers will still be affecting the costume, just as they pick up the discarded jargon of the adolescents a couple of years later. The older youths remaining in costume will be the ragtag and bobtail of hoodlums, sadists, oddballs, paranoids and perverts.

But, cultural lag being what it is, the public will continue to condemn something it calls the "hippie movement" long after its core has disintegrated. For it offers an easy and obvious target, a safe means of discharging aggression and frustration and anxiety and hate. In different ways, the movement has not only been a boon to the misfits, it has been a blessing to the perplexed public, who otherwise might have been forced to look inward for the causes of our troubles.

What conventional schooling does mainly is replace curiosity with conformity, vitality with docility, and honesty with hypocrisy — and what is so surprising is that young people didn't rebel against this distortion of the educational process generations ago.

*

It is a dangerous half-truth to suggest that children become "spoiled" by "giving them too much"; they become spoiled only by giving them too much of the wrong things as a substitute for interest, attention and intelligent supervision; it is bribery that ruins a child, not the mere bestowing of material things.

Don't Trust Anyone over Sixty-five

MOST OF US live in mentally airtight compartments; the left hemisphere of our brain doesn't know what the right hemisphere is thinking.

Our luncheon table the other day included the head of a large company, who was complaining about the present generation's lack of respect for age. He compared it with his own time, and deplored our modern youth's contempt for anybody middle-aged or older.

Yet this same man defends a rigid policy at his company which compels employees over sixty-five to retire, no matter how active, bright, healthy or capable they are.

And, while it is not official, his company will not hire anyone over forty-five for a middle management position, because it would put too much of a strain on the firm's pension and welfare structure.

This is the attitude of most companies in our time — which is not only psychologically, socially and economically devastating for many men of sixty-five who still have a decade or more of productive life in them — but also increases the "dependency ratio" of nonproductive people who are being supported either by the government or by the employed portion of the population.

If we callously discard older people regardless of their individual worth, we are obliquely saying to young people that they are right in their disdain for age.

We are confirming their belief that people get "useless" as they get older, and thus undermining the sort of respect for pickled wisdom that has sustained all traditional societies in the past.

Young people today, who reject the past out of hand, who

have no patience with "tradition," seeing only its negative and not its positive aspects, take their leaf from our practices, not from our preachments.

If we profess individualism, but cut people off the payroll collectively at the same age, regardless of individual competence; and if we pay lip service to "maturity" but deny responsible employment to people over forty-five, youth will pay more attention to our acts than to our words.

And, as we put older people out to pasture, instead of drawing on their experience and judgment, we are disvaluing age and tacitly concurring in the contemptuous attitude of youth toward its elders.

Such contradictions within our socio-economic system play hob with all our pious platitudes about "reconciling the generations." By our own refusal to give status and dignity to older citizens, we lay the groundwork for the widespread contemporary heresy that youth is all.

Most of the trouble between couples occurs because the man won't express what he feels, and the woman won't refrain from expressing what she feels; if the traditional roles could be reversed for an hour or two, they both might learn something.

*

Interesting (and depressing) how the word "intimate" between persons of opposite sex has come to mean wholly sexual; but a truly "intimate" relationship is one in which persons reveal themselves to each other, in all their weakness, without fear; and this kind of intimacy is becoming rarer all the time.

Help Stamp Out Fourth Grade

How DO YOU get an institution to change without putting a firecracker under its tail? If our colleges and universities had changed when, and in the way, they should have, the riots and disturbances of the late sixties would have been not only avoidable, but unnecessary.

This same discontent is now seeping down to the high schools, and the dead hand of institutionalization will soon be lifted by force if it is not raised by consent. For the quality of education is even worse in most secondary schools than it is in colleges and universities.

We could go right down to the elementary grades for an example of administrative paralysis in the face of modern educational knowledge. For instance, it has been known for more than twenty years that young children cannot be best educated by the present "grade" system of keeping them in the same class for all subjects.

That is, there are no "fourth grade" children. Students of the same age have differing abilities in different fields, and cannot be effectively schooled on a mass assembly-line basis, as they are almost everywhere today. Individual differences must be taken into account.

A child who is in fourth grade in English should not necessarily be doing fourth grade math, but third or fifth. Another might be doing sixth grade art and second grade music. A few might be working at the sixth or seventh grade level in history.

The fiction that abilities are roughly even at comparable ages makes for badly taught pupils and frustrated teachers, but eases the path for administrators, paperworkers and schedule planners. And, of course, the schools are mainly

run for the benefit of these people, not for drawing upon the
fullest potentialities of teachers or pupils.

All educational experts who have seriously studied the matter agree that the kind of "grade regimentation" we have in
the public schools is regressive — this is why so many pupils
entering high school have to repeat the last year or two of
grade school, and why so many entering college are simply
repeating the last year of high school. The "water" in the
educational system must be wrung out.

But it will not be wrung out until parents and teachers begin to attack the status quo as expensive, time-consuming and
ineffectual. Necessary reforms, however, are rarely im-
plemented by the people who find it simpler to keep the old
machine running in the old way; and this is what foments
revolutions. An institution that has lost its capacity to be
self-correcting invites its own eventual overthrow.

*When a married woman thinks she needs a lover, she usually
needs just a few more loving words from her husband; much
of what passes for sexual abandon is just injured vanity.*

*

*Why don't the beauty and glamour magazines tell their
feminine readers that no amount of flattering makeup, fascinating hairdo or fashionable clothes can make a woman appear
attractive if her mouth is tight and bitter, her eyes are hard
and calculating and her whole demeanor is tense and anxious
— as so often is the case with impeccably turned out women?*

*

*Unrequited love generally lasts longer than any other kind,
because it is never forced to confront reality.*

Parents Must Make Minds Up

PARENTS want two opposite things at once: they want their children to excel, and they want their children to be docile. But the two don't go together, and never have.

Every study made of "achievers" in a genuinely creative sense — that is, people who were truly innovative, whose existence made some positive difference for the human race — has shown that as children these people were anything but docile and conformist.

Almost all were independent, in mind and spirit, if not in body. They began thinking for themselves at an early age, and either rejected or modified their parents' code of conduct and scale of values. Many were not popular with their peers, and most of them were found either "stupid" or "difficult" by their teachers.

Actually, when parents say they want a child to "excel," what they customarily mean is that they want him to be successful and to be popular. But genuine achievers are often those who fail for a long time, and who rarely attain popularity outside a small circle. And they have often had severe educational problems, from St. Thomas Aquinas, who was called a "dumb ox" at school, to Thomas Edison, who received depressingly poor grades and left school before the age of twelve.

A creative and imaginative child is a great burden to the ordinary parent, and this is why a repressive society produces so few of them; the weaker spirits are crushed, and the hardier ones often overreact in a way that turns them into delinquents, or actual criminals if they happen to live in a squalid environment.

As adults, most of us do not care to tolerate the kinetic

qualities of children. We want them to stop wriggling or jumping or sloshing through puddles or dangling from fence posts; and in the same way, we resent agile minds and mercurial temperaments. We don't like to answer silly questions, to respond to anxieties that take fantasy form, or to acknowledge the deeper life of the child's spirit.

He is to be quiet, tractable, unquestioning, unthinking, and invisible if possible. Even the so-called permissive parent is doing the same thing in a different way — giving the child too much money or too much false freedom in order to get him out of the way, to leave time and energy for adult pursuits. The TV set is now what the Bible lesson used to be, only more seductive and more effective.

Nothing in the world is harder than rearing a child who will make a difference to his society. But nothing in the world is more worthwhile, if we are breeding for improvement and not just for dumb survival.

Far more single than married persons commit suicide; this is because in a marriage you always have someone else to blame when you feel you aren't living up to your capacities; the single person has no such source of consoling illusion.

＊

The best and briefest advice for youth and age alike today was given some years ago by James Thurber, when he urged, "Let us not look back in anger or forward in fear, but around in awareness."

＊

Men dress well to feel equal to other men; women dress well to feel superior to other women.

It's More Than a Generation Gap

WE MAY BE TAKING too short a view of what is popularly (and thoughtlessly) called "the generation gap." What is happening between parents and children today may be the end result of a longer process than we have considered.

Around the beginning of the twentieth century, the traditional "extended family" started to be replaced by the modern "atomic family" for the first time in human history — an event almost unmarked and unobserved, except by a few specialists in sociology.

I was the last of my family, for instance, to be born in an "extended" setting — in a house inhabited not only by my parents, but by grandparents and uncles and aunts as well. At that time — by the end of World War I — families were already being atomized.

That is to say, young people were marrying and setting up their own households, free from parental and traditional restraints. The "family" came to consist of a mother and father and several children, whirling around together in a constellation that was uniquely new in human society, replacing the tribe and the clan of the past.

This has become the prevailing pattern for the past couple of generations (as generations used to be measured in thirty-year spans), and perhaps it is time we examined its viability. The benefits of marital independence were immediately obvious to young couples; the strain of rearing children in an isolated family constellation was not.

Is it possible that much of the conflict and tension and rebellion of youth in our time springs from the social and emotional insufficiency of the atomized family? Are a mother and a father alone enough to handle a child, much less several children? Is the double burden of exclusive propinquity with each other, and isolation from other families, too heavy for parents and children to bear?

We must at least begin to ask these questions of ourselves. In the past, children were reared by many adults. They could go from one to the other, seeking consolation or understanding, and finding different responses from the varied adult members of the extended family.

The pressure was not nearly so great on the parents alone; decisions were balanced, and authority was diffused. Grandparents both softened the rigors of growing up and sustained family unity. Even though they had difficulties and conflicts, possibly the net result was supportive for the parents and satisfying for the children. Maybe no family, like no man, was meant to be an island, either.

Children know how to be children far better than old people know how to be old; the former is an instinctive reaction, the latter must be a learned response, and too few take the trouble to learn grace in age.

*

The best reason for letting a child sleep overnight with a friend at an early age is that he soon learns other parents get along no better than his own do, which relieves young fears and provides a more realistic recognition of the hazards of family life.

*

Experience is often no teacher at all. At the age of fifty, we have slept about seventeen years, but we don't do it as well as a baby with no experience whatever.

Our Youth Give In to the Group

SPEAKING of young people, as I was recently, reminded me of the statement by a twelve-year-old heroin addict in New York: "I started using dope because my friends were using it, and I didn't want to be left out."

Most kids begin experimenting with pot as a way of demonstrating that they belong to the "in" group, that they are "with it," that they march in the vanguard of young modernity. Children are the greatest conformists in the world, and nonconforming to the Establishment is the way they now conform to each other.

In commenting on this problem, Professor Raven McDavid of the University of Chicago makes an interesting and pertinent point in a recent educational bulletin. He suggests that our emphasis on "group activities" has stimulated the tendency of youth to copy one another even more than they normally might.

"It seems to me," he writes, "that one of the shortcomings of present-day education, on almost every level, is the emphasis on groups at the expense of individuals. Part of the process of growing up . . . is learning to take groups with a certain amount of skepticism, and acquiring the power to walk away from them (those who are loudest in asserting noncomformity are often the most tyrannical in imposing their own kind of conformism)."

I was struck by much the same thought not long ago, when I attended a film showing at my children's school. Five high school youths were standing up in the aisle behind me, talking to friends, and each was identically barbered and attired in hippie style, so that they resembled ludicrously overgrown quintuplets. They were just as regimented as if all had been wearing the same Brooks Brothers suit or military school uniform.

It is hard not to agree with Professor McDavid that our educational (and social) emphasis on group activities has unwittingly subordinated the individual to his peer group and made him more ashamed than ever before to be his own person.

Admittedly, there are many other factors moving young people to pot, and its even more dangerous sequelae. But the high sanction we confer on group activities and the censure we give to the individual who prefers to go his own way surely must contribute to the growing problem of addiction as a form of imitative peer conduct.

It is ironic that a nation that preaches individualism so ardently in the marketplace is so intolerant of individualism in any other area of social life, looking with approval upon the "joiner" and with suspicion upon the "loner." Since all revolutions take on the color of the regime they want to overthrow, it is scarcely an accident that our youth dissidents enthusiastically "join" in the pot parade.

A newly married man doesn't begin to know his wife until the first time he unexpectedly brings a friend home to dinner.

*

The strength of the male is as deceptive as the weakness of the female: many a woman has married a man she thought was "strong," only to discover he was infantile, just as many a man has married a woman who leaned on him, and learned that she was really pushing, not leaning.

Don't Keep Boys, Girls Segregated

SEVERAL of my fifteen-year-old son's friends are transferring to prep schools this fall, and some of their parents have asked me why we're not doing the same. In my view, adolescence is precisely the time when boys and girls should be together, under normal daily conditions, not placed in separate schools.

I think the whole idea of the sexually segregated school is a bad one — for boys and girls alike. It has not worked well in England, on many levels, including the high incidence of homosexuality among the upper classes who sent their boys away at a vulnerable age.

Men's and women's colleges are moving together, which is a healthy sign, and it seems to me that prep schools (if they are to survive) must likewise become coeducational. For they have the opposite effects than were originally anticipated and intended.

It was thought at first that being in separate schools would take the young people's minds off the opposite sex and allow them to develop their skills and strengthen their characters more freely. This may have been true (at least in part) in the last century, but modern times quickly made the whole notion obsolete, since exposure to sexual stimulation was found on all sides at all times.

It turned out that the girls at girls' schools thought of little else but boys, and the boys at boys' schools thought of little else but girls. The subject becomes overemphasized through being de-emphasized; the lack of natural contact with the opposite sex leads either to a frantic overstressing or a grim denial — neither a wholesome reaction.

Actually, our relationship between the sexes is almost as

abominable as our relationship between the races. And for much the same reason — lack of normal, easy contact during the important years. We have narrowed the concept of "sexuality" to the physical, and ignored the psychological and social connotations of both the similarities and the differences between the sexes.

What young people want and need is "intimacy" — but if it is not obtainable through the full spectrum of feelings and conduct, then they will grasp for it at the most transient, elusive and accessible level: the sex act alone, which satisfies drives without serving real needs, and which by itself can move couples further apart, not closer together.

Adolescence is a time for exploring one's feelings, and learning how to control them; for grasping the *humanness* of the other sex as well as its uniqueness; this informal "prepping" for marriage surely must take precedence over prepping for college, or any career.

It's strange how the people who regard it as an infringement of personal liberties if society should decide to limit the number of children we might have, don't at all consider it a loss of freedom that we are permitted only one husband or wife at a time; but if the state has the acknowledged right to enforce monogamy, why not the number of progeny? (And please don't quote the Bible at me, in defense of "multiplying"; all the Old Testament patriarchs had numerous wives, but that didn't stop ecclesiastical authorities from eventually banning polygamy.)

*

When a man speaks of "lean years," he is speaking fiscally; a woman, anatomically.

They Picked Up the Drug Habit from Us

IT IS HARDLY ACCIDENTAL that the same word, "drugs," has two meanings in our culture. It means pharmaceuticals and medications; it also means addictive narcotics.

There is not the gap between the two that we like to think: we are pre-eminently a drug-oriented society in the first sense of the word, and so the second sense should not be such a shock to us.

Not long ago, in an article in the *New York Times*, I read a cautionary quote by Dr. Judianne Densen-Gerber, who is both a psychiatrist and a lawyer, and also the founder of Odyssey House, a narcotics treatment center for youngsters in Manhattan.

Calling for the pharmaceutical industry to police itself more vigilantly in advertising, she said that "programming our children to believe that there is a pill for every problem is a bad way to educate them." And advertising, even for headache remedies or stomach upsets, "should avoid the language that reinforces a drug culture."

Nonprescription sedatives and nonprescription pep pills, as well as their more dangerous prescription prototypes, are often offered to the public in such a way as to seem to be problem-solvers, when at best they only relieve symptoms and may actually do harm by masking some serious disturbance below the threshold of consciousness.

In that same day's issue of the paper, as it happened, there appeared a long and sympathetic interview with playwright Tennessee Williams, who had just been released from a long hospital confinement, part of which was spent in the psychiatric ward.

Williams confided that for the last seven years he had

nearly killed himself with liquor and sleeping pills, adding that, "All I want, all I really wanted, is to get a good night's sleep and get up in the morning to do my work."

This is all most people want, but if they cannot get it — usually for emotional reasons that will not respond to drugs — then they think nothing of taking a pill to sleep at night, and another to keep alert during the day. The annual consumption of "up" and "down" pills in the United States exceeds that of the whole rest of the world put together.

What we consider our "innocent" drug culture, however, does much to breed the culture of addictive narcotics among young people, who are only going a step further — but a fatal step down the chasm. Pills, unless absolutely prescribed and rigorously supervised, are just a way of avoiding a confrontation with one's deeper problems; but the price they exact is far more than the pharmacist's bill, not only for us but for the generations to come.

The man who prides himself on being "brutally frank" is secretly more gratified by his brutality than by his frankness.

*

For a shrewd understanding of feminine psychology, it's hard to beat J. B. Priestley's observation: "She was not pretty, but she might have been handsome if somebody had kept telling her that she was pretty."

*

Women tend to find conversation between the sexes generally so unsatisfactory because they can listen so much faster than men can talk.

Angry Students Show They Care

A HIGH SCHOOL HISTORY TEACHER was saying the other day
that he wished he had a few "troublemakers" in his class. "The
problem with most of my kids," he said, "is that they're too
passive and uninterested. They don't seem to have any particular values at all."

I think he is right, and we ought to be grateful for our dissident students in the colleges — who, after all, are deeply
concerned with values and goals, even if they don't happen
to be the values or goals of the Establishment.

The great majority of students are not so much dutiful
as they are unconcerned. Most of them are disenchanted
with the educational and social structure they have grown up
in, but they aren't looking for ways to reform or improve it
— they live in a moral and intellectual void, trying to get
decent grades and then a satisfactory job.

But that isn't enough these days. Whatever the faults of
the college dissidents — and there are plenty — they at least
recognize that time is running out on the world, that it is
not realistic merely to reject old standards without proposing
some positive substitutions. To make no choice, as William
James said long ago, is itself a choice.

One of the Establishment leaders who seems to understand
what the college rebels are expressing is Edward E. Booher,
president of McGraw-Hill, who remarked recently:

"I believe that they (college students) are questioning the
basic values, or rather the lack of values on the part of many,
if not most, businessmen of my generation, other than the
usual regard for growth and profits. It is, in my opinion, our
failure as businessmen to recognize and emphasize individual
rights and the need to improve the quality of society that

closes channels of communication between us and the generation whose support we need and must have."

Whether we agree or disagree with the dissenters, it is a fact that they *care* about society, about the future, about war and poverty and prejudice. Their tactics may be distressing, or their solutions wrong, but they are filling a vacuum that no other segment of society is concerned with. It is up to us to channel their energy and idealism into productive paths, not to sneer, to scorn, or to shut them up.

Our real threat comes from the uninvolved, the disengaged, the blank-eyed students who simply go through the motions of conforming and believe nothing — who cynically reject the values of the past without embracing any standard for the future except safety, security and self-satisfaction. *This* spirit is treason to the American dream.

One thing a husband finds hard to understand is how a wife who "hasn't a thing to wear" to a party will try on six different dresses before coming to that dismal decision.

*

Most fatigue is not physical, even when it seems to be: a man can play three sets of tennis without tiring himself, but once around a museum with children in tow gives him intolerably aching calves.

*

Many people have a sadly deficient idea of "maturity" — they imagine that adulthood constitutes a renunciation of childhood, when actually it must include and accept the good (and easily lost) values of childhood, and build upon them.

Why Grades Should Be Abolished

A TEACHER I know has sent me a recent book called *Making the Grade*, which is a nice pun in itself — for young people today can't make the grade unless they make the grade. And the grade has become more important than anything else in the educational process.

For many long and wearisome years, I have chanted the refrain that grades should be abandoned in the school system. Everything they accomplish is negative, and they have absolutely no meaning outside the narrow framework of the course or the school.

In *Making the Grade*, the three authors — all educators, by the way — after examining possible alternatives and compromises, finally recommend the complete abolition of the grading system. Their main charges against it are five in number:

First, it "institutionalizes" the students, and moves them through the college anonymously, like beef stamped on the butt and processed in a meat-packing plant.

Second, it focuses course work around the goal of earning a grade rather than learning the subject. The grade, which is just a symbol, becomes an object in itself, and distorts the learning process.

Third, the relationship with the faculty is determined by the struggle for a good grade; there is little dialogue and less searching for wisdom, but merely memorization and playing back to the teacher his own set of values, preconceptions and criteria — which may differ vastly from teacher to teacher in the same general subject.

Fourth, study habits vary, depending upon how much the student wants to get a good grade, or how much of a "snap course" a certain subject is; it may be easier to get an A without working in one course than to get a C when working hard in another. This bears no relation to the intrinsic merit of the subject.

Fifth, student morale is depressed by a growing awareness, throughout college, of the whimsical and arbitrary ways in which grades are awarded by different teachers and different departments. For this reason, scholarship is replaced by gamesmanship, and even the awarding of the ultimate degree becomes cheapened and trivialized in the eyes of most students.

Of course, the trouble begins in the early school years, when young pupils are invited to compete with one another for gold stars and high grades, instead of cooperating with one another and with the teacher to bring out the optimum resources of each pupil. As long as schooling is considered a "contest," education must suffer.

Beyond a certain age, a woman's chief social satisfaction seems to consist in spotting other women in her age-bracket who are heavier than she is.

*

The trouble with skepticism is that eventually a man doesn't believe anything he hears, even when he says it himself.

*

Many people marry largely because they are afraid of loneliness; unaware that the loneliness within an ill-considered marriage is the most bleak and solitary of all.

An "Interesting" Child Is Best

WHAT WOULD you consider a fine compliment paid to you about your child? That she always looks neat and clean? That he has good manners? I wouldn't mind hearing any of this — but what really pleases me most is when some adult happens to mention that a child of mine is "interesting."

And this seems to be a trait that many parents overlook altogether. They feel responsible for giving the child wholesome food and warm clothing and setting a good moral example — but pay little, if any, attention to turning out a human being who is an interesting personality.

Thus, the world is filled with dullards who have been given wholesome food and warm clothing and sent to Sunday school and instructed to say "Please" and "Thank you" — and have been bitterly neglected and underprivileged in the area of true personality development.

This is a tremendous disservice to the child, for every baby born without deficiency is a merry, curious, humorous bundle of interest. But within a half-dozen years, by the time the child begins first grade, much of the curiosity has been knocked out, the humor repressed, and thereby the learning process has been severely inhibited. (And, of course, the wrong kind of teacher, who is in the majority, compounds this growing stultification.)

Our first obligation as parents — beyond the bare subsistence needs — is to turn out children who are interesting, to themselves and to others. This means children who are interested in the world, who are confident of their abilities, who are unafraid to question, who are willing to experiment and be wrong and accept their knocks.

Instead, most parents want children who are quiet and

neat and well-behaved and dutiful — but then who rebel in their teenhood, when they discover that society is a far larger, more exciting, more colorful and more complicated structure than they had been led to believe. Indeed, it is usually the *least* sophisticated who get into the most trouble at that age, not the ones who have been exposed to the world.

The only way to be interesting is to be *interested;* and when you are interested in external reality, then you are not bored or disaffected, and you have a focus for your activities. It is this lack of focus that makes so many teen-agers restless and ready for rebellion. If you can't raise yourself, all you can do is raise the roof.

Dull, flat, constricted and uncreative personalities clog this earth of ours, through no fault of their own, for God has breathed into each soul the spirit of wonder, of exploration, of humor, of charm. What parents *do* for their children is not nearly as important as what they *fail* to do in fanning that tiny spark of expressiveness.

It may be true that the child from the "broken home" is unhappier and more delinquent, but it must not be supposed that the "broken home" consists only of divorced or separated parents; it also includes those families where communication and genuine interest are lacking, no matter that the family are all smiling together on the Christmas card.

*

That "awkward age," for parents at least, is when a child is still dependent, but no longer deductible.

Putting Sex in Proper Perspective

"ONE THING I find it hard to forgive my parents for," said the woman next to me at the dinner party, "is their failure to tell me how important sex would be when I grew up, especially in marriage."

"But isn't that true of most parents?" I interposed.

"I suppose it is," she said, "but it's a dirty trick to do to kids. And even when parents are enlightened enough to tell you the biological facts about sex, they still underplay its significance — because, I guess, they don't want to get their children hipped on the subject."

"It's an interesting example," I said, "of a self-defeating principle at work. Sex is something set apart, a special subject, veiled in all kinds of mysteries, and pulled out of the normal, natural orbit of life. Even when we present it clinically, or hygienically, as in classrooms, it's taken out of emotional context and turned into a 'function.'

"But, of course," I went on, "sex is much more than a function. It's physical, it's psychological, it's social, it's symbolic — it's a complex of actions and reactions, emotions and repressions, all of which have to be working fairly well together in order for the process to fulfill itself as it was meant to."

"You make it sound so difficult," she said.

"It *is* difficult, the way most civilized societies approach it," I replied. "By making sex a thing apart, by seeming to diminish its fundamental importance, we actually succeed in enhancing its importance to people as they are growing up.

"That's what I mean by a self-destroying principle at work. Our aim is presumably to dampen down, or restrain, young people's sexual ardor until they are old enough to cope with their feelings. But when we do this, we give it a special place, and in a certain sense we overemphasize its importance to them.

"Sex has become so important in our society, from pre-adolescence right through to old age, because of all the taboos that surrounded the subject when we were children. Primitive societies don't have all our sex problems, including our shocking record of rape, because they accept it as a natural part of life from the child's earliest years."

"Are you suggesting," she asked, "that we adopt the sexual practices of primitive tribes — wouldn't that be a step backward?"

"No," I said, "we don't have to adopt anybody else's practices; what we have to do is teach our children, at an early age, that sex is important, is joyous, and is a learned activity as well as a natural impulse. If we put it in the right perspective from the first, it wouldn't become so distorted and so disproportionately important later."

A husband who "doesn't look at other women" generally doesn't look at his own very much either.

*

For every one man who is working hard in order to get ahead, ten are working hard in order to get along.

*

Some personalities are shaped by what they admire; others are disfigured by what they hate; this is why giving a child a model he can look up to is the most important element in his education.

Age Isn't Only Difference

WHAT IS DISTINCTIVELY NEW about the new generation is not simply its youth, or the mere fact that it is later in time, as a car is new if it is this year's model compared with last year's or the year before's.

There is a *qualitative* difference in young people, not just a *temporal* difference. And this quality can best be described, in Maslow's term, as "self-actualizing."

If you cannot understand this, then you cannot understand what young people are thinking and feeling and desiring and groping toward. "Self-actualizing" means *becoming who you are*. It is the highest and final step in human development, and it has become possible for many people only in recent times.

The human personality has certain basic biological needs that must be satisfied — hungers that must be fed, fears that must be allayed, physical demands that must be gratified.

After this, there are certain social and emotional demands made on, and by, the personality — for learning, for status of some kind, for group identification, for survival and support as a social being. These earliest and "lower" needs must be at least adequately met before the individual can concern himself with other levels of being.

"Self-actualization" is what the person wants to become with himself, not as a biological creature or as a unit in the mechanism of his society, but in the very core of his personal existence — so that his particular life has point and purpose and gives expression to values that are more than biologically or culturally determined.

In most societies of the past, there has been little chance to do this, or even to think about it very much; the struggle for mere physical existence was so intense and protracted that the individual organism fought all its lifetime for mere survival and equilibrium. Its higher, and distinctive, needs were necessarily subordinated to its primitive demands for life, for a kind of liberty, for a measure of security.

It is no accident that the most questioning and dissident youths today come from upper middle class families, whose "future" within the framework of conventional society seems most assured. They do not want to fit into a mold, do not want to accept the values of their caste, do not want to become like their parents or their parents' friends.

They are asking that our affluent society provide more than a plenitude of material goods; that it open new vistas for the realizing of individual potentialities, not in the economic realm, but in the realm of moral values, sensory experiences, creative expression and personal fulfillment. Their tactics are childish, but their ends mature.

The upper classes in American life are characterized chiefly by the emasculation of the men and the embittered dominance of the women, which seems an uncommonly high price to pay for affluence and status, and may explain the staggering and stultifying consumption of martinis at this level.

*

When a great deal is expected of a child, he either rises to the expectation or is crushed by it; and this is why an expectation that is not realistic can cripple a child as much as depreciation does.

Abolish the Summer Vacation

MOSTLY FOR ECONOMIC REASONS, some school systems are starting to stagger their pupils' hours. I was lecturing in a town recently, where half the kids attend high school in the mornings, and the other half in the afternoons.

Eventually, I think, we are going to have to do away with the old-fashioned three-month summer vacation for school-children, which is just a holdover from the days when America was largely a rural nation and the kids were needed in the summer to help with farmwork.

A month or six-weeks vacation would be plenty — perhaps with longer periodic vacation breaks during the rest of the year — and it is absurd for school facilities to be unused for so much of the time. More efficient use of time could also get students through school in fewer years than it now takes; there is too much "water" in the system.

When these reforms take place — and they are coming sooner than most of us think — it would be wise to "stagger" the school year as well as daily schedules, for the benefit of parents as well as children. Doing away with the enforced "summer vacation" would be a blessing to everyone.

Up where I spend my summers, for instance, the merchants have to "make it" in eight or ten weeks, because come Labor Day all the families fold their tents and slink back to town for the beginning of school.

Actually, the fall season there is lovelier than the summer, and if a considerable portion of parents had children with September and October vacations, they would be delighted to rusticate there in those months — especially since the spreading-out of vacation times during the whole year would relieve the unholy tourist congestion in July and August.

More and more Americans have become skiing enthusiasts the last few years, and millions of families would welcome a long winter school vacation rather than a summer one. Still others would prefer spring, which is the finest season for leisure in some areas. It is ridiculous that the antiquated school semester system regiments all parents into taking long holidays at approximately the same time.

Summer places get more congested, and thus more unattractive, every year, as more and more people crowd into them. Prices are high because people who cater to tourists know that the post–Labor Day slump is arriving. This hectic and artificial pattern of vacation-taking is stupid, uneconomical and irrational. When the changes come, they ought to benefit everyone, not just the school administrators.

Perhaps the only way to change our rotten educational system for the better is to convert all schools into private schools, giving families allotments to pay for education, and letting them freely choose where they want to send their children, among schools that are competing to provide the best education, as other institutions must compete for customers and clients.

*

Perhaps the real difference between us and all other animals is that we alone pass down acquired attitudes toward our young; other species pass down only instinctive behavior which tends to safeguard the species, while we transmit emotional distortions that tend to emperil the species.

Telling It Like It Is at Christmas?

SINCE IT TAKES US about a month to get rid of the Christmas tree, you can believe that we only now got around to tossing out the mound of Christmas cards. And the ones I most gladly parted with were those long, rambling recitals of "what the Guck family has been doing" all year.

These invariably come from families we hardly know, or have long forgotten, and we have to remind ourselves who these people are and why they feel driven to broadcast all these precise biographical details.

But what I most object to is their uniformly warm and cheery tone. They try to give the impression of being a model family, busy and creative, having gobs of fun, winning honors, enjoying jolly family reunions and going on yachting vacations at the drop of a hatch.

Maybe a few of these chatty Christmas notes vaguely approach the truth, but I doubt it. None of the families we know well would dare send us such literary treacle, because we are acutely aware of the scars and schisms in the family circle, from Papa and Mamma down to the littlest sibling who happens to be in intensive psychiatric care.

How refreshing it would be, for a change, to receive a dour and candid Christmas missive that more closely approximated the facts of family life, something on this order:

"Hi, friends across the continent. We're Jim and Betty Glum, and our three children, Ham, Shem and Impetigo, who used to live your way before Jim got demoted and his company moved him to the paraffin factory in Moose Jaw, which is the end of the business road for him.

"Well, we're still hanging on, folks. Last month marked our twentieth wedding anniversary, and we hardly thought we'd make it. But Jim found a new mistress up here, and Betty keeps herself busy as a Nurse's Aide, so the marriage keeps rubbing along, God knows how.

"Our oldest boy, Ham, was thrown out of three schools before we found one that allows pot-smoking in the dorms. He was briefly engaged to a little tart from town, but fortunately she became pregnant and married the milkman's son posthaste.

"Shem, our second boy, is still sleeping all the time, and keeps promising to look for a job 'tomorrow.' He's become the world's leading expert on afternoon TV soap operas.

"Impetigo, our dearest young daughter, writes that she's happily weaving burlap loincloths in Haight-Ashbury and intends to come home for a visit in two or three years.

"Jim's job looks more precarious than ever, and we haven't been asked anywhere very much since Betty started drinking and crying at parties. Merry Christmas, and the same to all of you!"

A father who wants his son to be a "credit" to him is unconsciously treating the child like an asset, and has only himself to blame if the boy rebels into a liability.

*

Bad horsemen use the whip because they have no skill in using the reins; the same is true of parents.

*

Masculine vanity is so great that the only flaw in being a grandfather, which most men enjoy, is the uneasy realization that one is married to a grandmother.

No Walk and All Phone Makes Flab

PHYSICAL TESTS given to European and American school-children have shown that the European children are far more physically fit than ours, despite our greater resources in food and our greater emphasis on sports.

There are two culprits here, I think: the automobile and the telephone. Unlike my generation, the American child today uses these as substitutes for his legs.

I must have walked ten miles a day when I was a boy; I doubt if the modern child walks ten blocks a week. And regular walking is probably the best and cheapest form of keeping fit.

One of the ironies of our time is that youngsters are provided with elaborate and expensive athletic programs at school and elsewhere — and then they are bused or chauffeured to the sites of their endeavors. If they walked back and forth regularly, they wouldn't need such involved programs.

The telephone, for all its usefulness, is another enemy of physical fitness among the young. I don't think I telephoned a friend more than once a month; if I wanted to see someone, I walked or biked over to his house. Nobody dreamed of chauffeuring me as a boy, and I rarely took a bus, except to go downtown once in a while.

In my early teens, my closest friend was Saul Bellow, the novelist. He and I lived about a mile and a half from each other, diagonally across a park. We would spend the late afternoon or evening together, and then walk each other home.

When we got to my house, we decided there was still more to talk about, so we would turn around, and I would walk him back to his house. And, often, we would turn around once again, and he would walk me back to mine. We would sometimes do this three or four times, and think nothing of it — and do it three or four times a week.

He was on the track team (an excellent miler), and I was on the tennis team; and we both got so much exercise walking that we were always in top form, without the necessity for calisthenics or special programs. Our school, in fact, didn't provide any.

It is absurd to spend so much for athletic and fitness programs today, and at the same time allow children easy access to the telephone, the car or the bus, when they could just as easily (and more healthfully) walk to school or to a friend's house. But they seem to have enormous energy for everything — except a simple six-block stroll down the street. The mere thought of that exhausts their imagination and brings on symptoms of immense fatigue.

Advising parents to "spend more time" with their children is not only pointless but also dangerous, if the parents' company oppresses the children rather than vitalizing them.

*

Neurosis begins when an infant is not accepted for himself, as he is; by expecting or forcing him to be different, *the parents inhibit self-acceptance, and "lose" the child before they know it.*

*

When someone under thirty says to us, "You've really got it made," we simply smile quietly and wait for them to grow older and learn that nobody has it really made.

Why College Kids Don't Go Home

I WAS SPENDING the weekend in a wealthy city in the Southwest recently, and two of the leading citizens complained that "our young people aren't coming back here after college."

"After they've been away at college a few years, they don't want to come back here and settle down," said one. "Even though they may have the best business opportunities here, through their parents and other connections. I can't understand their reason, when they know this town needs young people so badly."

What could I say to him? I knew the reason, of course, since I visit dozens of colleges and universities throughout the year. The young people don't want to go back because they can't stand the atmosphere of their hometown, when it is smug and provincial.

This is an atmosphere the older citizens cannot feel, the way a fish does not feel water. If you have lived in a specific environment all your life, it is not an "environment" — it is what you call "life." But to the young people it is suffocating, unreal and unutterably dull, both in spirit and in substance. This is why so many gravitate to large, cosmopolitan communities.

Having talked to college students about this subject, across the whole country, I find that these are their chief objections to going back to the town or city they grew up in:

It is deadly conformist, in its thinking, feeling and acting.

It is static in its beliefs, and reactionary in its activities.

It lives by clichés and platitudes that bear no relation or relevance to the twentieth-century world.

It is totally self-delusive, thinking itself to be the repository of all virtues, while wholly oblivious of its defects of vision, imagination, flexibility, tolerance and social responsibility.

It lacks verve, humor, insight and, most of all, a capacity for genuine self-criticism which alone could change it in the future.

The virtues it pays homage to are riches, respectability, power and acquisitiveness; it has little or no use for the energies of the mind and spirit unless they are harnessed to conventional civic goals. This, right or wrong, is what many of the brightest and best college students think of the communities they come from. If they are right, they should not go back; if they are wrong, how did they get these notions?

This is what the town fathers should be asking themselves, instead of scratching their heads and sighing in perplexity.

Nature itself has made women "unequal" in that they alone are charged with the responsibility for bearing children; and all efforts to achieve parity are simply attempts to redress this biological disparity between the sexes.

*

The highest parental art is to rebuke effectively without wounding.

*

It is harder to understand why things work smoothly than why they work badly; and we need more studies of good function — such as in families — than of dysfunction, in order to learn as much about health as we know about disease, mentally, physically and socially.

Do We Need a Brake on Marriage?

"I'll tell you what the trouble is," said a friend, as we were chatting after dinner. "It's too easy to get divorced these days. That's why all these kids make such crazy marriages."

"That may be so" — I nodded — "but I think you're putting the cart before the horse. It's too easy to get *married* — that's the trouble.

"Society," I continued, warming to my subject, "puts up qualifications for everything, but not for marriage. You can't even get a driver's license unless you know how to handle a car, understand the rules of the road and have no gross physical defects.

"But any idiot can get married, almost on the spur of the moment, as long as he can scrape up five dollars, or whatever it costs to get a license in your state.

"There is no preparation for marriage in our society, no training for domestic responsibilities, except a few half-hearted college courses that come too late and say too little.

"You might protest that other cultures throughout history haven't set up any qualifications, either, but there is one big difference — this is the first time in the history of the world that romance, and romance alone, has been the criterion for making a marriage.

"Until the twentieth century, in our country young people largely married for economic motives or because the families wanted them to, or for other practical reasons that might or might not have been justified. But at least they knew there was a reason for getting and staying married.

"If we are going to allow our young people to marry on a romantic basis, the least we can do is insist that they recognize what a marriage entails — the responsibilities, the emotional demands, the *givingness* and not merely the *takingness*.

"But instead, the films, the popular magazines, the best-selling novels, all lead up to the altar, and drop the young people there on their own. Our society emphasizes sexual attraction more than any other in the history of the world — and then we are surprised when our young people find that sexual attraction is not enough to hold a marriage together, and we blame them for breaking up.

"Divorce is a serious problem, a messy business, and I don't think young people take it lightly. But as long as we present marriage merely as a matter of moonlight and roses, they will rush into it headlong. If we made the qualifications for marriage half as difficult as the qualifications for any other job, we'd be attacking divorce where it begins — at the altar."

Erotic love between the sexes is possessive, but parental love must convey the gift of freedom; and whenever parental love is possessive, it indicates an ungratified erotic love on the part of the parent, who is transferring to the child an illicit share of the conjugal relationship.

*

Sex, in our society, has been hypostatized as a substance or object, which it is not, rather than regarded as a process, which it is; thus, we mistreat it as something to be achieved rather than to be realized.

*

Children are never fooled by what is going on in a home; they merely pretend to believe what they are expected to believe; and it might be said that children delude their parents more than the parents delude them.

3

OF THE SOCIAL ANIMAL

Goal of Age: the Older, the Better

WE OLDER FOLK like to prate a lot about the "duties" and "responsibilities" of young people, but have we ever thought of the obligation that is entailed upon us by growing older?

I don't mean the financial and social and family obligations, which we all accept and understand, but the obligation to become more appealing on the inside as we become less attractive on the outside.

An older person who gets all dried up and brittle and wrinkled and full of complaints is just a total drag, no matter how rich or influential he may be. Most people allow age to do awful things to them.

It seems to me that growing older imposes a duty upon us to get more like a peach on the inside as we get more like a prune on the outside; otherwise, what's the point of it all?

We have to get cuter and funnier and mellower and more tolerant and more perceptive and wiser, simply to compensate for the external ravages of the aging process. Instead, most older people allow themselves to become more rigid, more disapproving, more psychically constipated, more narrowly opinionated and more querulously self-centered as they pass from childhood to senescence without ever having arrived at maturity.

Actually, young people have a natural love and affinity for oldsters who have maintained the spirit of youth within themselves; what they reject and resent are old people who have forgotten what it was to be young, who have discarded their earlier stages of life instead of incorporating them into the total personality at some deep and permanent level.

Our desperate quest for youth must be turned inside out; an older person who tries to look and act and dress like a junior is simply an object of fun or pity. Youth is an emanation from the inside, not a cosmetic application, and it is the inner spirit of the person that youngsters respond to, not the surface appearance.

Old people who feel alienated from the young tend to blame the "changing times," when in reality it is their own inability or unwillingness to deepen their perceptions and broaden their sympathies. Most of us get worse as we get older, when we should get better — we settle into our individual deformations, instead of emerging from the hard shell of self to meet the new world at least halfway.

There is no more delightful person in the world than an octogenarian who is both childlike and wise, spirited and supportive, more willing to learn than he is quick to advise. Socrates began taking dancing lessons at seventy; most of us just take dying lessons.

Why do we complain about the slowness of mail service, when most of the mail we get consists of letters we don't want to read, complaints we don't want to answer and bills we don't want to pay?

The Profit System's Excesses

How CAN CAPITAL preach incessantly that profit is the main driving force of society, and then expect labor to act otherwise? It seems to me that capitalism has been hoist with its own petard, philosophically and practically.

Workmen don't care about the quality of their work. Laborers goof off from their jobs. All they care about is getting more for doing less. The ultimate survivability of the company doesn't interest them.

These are all charges made by capital against labor, and they are in large part true. But why are they true? What has happened to the "old virtues" of reliability, loyalty, craftsmanship, scrupulosity?

What has happened is that the workmen have been thoroughly indoctrinated with the philosophy of profit above all, profit here and now, and damn the consequences. They are just practicing what has been preached to them from the other side of the hall.

Capitalism is an economic system that works well within carefully defined limits. It is not a social system. It is not a philosophy of life. It is not a gospel. It is simply an arrangement of working, owning and producing; and like any other human arrangement, it has its own built-in flaws that must continually be corrected and rectified.

But if you convince people that profit, that the desire to get more and have more, takes precedence over any other set of motivations — and if you elevate this to a principle of life, not just an economic doctrine — then it is hard to blame them for acting on that principle.

If getting the most you can is what counts, labor will try to get the most it can. If buying low and selling dear is the first axiom of capital, then pulling down the highest wages for the smallest expenditure of effort becomes the first axiom of labor.

It is ironic that most American businessmen are much closer to Marx than they know. Marxism is a purely material- istic philosophy, holding that economic considerations dom- inate human history. If capitalists agree with this view (as most of them seem to), then they have capitulated to a doc- trine that will ultimately destroy them.

Our nation was founded on the belief that man is a social and moral creature, and not just the victim of his appetites; on the belief that justice and honor and fidelity and the com- mon welfare are more important than gain. When the profit motive becomes the mainspring of our society, it signals an ideological triumph for Marx, even though it goes by the name of capitalism.

Considering our annual crime bill, it seems to be the only commodity in the country for which we are getting our mon- ey's worth.

*

The layman is invariably scornful of what he calls "legal language" — until he is victimized by a will that was written so loosely and imprecisely that he loses a bequest.

*

There is an optimum distance for viewing any object in order to understand its proper place: a mountain viewed from a distance looks like a grain of sand, while a grain of sand viewed up against the eye looks like a mountain; in making judgments, perspective is all.

Struggle Is Fine — in Moderation

ANYONE who knows the least bit about propaganda and persuasion is aware that a half-truth is more dangerous than a lie; a lie can always be exposed, but a half-truth can be manipulated so that its obverse side remains concealed to the spectator.

In a recent issue of the little magazine *Quote*, I ran across a perfect example in the statement by B. C. Forbes: *"Strength comes from struggle; weakness from ease."* There is just enough truth in it to make it a deceptive generalization.

Nobody would deny that a *certain amount* of struggle is necessary for the development of strength; but too much can be as bad as too little. Struggle may strengthen us, but if the odds are too uneven, it may also overwhelm or cripple us.

And, likewise, nobody would deny that *too much ease* makes for weakness; without some challenge, we sink into torpidity and softness. But it is worth remembering that only those civilizations where the people had a broad margin of ease contributed a culture and a technology. Countries where everyone struggles all the time remain brutal and backward in the arts, the amenities, the very flowers of what we are pleased to call "civilization."

The most productive societies manage to achieve a *creative tension* between struggle and ease: enough competition to keep us on our toes, but not so much as to force us to our knees.

Men who have had to struggle ferociously from an early age acquire weaknesses as well as strengths; they tend to become harsh, rigid, contemptuous of any values but conflict and victory, and incapable of adjusting to changing times and conditions. Since such men tend to rise to the top, they generally lead their countries into inappropriate combat, like a Napoleon or a Hitler.

Everyone is aware of the perils of too much ease, but it is not as clear at first that struggle itself can be damaging if the handicap is so great that a man must sacrifice a large part of his personality in order to make King of the Hill. This is why so many public "successes" are private failures.

One of the main objects of struggle is to attain relative ease, so that other and higher values may be aimed at; but when struggle is too relentless, it becomes an end in itself, overwhelming and obliterating the cooperative aspects of living together.

A Keats or a Mozart died tragically young from struggling against insuperable odds; a society which would have made it a little easier for them to give us more of their genius ought to be our object.

The "seniority rule" in Congress — with no retirement age — means that the older, the more rigid, and the more out-of-touch a Congressman gets with contemporary problems, the more power he exerts over key committees; surely not a system envisioned by the founders of our country, when the average age of the signers of the Declaration of Independence was under 45. (Thomas Jefferson was only 33 at the time.)

*

The same Americans who are arguing for segregation today would have been arguing for slavery a century ago — and the only reason they fail to do so now is that they are ashamed to face the logical consequences of their beliefs.

Why Frown on Women M.D.s?

I HAVE WRITTEN about this before, a dozen years ago, but the situation is now worse than it was then, and still nothing much has been done. I refer to the shortage of doctors in the United States, and our provincial prejudice against women in the medical profession.

Our country could use another quarter-million doctors, but many young men are not able to go through the lengthy and expensive period of medical education; on the other hand, hundreds of thousands of college-trained women could take up the profession if they were encouraged to do so.

The majority of doctors are women in Russia, and in the Scandinavian countries and throughout Europe generally there are many times more women doctors than we have in the United States.

Male chauvinism does not run nearly as high in those countries as it does here. Even female lawyers are frowned upon in the United States (both inside and outside the legal profession), are paid less, given more menial assignments and rarely elevated to positions of any real responsibility in public service, as their male counterparts are.

It may be a plausible (though not, to me, persuasive) argument that women lack the toughness of fiber to make first-rate lawyers; but surely no similar argument applies to their potential abilities as doctors.

In the first place, women tend to be natively more sympathetic to physical ailments than men; women are more aware of their bodies, more sensitive to biological processes; more emotionally engaged in the arts of nursing and nutrition and conservation of health.

Secondly, and just as important, women have a naturally

deeper understanding of psychosomatic ailments — which are at the bottom of more than 50 per cent of all cases seen by doctors — because their own minds and bodies are so intimately related, so delicately interpenetrated by one another.

And, so far as the technical skills of medicine are concerned, these can be learned by any competent and ordinarily intelligent person of either sex. What chiefly distinguishes a good doctor from a mediocre one is precisely the area in which women excel: the ability to *identify* with the patient, to *communicate* and *interact* on a level beneath the merely verbal and intellectual and clinical.

It is one of the scandals of our society that we fail to extract the vast potential from our women, and still condemn them to second-class citizenship in the profession that needs them most.

The things we need most, as a community, are "public goods," but the way men get elected to office is by offering "private goods" to various groups, who vote for the self-interest of their own segment; and thus the general welfare is customarily subsumed to special needs whose conflicting costs cancel out each other and leave the community no better off than before, and considerably poorer.

*

The next hardest thing to giving up smoking is to avoid substituting something for it, like smugness.

*

Idealists thought widespread "communication" would put feet on brotherhood; instead, it has merely given wings to envy.

The Reason Extremism Pays Off

ONE OF THE VERBAL GAMBITS we are fondest of invoking when we possess institutional power is to call for "responsible criticism," as opposed to "irresponsible criticism."

What we generally mean by responsible criticism is the same thing we used to mean by "constructive criticism" (a phrase that has perished through hypocritical misuse) — and that is, nothing that will make us look bad or threaten to topple us off our thrones.

Unfortunately for the possessors of power, a careful reading of history seems to indicate that fundamental and necessary changes are usually brought about precisely by irresponsible criticism, and that the responsible variety accomplishes nothing, or its effect is so slow that mild reforms lag far behind massive injustices.

Anyone who has seriously studied the American Revolution, for instance, is aware that the colonists kept making the most responsible criticisms for years that had absolutely no effect on the British crown. The last thing the American leaders wanted was to declare independence or go to war against Britain; but every responsible petition for reasonable change was ignored or contemned.

Recently, the American public has been stunned by a series of prison outbreaks, which are going to become more widespread and possibly more violent, as I predicted a couple of years ago. These insurrections — they are no less — spring directly from the failure of all responsible criticism to change our penal system.

For many years, everyone who has objectively assessed the way we handle prisoners has urged some basic reforms, and warned of what might happen otherwise. But the penological establishment in the United States has been more concerned with maintaining its authority than with making any concessions to realism or humaneness — and the Attica slaughter was the inevitable result of such obduracy.

We pay little attention to critics who are soft-spoken, logical, reasonable and moderate; it is only when they begin to snarl, scream and strike out that we hasten to make changes long overdue. It is only because our response to reason is so negligible that critics take recourse in extremism.

What we fail tragically to recognize is that extremism is *always* a symptom of failure in the feedback process of an institution, and not a cause of anything in itself. It is like blaming the fire for our lack of sensing devices in the alarm equipment. To be effective, responsibility in criticism must be assured of a quick and fair response.

Urging people to "get out and vote" who have not taken the time to study the issues or the candidates, represents subversion of democracy more than support of it; for the larger the number of ignorant persons who vote, the less the chance of a rational result.

*

"Tribalism" is, and has always been, the greatest enemy of civilization — the fear and dislike of the "outsider"; and only when we recognize that the true outsider is the man who places his tribe above the welfare of civilization will we be able to construct and maintain a workable social order for all mankind.

Provoking Radicals Is a Tyrant's Trick

NOT ONE CITIZEN in a thousand, perhaps, knows what is meant by the French phrase, *agent provocateur* — although most Europeans have been aware of it for long and cynical years.

Most people who have heard of it think merely that an agent provocateur is some sort of spy or secret agent planted amongst an enemy group. But he is far more than this. He is a man in the employ of the police or the military or the intelligence agency who penetrates a "suspicious" group and tries to make it act worse.

The agent provocateur does not merely become a member of some dissident organization and pass back information to his employers; he becomes the most violent, extreme and revolutionary member of the organization, and tries to involve it in incendiary plots which will enable the officials to crack down on the group.

This has long been a favorite trick of Hitler, Stalin and other such despots — using their own man as a Judas-goat to lead opponents to slaughter. The famous Reichstag Fire, which gave Hitler his rationale for seizing power, was set by a Nazi agent purporting to be working for "the communists."

There should be no place in the United States for such nefarious activity. Surveillance of extremist groups is one thing — and, even here, we need the most scrupulous definition of "extremist" — and inciting groups to criminal action is another. Such incitement should itself be liable to criminal prosecution.

Most dissident groups are by their very nature unstable, ill-organized, susceptible to emotional appeals, because their members feel so deeply on the political and moral issues involved. One firebrand can steer the organization into a violent action it might not take if calmer heads prevailed. When officials provide such a firebrand, are they not engaging in a conspiracy to break the law themselves?

One obvious reason they do this is to persuade the citizens that such groups are truly dangerous, to point up the "need" for increased security measures, and thereby to obtain more funds and support from a frightened public and a concerned legislature. It is like putting a puncture in an automobile tire to convince the motorist he needs to buy a better set of tires.

The agent provocateur runs against the grain of the whole American tradition; it is an importation of the worst of European totalitarianism. To use it to combat extremist groups is to fall victim to their own repulsive practices and to become the mirror-image of our enemies.

Against all sense and reason, it's nearly impossible to refrain from shouting at a foreigner with a weak understanding of English — as if it were a defect of hearing rather than of language.

*

One of the curses of "bigness" in society is that keeping the records straight soon becomes more important than keeping the customer satisfied; and whether one is in a hospital, restaurant or shop, the nurses, cashiers and clerks are much more concerned with their paperwork than with the human beings who make the work possible.

*

Sometimes the best, and only effective, way to kill an idea is to put it into practice.

We Cannot All Enjoy Good Life

TOOLING AROUND the Wisconsin village where I spend my summers, I was thinking this morning about John Maynard Keynes' "paradox of the aggregate." This paradox is obviously at work in every summer resort.

Keynes pointed out long ago that as nations prosper and their standard of living rises, what is "desirable" for the individual turns into something intolerable for the aggregate.

Suppose, for instance, we become rich enough to afford a high-rise apartment on the beautiful skyline of a big city like Chicago or San Francisco. If enough people are likewise affluent, they too will seek such a view — and so the whole skyline becomes cluttered with towers in which the tenants stare out of their windows into adjoining windows.

The automobile is another prime example of the "paradox of the aggregate." When autos are relatively scarce, it is a luxury and a convenience to own one; when the economy permits nearly everyone to drive his own auto, then the traffic jams and parking problems turn a convenience into a nuisance and nobody really enjoys the "luxury" anymore.

The finest resort places in the United States and abroad have been "ruined" in the last decade or so by the mounting affluence of families who take them over in the summer. Thus, the things we can afford lose their value simply because the numbers taking advantage of them cancel out the pleasure.

A few miles away from my house there is a lovely state park with facilities for camping. But so many people now possess elaborate camping equipment that tents are pitched cheek by jowl and the whole place resembles a rural slum. In fact, the density of population among these people who want to "get back to nature" is higher than in the city.

Nowhere is the paradox of the aggregate seen more clearly, and more depressingly, than in suburbia — where families have left the city to enjoy the amenities of "easier living" and found that so many others have done the same that many of the urban problems have been dragged along with them. A "crowded suburb" is as self-canceling as a convention of hermits.

In an impoverished society, no one can enjoy luxuries. In an affluent one, the very affluence destroys the exclusivity of pleasures and possessions. When everybody can afford to go skiing, the line at the lift gets longer, and everybody enjoys it less. The paradox of the aggregate is what turns prosperity into a sour joke.

It is a fitting retribution that the man who lives for himself dies without ever getting to know himself; for it is only in the free give-and-take of social commitment that we can ever realize our personalities.

*

If I were a workman, I'd be more inclined to trust an employer who inherited his wealth to treat me fairly than a self-made man who rose from the ranks, and would like to forget it as fast as possible; a real sense of social obligation usually takes a couple of generations to develop.

*

America is one of the few countries in the world where two men in their fifties will meet, after an absence of years, and talk at length about their college days as perhaps the most memorable of their lives; does this nostalgia not say something about the bleak quality of middle-aged life in our society?

"Practical" Pol's Ethics All His Own

ON THE VERY DAY that the United States Senate was to vote on the SST bill, Senator Margaret Chase Smith received a letter from President Nixon informing her that the Portsmouth Navy Yard, which had been scheduled for closing, was going to remain open.

The Johnson administration had cut off funds for the Yard, effective in 1974. The Nixon administration reversed this decision and notified Senator Smith on the day of the SST vote — hoping that, since the Yard employed many workers from her state, she might support the bill.

What makes the American electorate more confused and cynical than anything is the sharp contrast between our private and our public morality. It is hard to understand why what is "wrong" in a private transaction is "expedient" or "practical" or "good strategy" in a political context.

Privately considered, the shipyard restoration might be called "an extraordinary coincidence"; it would more likely be seen as a "bribe." The Senator from Maine was offered a considerable economic inducement for her area at the most crucial moment her vote was needed to support a bill. Can you imagine the furor if this inducement had come from an individual or a corporation, instead of from the government?

Now, do not construe this as a specific slur against the present administration. It has been true of all administrations of both parties. It is the way the game is played in Washington: You dangle bait before a Congressman in order to get his vote on something else you want. This is what "pork barrel" means — everybody gets a little something by trading off, and the taxpayer gets it in the neck.

If a Congressman represents his district, and a Senator represents his state, who in the legislative branch represents *all the people* of the country? If the prevailing ethos is "You give me this, and I'll give you that," then the new post office or highway or dam is costing us far more than we imagine in total expenditures for projects everywhere.

I have long advocated that defeated Presidential candidates be given permanent seats-at-large in the United States Senate, where they could (theoretically, at least) guard the interest of the nation as a whole, and speak out frankly without fear of alienating their constituency or losing re-election. Someone has to care most about the general welfare.

The "game" of politics is a matter of trade-offs and influence peddling, but these trade-offs are too often at the expense of the public and not in their long-term interest. As long as the two parties can keep us excited about being Democrats or Republicans, they hope we won't bother to notice they're both playing the same game.

Until the disinherited achieve a genuine vested interest in the goods of the community, no social system can be assured of stability without recourse to "official violence" from time to time — and in increasing severity, as greater expectations are rebuffed by greater force.

*

The only happy men, vocationally speaking, are those who would be willing to do their jobs for nothing if they could afford to.

The Best Argument for Democracy

No MATTER how smart you are, there is always at least one thing you are not clever enough to do. For instance, either you can tie a knot that you cannot untie, or you cannot.

The sentence above is a pure exercise in modal logic. If you can tie a knot that you cannot untie, then the untying is the thing you cannot do. If you cannot tie a knot that you can't untie, then the tying is the thing you cannot do. In either case, there is always one thing you cannot do.

But there is somebody else who can. Somebody who can either untie your knot or tie one that you cannot untie. No matter how smart you may be, there is always something of this sort that somebody else can do better than you.

This is much of what Mark Twain meant when he said: "There is somebody who is smarter than Anybody, and that is Everybody." Without knowing the term, he was expressing a basic principle in modal logic.

Yet, many institutions and organizations, at the top, do not recognize this principle in their operations. They may pay lip service to "cooperation" or "teamwork," but the authorities too often imagine that they alone are able to untie every knot that they tie.

No man, no matter how smart or skillful, can stand in one place and see the Eiffel Tower in the round. Sometimes one man, working alone, can solve a problem. Sometimes it takes two, working from opposite ends. Often, it calls for the multiple vision of a group, whose collective intelligence is greater than the sum of its parts.

Every permanently successful institution or organization needs to maintain a delicate and sophisticated equilibrium between the individual and the collectivity, between the Gen-

ius and the Group. The Genius may be able to tie the
greatest knot in the world, but it takes the Group to untie it.
Or the other way around. There is always something each of
them cannot do that the other can.

And, of course, this is the most forceful argument in the
world for the practice of democracy, from a logical and
not just a sentimental or moral standpoint. The leader, no
matter how brilliant or decent or well-meaning, is never clever
enough to both tie and untie the knots.

Sooner or later, if his authority is not balanced by the group,
he must fail either in the tying or the untying, and the whole
society will come apart in his hands. There is no more realistic
repudiation of dictatorship than this simple exercise in modal
logic.

*To those who have lived by routine all their lives, leisure is
far more menacing than work; it is frightening to have to plan
one's own time creatively after decades of having time laid out
on a rigid pattern; and many men die soon after retirement not
because they have lost their work but because they have never
found themselves.*

*

*The main difference between depression and prosperity is
that in the former you wonder where your next dollar is coming from, and in the latter you wonder where your last dollar
has gone to.*

*

*There is possibly less rectitude, honor and common decency
in the "business side" dealings of the entertainment industry
than in any other enterprise in society, including the rackets.*

How We Can Master Our Technology

FIRST we invent something. Then we put it into production. Then we buy it and use it. Then, and only then, do we begin to wonder if we haven't been too heedless and hasty.

It's happening now with the snowmobile, as the latest and most dramatic example of this process, but by no means the most important. Only now, after millions have been produced and bought, are we starting to recognize and control the possible damage they can do.

If we are going to become the masters of our technology, however, and not be dominated or overwhelmed by its consequences, it is imperative that we set up a new agency to work alongside the old United States Patent Office, to determine the "social utility" of new devices.

The Patent Office decides only whether a gadget or process will work and whether the applier is entitled to an exclusive right. The new agency should have the power to determine — after the broadest public hearings — whether any invention should be permitted to go into production before its social costs and consequences have been adequately worked out.

This would slow down our rate of technological progress — which is not a bad thing in itself — and would also give us time to prepare for the environmental impact of industrial changes.

While the snowmobile is both a boon and a blessing to winter-bound citizens in many areas, it is already a blight and a menace in these same areas. It came on the market unregulated, without strict registration or licensing, and has been dangerously abused by thousands of idiotic and unqualified operators.

No rules were set up, no trails laid out, no speed limits established. Snowmobiles have chased animals to exhaustion and death, have killed off plantings of seedlings in forests and have upset the whole ecology of wildlife and wilderness in places never before touched by human predators.

This, as I said, is only a minor example of our past indifference to the social consequences of new technology, but one we can see quite vividly. There are others, more obscure and more dangerous in the long run, which must not be allowed to proliferate before it is too late to take anything but the most drastic measures to curtail them.

We have treated our future with the utmost contempt, using our world as a place to plunder, to pollute, to create massive problems for short-term gain. And we have consistently failed to calculate the social costs of these "advances" — for which we are paying, not only through the pocketbook but through the nose, eyes and lungs as well.

"Urban redevelopment" in the past has largely meant relocating the poor where their presence doesn't embarrass the development of the prosperous.

*

Our housing and city planning programs are failures, among other reasons, because they neglected to take into account the ethnic differences of the groups they were dealing with, preferring to pretend they did not exist or would go away; but a social project, to be effective, must start with reality and work toward the ideal from that base.

Stop the Madness on Our Roads

THE HARD-HEADED, hard-hatted and hard-nosed "law and order" people would gain a lot more credibility in my eyes if they started with themselves and applied the same rigorous standards to their own conduct that they demand from muggers, rioters, dopesters and delinquents.

The most "criminal" and least punished element in this country is the reckless and drunken driver. We so-called good citizens kill more than 55,000 of our neighbors *each year* on the highways — more than the total number of Americans killed in Vietnam *in the last ten years.*

And more than half of these fatal accidents involve the abuse of liquor. Every public official knows this; every motorist knows this. Yet where is all the clamor for "stiffer" and "tougher" laws against our nation's biggest killer of all, the drunken driver?

I don't hear any, except on the part of the National Safety Council and the insurance companies. Most of us "decent" and "law-abiding" citizens don't want sterner highway laws, because we are vulnerable to them. We only want tougher laws against crimes we know *we* won't commit. And against the kind of people we know we aren't. This attitude is a travesty on what "law and order" ought to be, and where it ought to begin.

I hold in my hand — as Senator Joe McCarthy used to say — a clipping from the *New York Times,* reporting that the Oregon Republican state chairman pleaded guilty to charges of killing a sixty-two-year-old woman while driving under the influence of liquor, on the wrong side of the street and with his lights out.

This man was given a suspended sentence. And he is the

rule, not the exception. Everyone knows a dozen horror stories like this — of boozed-up kids racing through a red light and killing four people in another car, and getting at the most thirty days for "negligence."

Yet most solid and respectable Americans oppose stiffer laws against inept or intoxicated drivers. Most states don't permit "Breathalyzer" tests to scientifically determine the degree of sobriety of a driver picked up by the police. Most citizens will resort to any lie, bribe, fraud or influence to avoid losing their driver's license. It is all considered "part of the game" — the most murderous game played in this country by the most players, inflicting the greatest loss of life.

All the muggers, rioters, dopesters and delinquents put together don't do as much damage as we do, or defy justice and decency more successfully. When we start a genuine and meaningful crackdown on the homicidal, alcoholic driver, I will start to believe in law and order.

The only excuse for work (apart from its productive value) is that it must be therapeutic for the individual worker; that is, it must provide an outlet for feelings unsatisfied in other areas of life, and charge up the psychic battery, rather than running it down; using this crucial standard, how many jobs in modern society fulfill this basic need?

*

The penalty for always trusting others may be occasional betrayal, but the penalty for never trusting others is certain decay; it is far better to lose something we have than something we are.

Pro Sport Is Mercenary Combat

"PROFESSIONAL SPORTS" don't interest me, because I think that the phrase is a contradiction in terms. An activity ceases to be a sport the moment it becomes professional.

Some months ago, I noted big black headlines on the sports pages, announcing the trading of a star football player from one team to another. The fans were shocked, but the coach said simply, "It's a cruel, hard business. But I have a job to do and I can't let sentiment enter into it."

It's a cruel, hard business. So is every professional sport — baseball and basketball and hockey and golf and tennis. It's mean and mercenary and basically dehumanized — when the whole idea of "sport" should be its humanity.

Recreation was devised so that men could find release from the grim business of making a living; so that they could glory in winning a contest *for its own sake.* The Olympic heroes of ancient Greece were crowned with laurel and given the highest honors of the state because they showed what men could do with no incentive but victory.

Take sentiment out of sports and you take away their reason for existence. Remove sentiment and you have cut the loyalty that clings to a losing team; and little is left but to raise the money that can buy a winning team.

It is good and necessary that men should work for a living. It is a monstrous perversion that men should play for a living. The whole purpose of play is to escape to a realm beyond necessity, to a glorious never-never land, where the skillful and the fleet and the courageous can find a happy ending that is too often denied them in the cold marketplace.

In true sports, the contestants are ranged against each other. In professional sports, they are all ranged against the public.

The ultimate object is to attract as many customers as possible. They are merchandisers and promoters and box-office accountants. And the basic loyalty is not to the city, the uniform, the team — even to the game — but to the contract. Their lawyers compete as ferociously as their coaches do.

Let us not pretend that what we have here is "sport." What we have is business, transferred from the counter to the stadium, with a deadly seriousness that has nothing to do with the pleasure men are supposed to take in their bodily prowess. This is not to say the players do not enjoy playing, or the spectators do not enjoy watching; but their enjoyment has lost the innocence it has for children — which means it has lost precisely the healing and redeeming quality that makes it good.

As the coach said, "It's a cruel, hard business." Sport began as a substitute for war, as a cleansing agent for the spirit of aggressiveness; it has turned into combat between mercenaries with a job to do.

If the "flying saucers" are indeed visitors from other worlds in our galaxy — and this cannot be ruled out — then possibly such visits have been taking place surreptitiously for thousands of years; which would explain our whole mythology of "elves" and "brownies" and "the little people" as rooted in some extraterrestrial reality rather than mere fanciful folklore or figments of the unconscious mind.

*

The main discomfort in being a middle-of-the-roader is that you get sideswiped by partisans going in both directions.

"What's So Special About a Tree?"

THE EFFICIENCY of your air-conditioner is best measured in BTUs — the British Thermal Unit that indicates the amount of heat required to raise the temperature of one pound of water one degree.

The cooling capacity of the average home air-conditioner runs from 5000 to 7000 BTUs. Even the larger window units, on a separate circuit, generally give out no more than 10,000 to 14,000 BTUs.

Now look at a large, well-watered tree. The *daily evaporation* from this single tree can produce the effect of *more than a million BTUs*.

Thus, the "air-cooling" effect of one tree is equal to a hundred or more air-conditioners, if the tree gets an adequate amount of rain. Multiply this by thousands and millions of trees, and you begin to understand the importance of preserving our forests, and tree life everywhere.

It is not just a sentimental, or aesthetic, or "nature-loving" attitude that impels ecologists to take such a militant stand for preserving and enhancing our national woodlands system. It is the most practical and sensible attitude one can take.

All that most people know is that a tree is pretty to look at and gives shade and wears a nest of robins in its hair. But it also has vast implications that dear old Joyce Kilmer never dreamed of.

The more we learn about the great chain of life on this planet — and we have learned more in the last two decades than in the last twenty centuries — the more we are forced to recognize that the simple everyday things we have always taken for granted are part of a web of immense complexity and sophistication.

Governor Ronald Reagan's famous dictum of a few years ago, "What's so special about a tree? You've seen one, you've seen them all," reflects an ignorance and indifference we can no longer afford to tolerate. If we pulled out air-conditioners as ruthlessly as we bulldoze trees, he and a few million other Californians would rise up in arms at once.

As Ray Hoague, the United States Soil Conservation Service man up in my neck of the woods, put it not long ago, most of us are familiar with the common uses of trees in manufacturing and production. But we forget their most important uses — protecting the soil from raindrop impact, stabilizing the water tables, lowering the peak flows and their ability to absorb polluted air and emit air richer in oxygen.

"Trees are essential to life on our planet," Hoague warns. "They have much to do with the moderation of temperature, noise, wind and water." And, of course, their cooling effect is what brings millions of visitors to the North Woods every summer. Without air-conditioners.

Well before this century is up, it is my semi-educated guess, the problem of obtaining sufficient quantities of pure water will overshadow all other technical problems throughout the entire world.

*

To imagine that there is a "political solution" to our social problems is the romantic delusion of the self-styled "realist"; every political solution creates its own problems, ad infinitum, and only when we advance beyond the realm of the political to the human and the personal is there a chance of breaking out of self-perpetuating systems whose means inevitably turn into ends.

Welfare System Hurts All

WHEN THE ORDINARY CITIZEN talks about "welfare payments," he is customarily thinking about the slum population in a big city, mostly black, and "unwilling" to work. This is the stereotype of the welfare client in the minds of those who know little and care less about the poverty problem in the United States.

Yet, last winter, Westchester County in New York State, regarded as one of the wealthiest and most exclusive areas in the nation, was given a proposed budget for 1970 of $193 million — of which more than half was earmarked for welfare spending.

Westchester County doesn't fit any of the stereotypes: it has no big cities, no urban slums, no considerable crime or racial unrest and a black population of less than 8 per cent. But it apparently needs more than $95 million for welfare spending this year.

Indeed, welfare costs in this affluent suburban area accounted for the largest increase in county expenditures in 1970, with "relief" payments alone projected at more than $87 million.

Out of a total population of 900,000, only 4 per cent receive welfare. Yet this 4 per cent, plus the administration of the program, will account for the largest single expenditure of the county budget.

And this is one of the main reasons that economists of both left and right are agreeing more and more that the whole present welfare setup must be junked and replaced with some kind of direct payments to the needy — either in terms of a "guaranteed annual income" or a "negative income tax" or some combination of the two.

126   FOR THE TIME BEING

It is an ignorant and mean-spirited libel that most people on welfare are equipped to work but don't care to do so. Every careful study made of welfare recipients has shown beyond doubt that more than 90 per cent of them are unable to obtain employment — they are too young, too old, too sick, too blind or crippled, too unschooled and unskilled for even the manual jobs that are no longer in large supply.

The present welfare system is not only expensive, wasteful, cumbersome and unworkable on the practical level; it is even worse on the social and psychological levels, where it acts only to demoralize the spirit, humiliate the pride and alienate the personality from any true participation in our communal life.

When one of our nation's most prosperous suburban regions can find itself hip-deep in budgetary quicksand because of its crushing relief load, then we must recognize that poverty is not just a city problem, a black problem, or a "lazy" problem — it is a human problem that will not go away until we begin to treat it humanly.

Nearly thirty years ago, Paul Valéry, the French writer, accurately defined the political malaise when he observed: "Politics is the art of preventing people from taking part in affairs which properly concern them."

*

If we insist upon putting certain groups of citizens into a position where they have nothing to lose by upsetting the system, we have provided them with a source of power — desperation — that they never could have obtained by themselves.

"*Let Them Eat Promises*"

IF YOU think you know something about poverty in the United States — or if you deny its prevalence — let me recommend one of the best books of contemporary reporting I have read in a long time: *Let Them Eat Promises*, by Nick Kotz, the Pulitzer Prize-winning Washington correspondent for the Des Moines *Register*.

It is a frightening book, though not a sensational one. Kotz is a bear on facts. He tracks down statistics to their ultimate lair, and discloses the raw human flesh behind the tables and charts. This is not a book on economics, or politics, or even sociology; it is a trail-breaking expedition right into the heart of starvation country.

The United States has officially recognized that about 16 million Americans are chronically hungry. President Nixon, not widely regarded as a bleeding heart, has said, "Something like the very honor of American democracy is at issue," in the problem of widespread poverty. Yet, while everyone deplores the situation, no one does much about it.

Why? The average American is ignorant or callous. Either he fails to realize the extent of poverty in the most affluent nation in the world, or he dismisses it with the ugly defamation that the poor are responsible for their poverty.

The average politician is even worse. He knows the problem, but he uses it for his own ends — to flatter the prejudices of his constituents, to enlarge his bureaucratic domain, to trade off votes and influence, to maintain the status quo even at the cost of riots and rebellion in the near future.

While the nation as a whole has got richer in the last twenty years — both absolutely and relatively — the gap has widened between the affluent and the poor. More people are better off than two decades ago; but the one-fifth who have not been able to find their way into the mainstream of industry are relatively worse off than before.

And, as advancing technology further trims away the need for unskilled and unschooled labor, these people face a bleak future. They are not wanted on the land, they are not needed in the factories, they are unequipped to enter the offices and stores and service businesses. Fifty thousand of their children die unnecessarily every year.

To tolerate this situation, to ignore it, to use it for political purposes, is to provide ammunition to the most militant critics of our system. The only effective way to disarm them is to prove, swiftly and conclusively, that we are willing to spend as much on fighting the crime of poverty in a rich society as we are willing to spend on fighting the crime that is in large part generated by these inequities.

It is hard for someone else to injure us unless we have first placed the weapon in his hand; most ill-treated people are in some manner accessories before the fact.

*

Most of the people who are against stricter gun controls are great proponents of "law and order" and supporters of the police force — yet every urban police force is in favor of stricter gun controls as the most effective way to combat armed crime.

*

A "mob" is simply a "group of aroused citizens" we have not yet seen fit to join.

The Real Threat to United States Justice

ALTHOUGH American newspapers do otherwise, I follow the practice of the British press and refrain from commenting on trials while they are in progress.

During the long trial of the "Chicago Seven," I was shocked, dismayed, disgusted and silent. Now that the tragic farce has ended, and we can look back upon it with a little perspective, several distinctive features seem to emerge.

First, it was not a legal trial so much as a political action. There obviously was no "conspiracy" — as the jury correctly decided — and all the defendants had in common was a distaste for the system.

Second, while the conduct of the defendants was outrageous, the conduct of the judge and prosecutor was inexcusable, both during and after the trial.

Third, the whole proceedings served no useful purpose — as former Attorney General Clark predicted — except to make the government look bad and to create enormous publicity for the most extreme and exhibitionistic elements among the defendants.

Fourth, and most important, it helped undermine the American system of jurisprudence far more than it clarified any issues at stake.

To me, the most melancholy aspect of the trial was the public reaction. Although we prattle about "freedom" and "democracy" more loudly and constantly than any other people in the world, we have a sadly limited idea of what these terms genuinely consist in.

We imagine that you have to like or approve of defendants in order to give them their fullest judicial and constitutional privileges. We wrongly assume that anyone who protests that these defendants were badly and unfairly treated by the government is in favor of what the defendants stood for, or condones the obnoxious way they behaved.

We seem incapable of separating form from substance; of saying, "We don't agree with these people in any way, and that is exactly the reason we must bend over backward to see that their rights are respected." This is a statement of the democratic doctrine; anything less is rhetoric, hypocrisy, ignorance, bigotry or malice.

I was delighted, subsequently, that all five active judges of the Federal Appeals Court unanimously reversed Judge Julius Hoffman's denial of bail to the defendants. His spite and partiality were nowhere more revealed than in this closing gesture of illegal vindictiveness — and exceeded only by the prosecutor's ugly attack upon the alleged "homosexual" proclivities of most of the defendants. These post-trial exhibits revealed, more eloquently than any comment I could have made during the trial, exactly where the threat to our system of justice really lies.

In any rational society, people who toss beer cans on public roads and parkways would be treated more severely than those who take pot privately; but in our system, the beer-tossers flourish unmolested while the pot-takers are punished far beyond the seriousness of their offense.

✱

The most shameful blot on the whole American governmental system remains the appointment, or seating, of judges on a political basis; a man involved in politics should be by that very reason ineligible for the bench, or the whole independent judicial process is tainted.

Regulators Are Cozy Fellows

WHEN A PRIVATE COMPANY hires a key management man in a complex and competitive industry, it often makes the man promise not to take a similar job in another company for two or three years after he has left.

This is to keep him from using his special knowledge and competence (not to mention trade secrets) for the benefit of a rival firm. It is a promise that ought to be elicited even more from key government officials than from private management.

One of the most distressing things that has happened in our society is the way in which "regulatory" agencies of government have tended to snuggle up to the very groups and interests they are supposed to watch.

Too many of the men appointed to such agencies take on the coloration of the industry they are obligated to scrutinize. Instead of being the guardians of the public interest, they turn into the willing tools of a special segment, and the laws are not enforced, or are enforced in a prejudiced and self-serving way.

Then, after a couple of years of playing footsie, these officials leave to take high-paying jobs in the very areas they were supposed to regulate. Some 2000 military and naval officers have been hired as expensive "consultants" by companies dealing in defense contracts.

Obviously, no government official above a certain level should be permitted to leave public service and enter the employ of a company or industry where his inside knowledge or influence would give it an unfair competitive edge. If he knows he can do this, he will be tempted to cuddle up to a company or industry he is supposed to be objective about.

Much of the "consumer revolt" we read about these days has been induced by the growing public realization that regulatory agencies are not regulating properly, that bureaus are not nearly as responsive to the needs of citizens as they are tender toward the sensibilities of the private interests they handle.

Cynicism is the most dangerous enemy of a democracy. The people will put up with a great deal so long as they feel that in the long run they will get a fair shake from their representatives in government. But when the feeling becomes widespread that these representatives talk one way and act another — then the constitutional fabric of society begins to dissolve faster than any radical action alone could account for.

Illegal and devious strikes by such decent and patient people as mailmen and airport controllers are fomented not by "agitators" but by the disillusioning recognition that government will ignore their legitimate needs as long as it is possible to do so, and until they put on the kind of pressure it should not be necessary to exercise.

It's almost unbelievable that one out of every three "housing starts" in 1970 was a mobile home; through greed and stubbornness, the housing industry is changing the whole demographic structure of the nation, and for the worse.

*

The singular, and perhaps unique, situation in which our society finds itself today is having plenty of room at the top — where talented managers are desperately needed — but no room at the bottom, where unschooled, unskilled and untrained people can no longer be utilized.

The Pagan Rites of Manufacturing

THE SILLIEST merchandising and manufacturing ritual in American society is the "annual model" of the automobile. It has been going on its own impetus for a long time, but the profits are beginning to diminish in proportion to the costs.

Why should a company put out a "new" car every year, especially when there are only minor changes in most years? And why invest so many millions in making new parts for the sake of newness and salesmanship and competition based on slogans more than on substance?

A new model ought to be made when some genuine and appreciable improvement calls for it. Then there would be a real competitive edge, and customers would be buying vehicles rather than erotic or aggressive fantasies, or status symbols that give little real status.

The frenetic annual race among the auto makers does nobody any lasting good. It increases expenses for the companies, and prices for the buyers, and the relative position is rarely changed. Perhaps more cars are sold than would be under a two-year change, but these cars can't be serviced satisfactorily, anyway, and the net result is disillusion if not disgust.

One of the reasons that foreign cars have done so well in the United States — beyond their economy and maneuverability — is their unwillingness (and no doubt their financial inability) to play this annual-model game. The Volkswagen, indeed, has one of the highest resale values on the market precisely because the old models are not made obsolete every year or so.

Our society is slowly, but perceptibly, changing from a "more and more" to an "enough already" kind of thinking.

We are becoming satiated with novelty for its own sake, and are ceasing to equate mere size and newness with value and quality. As the consumer becomes more sophisticated (and there can be no doubt that he has made a quantum-jump in sophistication in the last decade), he becomes increasingly suspicious of merchandising techniques that do not reflect substantial improvements in the basic product itself.

Manufacturers, like nations in an arms race, are caught up in custom and tradition, and often themselves become the victims of practices they might like to abandon but are afraid to be the first to jettison. The proliferation of products, like the escalation of weapons, then becomes an end in itself, without any rational relationship to the needs of the people — or even to the best interests of the competitors.

A suburb is that self-delusive community where a white-collar homeowner calls in a blue-collar "workman" who earns more than he does.

*

A teacher who displays favoritism must be prepared not only for the dislike of the less-favored pupils, but also for the contempt of the favored, who secretly know they don't deserve it.

*

Just as illness has the power to spread, while health doesn't, so on the psychological level, pessimism seems contagious, while optimism remains limited. (Likewise, "mob spirit" has never prompted any group to rush across town to perform a good deed.)

"Outside Agitator" Hogwash

IT HAS LONG PUZZLED ME why authorities seem to feel that a bad situation can be made to look better by blaming it on "outside agitators." What does it really matter where the agitation comes from?

In most cases, of course, the allegation isn't true. When a demonstration erupts, or a riot explodes, it's usually because the pressure has burst from the inside, and no safety valve has been provided.

Agitators can agitate successfully only when the community supplies no realistic alternatives. Communists have been agitating in the United States for 50 years, and have not succeeded in recruiting as much as one per cent of the population into party ranks.

Indeed, one of the great testimonials to the loyalty and basic trust of the American Negro was the fact that he — who might have been thought to have the least to lose and the most to gain — never succumbed to communist enticements even during the darkest days of the Depression. Here was a pure "proletariat," and it did not respond.

It was not until the Negro realized that America's promises outran its performance that he changed his name to black, and took on an air of militancy. And, even here, the Marxist influence is negligible.

When the blacks, or the students, or any other group, begin to engage in civil disobedience, the first reaction of the authorities is to blame those "outside agitators." The implication being that without such inflammatory aliens, the natives would be happy and passive.

Obviously, that is a lot of hogwash. If strangers can come into a community and incite the residents to social action, all this means is that the fuse was there waiting to be lit. In fact, it is a bigger insult to the authorities that outsiders have a more decisive influence on their people than they do.

If I were a mayor or a governor, I would be ashamed to admit that a few bedraggled orators were able to lead my constituency into militant opposition; it would imply that I had done a rotten job of tending to their needs, responding to their complaints and assuring their rights.

A good and decent administration would inoculate its people against such agitators — not by banning or jailing them but by making sure that grievances are promptly and justly taken care of, that lines of communication are open, that the instruments of law are equally available to all segments, not used by one group against the other. When peaceful alternatives are available, nobody but a nut will listen to the voices of violence.

Nobody ever imagines that he is, by double-parking and forcing a stream of traffic to go around him, in any way contributing to the disintegration of society; and yet it is precisely in such tiny ways that the fabric of the community is torn asunder, with each person blaming some vast abstraction called "They," and defending his mild transgression as merely a necessary part of "the struggle to survive."

*

The worst evil of our age is not the passion, violence or conflict of opinion, but public pococurantism — *the indifference to social problems until they break out in virulent form and can no longer be contained by laws, neglect and a conspiracy of silence.*

The Will's Missing, Not the Way

THE CONVENTIONAL WISDOM of our time keeps pointing to our space program as an example of what we *can* do, contrasting it with our social policies, as an example of what we *can't* do.

But conventional wisdom, as usual, is wrong; we could do far more on earth than in space, if we wanted to and decided to. It is the will that is missing, not the way.

Don't write this off as the wishful thinking of some fuzzy-minded idealist. It was several years ago, in fact, that the manager of the RCA Systems Development Center told a conference of marketing men that attacking our social problems was much more important than the nation's space program — and that we already had the systems-engineering capabilities to do it with.

The same methodology used in aerospace systems, he pointed out, can be used to overcome the social ills of "poverty, rotting cities, the need to conserve natural resources, improve health and education." But he wasn't very hopeful that this was going to happen for a long time.

We apply our scientific knowledge mostly toward the things that pay in the short run — to specific, objective, material and quantified goals. Our incentive system is focused almost exclusively on converting knowledge into profit.

Yet the unmet social needs of the nation — and, even more, of the world — represent a tremendous loss, not merely in unfulfilled productivity, but in paying for random remedies and symptomatic treatment that never get to the root of the ailment. What does it cost us for poor educational policies, for ineffective welfare programs, for indigent medical care and all the rest of these patchwork palliatives?

As the man said, "Our problems are closing in on us. The time for improvisation is past." Obviously, we need what he recommended: a systematic, planned, industrial-academic-government approach to social therapy as a whole. Treating the parts separately results only in conflict, confusion, contradiction and continuing futility.

If you're puzzled about the kind of methodology used in aerospace systems, let me recommend a good new book for the layman, *The Systems Approach* by C. West Churchman (Delta Paperback, $2.25), which explains in nontechnical terms how this revolution in approach and planning can be efficiently applied to social problems.

This is not to say that science can do it: first of all, the public must recognize the gravity of the situation and the incapability of any political doctrine to cope with our ills. When we want to build as sound a society as we do a spaceship, our technology is able to lead us. Only, first, we must be willing to lead it, and not be led.

Progress is wonderful — before the mechanical age, people used to run into debt; now they ride around in it.

*

Successful people should always pursue one hobby they don't do well at — simply to remind themselves that ability in one kind of endeavor does not guarantee infallibility in other areas of thought or action.

*

Technology was devised in order to meet the demands of people; now people are manipulated in order to meet the demands of technology.

President Hoist on His Perquisites

ONE OF THE BOOKS I have been reading lately is George Reedy's *The Twilight of the Presidency*, by the man who served briefly and bitterly as President Johnson's press secretary. What emerges from this book is the absolute conviction that we have to "ventilate" the White House. We need to let in more air and light and the hubbub of public controversy.

Despite more facts at his finger tips than any other man in the world, the President — whoever he may be — remains one of the most insulated men in the world. He is protected by his advisers, toadied to by his sycophants, pampered by his staff and shut off from the fresh breezes of public sentiment.

This has always been true. President Garfield, nearly a century ago, remarked that "The President is the last person in the world to know what the people really want and think." Since then, the White House has become even more remote from everyday life, as experts multiply, administrative bureaus flourish and the whole panoply of power armors the Chief Executive against the rude winds of popular feeling.

How otherwise could so shrewd a politician as Lyndon Johnson have so misjudged the mood of the nation that a hastily organized campaign of college kids succeeded in dislodging him from office? How else could so facile a compromiser as Richard Nixon make two successive mistakes in selecting nominees for the Supreme Court?

Presidents are told what they would like to hear. Their whims are indulged, their immaturities catered to, their circle is confined to ego-massagers, sweet-talkers, and likeminded men. It becomes easy to believe that this select, selfserving group represents "the country," and understands the temper of the times.

It is a para-political problem, going beyond parties and issues. It is a matter of getting the President out of his gilded cage and into the mainstream of society. To confer upon him such immense power, without at the same time seeing to it that he is responsive to all the complex and conflicting needs of society, is to erect a kind of modern monarchy as myopic as the one we overthrew.

It should not be so necessary for the Court to rebuke, or the Congress to revoke, what the White House proposes. It is not the power of the Presidency that corrupts, so much as the pride, the privileges, the perquisites of office that seal off a man from the ultimate reality of his age.

It's been a long, long time since I met a person who didn't know what this country needs.

*

Society, and the law, should differentiate between crimes where there are victims, and crimes without victims; in the latter cases, such as marijuana-smoking, there should be different procedures and punishments (if any) from crimes where there are victims.

*

There is only one respect (apart from speed) in which the computer is superior to the human being operating it, and that is its ability to monitor its own performance and know when it is behaving defectively.

What's Wrong with Police

WHENEVER a mayor or a police chief in a big city is confronted with evidence of connivance or corruption in the police force, he brings out his familiar barrel of apples.

"There's always bound to be a few rotten apples in any barrel," he pronounces, with an air of profound philosophic discovery. This is supposed to excuse, if not refute, the ugly charges. But it misses the point.

What if the barrel itself is rotten, so that even when you throw good apples into it, they sooner or later become contaminated? It is not the isolated individual cases of crookedness on a police force that bother anybody — it is the feeling that corruption may be built into the very structure of the organization.

Temptation being as great and omnipresent as it is for these lowly paid and sorely tried men, there will always be a certain number who succumb to it; this is understandable, and statistically acceptable. It is only when crookedness is sewn into the very fabric of the police organization that the public has a reason, and a right, to worry.

And, in most big cities, the plain fact is that there are not enough internal or external checks on the integrity of the force.

Part of this is due to the alliance between politics and the police, when privileges or promotions can be granted or withheld by powerful figures in the party councils. But even when this is not true — as in New York City under Mayor Lindsay — there still remains a stubborn obstacle to effective policing of the police.

This obstacle is the relative autonomy of the force itself. Although nominally subordinate to the mayor and the city government, the police often operate as independently as the Pentagon — and are as resistant to direction or reform from the outside.

The basic loyalty of the police is to the organization itself. Police will not "snitch" on one another. If they won't get in on the graft personally, they maintain a discreet silence about it. Their "internal security" tends to be far more self-protective than self-regulatory. They resent public intrusion, and look upon their conflict with lawbreakers as a private matter.

Such a police force is really a legalized gang, with its "code of honor" turned wholly inward. In such a setting, good men quickly become either corrupted or cynical. The problem for the new urban society is not so much getting rid of the few rotten apples as changing the shape of the container they are tossed into — and making it, for one thing, more transparent to public scrutiny.

Obviously, our whole penological system is a failure, either as deterrence or as rehabilitation: the rate of "repeaters" is distressingly high, perhaps increasing, and as Judge Thomas McMillen remarks, "It has been said that a youthful offender has a better chance for rehabilitation if he is not caught."

*

Unions began, necessarily enough, to protect the workingman from abuses; but now, in too many cases, both the producer and the public have too little protection from the abuses of the workingman. (A classic example of the way in which the remedy for one set of evils results in the opposite set.)

Better When It Wasn't So Good

WE SPEAK glibly of "the marvels of transportation" in this modern age, but I think a good case can be made out that the average traveler is *worse* off than he was thirty years ago, not better.

The average traveler doesn't fly from New York to Los Angeles, and it is the long cross-country trip that has been enormously shortened by jet flight. The average traveler goes from 300 to 500 miles, and here he finds the airplane a dubious advantage over other forms of locomotion.

One day this summer I had to fly from Green Bay, Wisconsin, to Pellston, Michigan, a distance of less than 200 miles almost directly across Lake Michigan. I won't bore you with the grisly details, but suffice to say I could have flown from Green Bay to Paris in less time — actually.

On second thought, I *will* bore you with the grisly details. My plane let me off in Grand Rapids, for a two-hour wait. Another plane put me down in Traverse City, for an hour's wait. I arrived at the Pellston airport later than if I had taken a nonstop jet to Chicago and transferred to another of the same going to Paris. And it was even longer getting back — a four-hour wait in the Grand Rapids airport.

Airplanes do not, and perhaps cannot, fill the place left by the disappearing railroad. Smaller cities and towns are ill served by them; and so, more and more people in such communities are driving their cars hundreds of miles and clogging up the highways to no one's advantage.

Some colleges I have visited are almost totally cut off from public transportation, even though railroad tracks run right through the towns. Planes don't land there, bus schedules are sparse and everybody has to have a car to get home for the holidays. In these many places, the air age has *isolated* people far more than bringing them closer.

Decades ago, such historians of technology as Lewis Mumford deplored and decried the massive government subsidies to highways and air carriers, predicting correctly that neither the auto nor the airplane could provide adequate substitution for the declining railroads. But nobody listened, and we have no national transportation policy that makes any sense for now or the future.

Rail transit, both within and between cities, is the most sensible, economic, efficient and comfortable way to travel. True "progress" should consist of supplementing one advantage with another — not of abandoning tracks for wings and then learning painfully that it doesn't pay to land a plane in Podunk, after the depot is dismantled.

To be concerned about "environmental quality" without being equally exercised about world population growth is like trying to put out a fire with one hand while squirting kerosene on it with the other.

*

There's plenty of space in the United States, but we don't utilize it sensibly; 100 million people, about half the population, are concentrated in 200 urban areas which would fit neatly into Lake Michigan.

*

Only the poor can be extravagant; the rich can be merely ostentatious.

The More Papers, the Better

A READER in Delaware wants to know why I haven't commented on the "underground press" that is springing up in cities all over the United States. The reason is simple: I haven't seen enough of it to form an opinion that would have any value.

But, as a generalization, I welcome the addition of any press, over or under ground, whether or not it happens to coincide with my views. In fact, I get more out of reading things that jolt my own point of view. They force me to re-examine my preconceptions and sharpen or refine my own defense of what I believe.

One of the problems with a democratic society that becomes so highly technocratic as ours is that only those with considerable funds can afford to own a newspaper, a radio station or a TV channel. Minority voices tend to be heard less and less, except through the charity or good will of those who control the mass media.

The emergence of an underground press is a reaction against this situation. It is, on the whole, a healthy reaction, even though some of the underground papers themselves (at least the ones I have seen) are scarcely any more reliable than the organs they protest against. But everyone has a right to be partial — as long as that partiality is openly expressed as such, and not disguised as "fact."

There is an odd irony involved in the rise of the underground press. While "Middle America" complains that the mass media are too sympathetic in delineating the activities of leftish and protest groups, the left itself complains that the mass media suppress or distort such events to the detriment of the protesters.

The conventional press today is caught between the hammer and the anvil; the twist of the irony being that, in my opinion, it is performing the best job it has ever done in my thirty years of newspaper experience. I happen to think that papers are far fairer, more balanced and more concerned with depth-reporting than when I started in the business.

Yet the attacks on them have never been greater, from all sides. This is not because they have become worse (they are, in fact, much better), but because public needs and expectations have risen so much in the last thirty years. They have improved absolutely, but not relatively in ratio to our expanded education, awareness and sophistication.

Every avenue must be kept open for every source of expression and communication — especially the ones we may happen to disagree with. If the overground press does not protect the rights of the underground as zealously as it defends its own, both will eventually perish at the hands of the twin paranoids of extreme right and left.

There are no "native" Americans, in strictly scientific terms; even the Eskimos and Indians emigrated to this continent from Asia, as evidenced by the fact that no humanoid prehistoric skeletons have ever been found in North or South America.

*

My favorite sensible answer to a stupid question was given to a reporter visiting a nudist camp who asked one of the campers, "How did you get to be a nudist?" and the camper replied, "I was born that way."

Why Waste Our Time on Shoes?

INTERNATIONAL TRADE is one of the dullest subjects it is possible to write about — unless the reader happens to make his living in an industry that is threatened by foreign competition.

The question of free trade versus protectionism is an old and badly scarred debate in the United States. Theoretically, the free traders have the best of it; but practically, the protectionists have usually won.

If we are genuinely a capitalistic country, and believe in free competition, then we must admit that other countries have the right to ship goods here and sell them at the lowest possible price. We can't be in favor of competition just for our own country.

Where the rub comes is that the cost of labor in many other nations is far lower than in ours. A textile worker in Japan, for instance, gets less than $100 a month, and an American producer can't compete with these low labor costs when his own employees make many times more.

This is the argument of protectionism. We have to keep the countries that pay "coolie wages" from undercutting our own high standard of living. It makes sense, as far as it goes, but this argument doesn't go far enough, as almost all economists agree.

The fact of the matter is that a nation like the United States should not be wasting its energy and manpower in the production of low-efficiency goods like textiles, or shoes, or such commodities. We are a high-efficiency society, and should devote our industrial efforts to producing the goods we can best produce at the fastest rate for the lowest cost.

Low-efficiency societies should be allowed to take over the production of goods that best suit their economy and fit their wage scale. If we want to see capitalism and free competition spread over the world, we cannot insist that other countries be penalized for sending their goods over here and selling them at the cheapest price they can.

To "protect" certain industries against foreign competition is a form of state socialism, no matter what else it may be called. It is a subsidy to inefficiency, because we should not be wasting our resources in turning out goods that we can buy cheaper elsewhere. Both politically and economically, protectionism is a slap in the face to world unity and to our professed creed of free competition.

It does not even make good sense to our short-term self-interest, for if other countries are limited in selling their goods here, they will not have the funds to buy our commodities, and world trade will shrink perilously. Our rejection of an open market would only confirm the communists' accusation that we manipulate capitalism for our own ends.

Industrial civilization makes things accessible to those who have no idea of the labor, thought and imagination that have gone into the making of those things, and thus tend to take them for granted; while in a primitive society, the value of products is accurately known and appreciated by all — which unifies the society in mutual respect.

*

Most shipwrecks occur near the shore, and most airplane crashes near take-off or landing; likewise, any venturesome enterprise is in greatest danger of failing not only at the start, but nearing its goal.

Why Jail System Fails Us

OF ALL THE TENS of millions of Americans who are perturbed about the breakdown of "law and order" in the United States, how many know anything or care anything about our prison system? Not one per cent at the most.

How many know or care that it is the most expensive, most futile and most self-defeating system we could employ, or that more than 70 per cent of the men we send to jail each year are repeaters?

The public's ignorant prescription for "law and order" is harsher laws and stiffer jail sentences, when every modern penologist knows that putting a man in prison for a long time makes him worse and does not deter others. And the longer we keep him out of circulation, the more we infect him with hatred of society when he comes back again.

Bernard Shaw said a half-century ago that nothing a criminal does is as unjust as what society does to criminals, and conditions have not changed since he said that. But even if the moral argument falls on deaf ears, the practical argument is irrefutable — our system of punishment doesn't work.

I would not be surprised if the next round of revolts moved from the college campuses to the nation's prisons. They are overdue for a thorough cleaning-out, and authorities will not reform them until they are forced to — if not by public opinion, then by a show of violence.

This should not be necessary. Even the cautious and conservative American Bar Association last year endorsed a drastic reduction in criminal sentences, with five years the limit, except for the most serious crimes. If a man is not rehabilitated in that time, keeping him in jail longer is a cruel and stupid act of vengeance.

There are no real opportunities for a man to change in jail. In most states, the prisons are politically run. The staff is ill-trained and inadequate. Psychiatric and medical care are minimal. The "vocational" programs are a sour joke. And ex-convicts have little chance when they get out.

We are not "soft" on criminals as a class. We are soft on those with money, connections, shrewd lawyers and political influence. But we are unconscionably hard on the poorest, the dumbest, the clumsiest and often the least culpable. So the aim of a lawbreaker is not to go straight, but to get big. Success is what buys him immunity.

England, with its low crime rate, metes out far shorter sentences than we do here. But punishment there is swift, fair and certain. Here, it is slow, discriminatory and dubious, depending on factors that have little to do with a man's guilt or innocence. As long as this remains true, our prisons are more a reproach to society than a rebuke to our criminals.

The most pressing need in America today is to transform our present political units into geo-economic entities, getting rid of our obsolescent "states" and "counties" and replacing them with units of self-government that have relevance to modern needs and conditions.

*

Those fatuous library boards and citizens' committees which are so fond of banning books for alleged indecency need to be reminded regularly that when Mark Twain's Huckleberry Finn *was published, the Committee of the Public Library of Concord, Massachusetts, banned it as "trash and suitable only for the slums."*

Helping More People to Starve

IN BOTH the Near and Far East, measles in children often prove fatal. With the advent of the newer vaccines, we are able to reduce the percentage of children who come down with the disease, and thus cut the death rate from this cause.

When we cut the death rate, we naturally reduce the high infant mortality rate in these areas, and thus increase the population where millions of people are already starving. The children won't die from measles, but from malnutrition.

Everywhere in the world, modern medicine is performing this same dubious miracle — redeeming overpopulated areas from disease, only to have the people succumb to starvation because there are more of them. It is a nice moral question whether pestilence or famine should be their fate.

This is one of the great and pressing paradoxes of "progress." The longer that science increases the life span, the more people we keep alive, the more babies we save through vaccines and antibiotics — the graver becomes the food situation in these underdeveloped areas, and the higher the possibility of mass starvation on a scale unknown in the past.

There is another pathetic paradox involved in this same situation. As long as the standard of living remains low, the birthrate remains high; it is only when the stardard of living goes up that the number of children per family goes down.

So that the less people have to eat, the more they breed, and then the even less they have to eat. And the more the people have to eat, the less they breed, so that they soon have enormous surpluses — so large in our case that the government will pay farmers not to produce certain crops, while two-thirds of the world goes to bed hungry every night.

Of course, this whole thing is not rational, is not sensible, is

not humane — it is like a fantasy invented by some black hu-
morist, or a satire beyond anything Swift could have imagined. Nor can we simply hand over our surplus food to
starving peoples — for this would threaten the "economic
balance" of world trade and upset the economies of some
countries.

So here we are, increasing the world's population through
science — and increasing it precisely where it should be de-
creased — while the mighty abstractions of "economics" and
"trade" and "government" prevent any rational disposition
of the world's food resources to those in most critical need of
it. Little wonder that young people all over the world find
us blind and paralyzed to the edge of insanity.

*As long as most people continue to value men by their ex-
ternal success or their fortune, no political or social system
can succeed in fully humanizing itself, no matter what ideology it professes.*

*

*How can two countries empathize with each other, when
in one most of the adults are starving, and in the other most of
the adults are reducing?*

*

*Man looks upon himself as the "conqueror" of the world.
But in actuality all animals — including us — are parasitic on
plants, for, using sun and earth, plants build sugar and starch,
which are the essential fuels for our vitality, and which we
cannot make for ourselves; and the brain of an Einstein is
dependent upon a blade of grain.*

But John Q. Just Doesn't Care

WHAT THE BULK of society really wants is for unpleasant people to go away and not bother anybody. "Unpleasant people" are the poor, the convicted, the mentally ill, the old and the troublesome young.

So-called poverty programs keep the poor just where they are, barely hanging on and discreetly out of sight. "Urban redevelopment" means putting the poor where out-of-town visitors can't see them.

Our jails and prisons are devoted to keeping unpleasant characters out of circulation as long as possible, providing minimum opportunities for their rehabilitation and then throwing them back into cells as fast as they get out and demonstrate their inability to break the law again successfully.

Our mental hospitals are grossly understaffed, relying on drugs to keep patients tranquil instead of positive therapy to make them well. We will spend millions for new buildings to put these patients in, but we won't pay enough for doctors, nurses and orderlies to establish a system in which hope, and not despair, is the chief climate.

Our old people are simply a drag. Many have no place to live, no income to live on, and little to live for. We scarcely even pretend to be concerned about this social problem, embarrassing though it is.

The troublesome young are told to cut their hair, brush their teeth, keep going to school (no matter how rotten school may be) and face the delightful prospect of being drafted at eighteen.

If they get into real trouble with the law, they are either put on probation and allowed to keep doing the same things until the boom is dropped, or else they are stuck into a "train-ing school" where they are trained to be professional crimi-nals in a short time.

Despite our massive programs, and our appropriations, and our public and private welfare agencies, the plain fact of the matter is that the average American doesn't give a damn about anyone outside the mainstream of our society — and every-body outside the mainstream knows it. So do the few dedi-cated people who work with them.

If we really cared, would we tolerate our Congress spending billions and billions for highways (with no relief of traffic congestion), and a mere dribble for decent, human-scale hous-ing? Or a fifth of our national budget to put a man on the moon (mainly for reasons of pride), while our whole school system is falling apart?

We ought to stop congratulating ourselves on our Gross National Product, and start reflecting on our gross attitudes toward the disinherited, the feeble, the troubled and the torn. They won't go away, and we can't build stockades big enough to hold them all.

If you're in a mood to complain about your income tax this year, consider conditions in the republic of India, which has nearly 500 million inhabitants, and only two million persons in a position to pay any income tax at all.

*

One of the best and briefest statements of our pollution problem was made by Professor John Platt, when he observed: "Endowed as we are in the technology of Doing, we are miser-ably poor in techniques of Undoing, which the progress of Doing makes ever more necessary."

We Cheat Our Craftsmen Socially

THE WEEKLY DIGEST *Quote* recently reprinted a paragraph by Hubbard Cobb, editor of *The American Home*. Cobb pointed out that not everyone can become a successful nuclear physicist or surgeon or businessman, and went on to say:

"The individual who can work with his hands is just as important to our society as the individual who works with his mind. A pair of skilled hands is more valuable to society than the output of a second-rate mind."

I couldn't agree more, but I would like to have seen how Cobb pursued this line of thought. Because it seems to me that our society may pay lip service to the skilled craftsman, but at the same time denies him any true social status — and this is why he is a vanishing species.

A good barber, for instance, is a necessary and noble creature; yet not one American barber in a hundred knows his business, and the only satisfactory ones I have found were European in origin. American boys don't want to go into barbering, because it lacks a certain social *cachet* we deem more important than pride of craftsmanship.

Good cooks are in desperately short supply in American restaurants, for the same reason. With the highest standard of living in the world, we have the most abominable cuisine, even in the biggest cities.

Nobody here wants to be a chef, just as nobody wants to be a barber. A truly skilled carpenter is increasingly hard to find, and a mason nearly impossible. Roofers can't recruit trainable employees, and any homeowner who has had spout-and-gutter trouble knows how deplorably low the standard of craftsmanship is in this important area.

The cult of the white-collar has been a self-defeating one

— for now that our affluent society can afford the best, we lack the people to provide it for us, or to service it after we get it. Because we look down on manual work, our tailors clothe us poorly, our cooks feed us vilely, our barbers crop us barbarously, our shoe-repairers are a dying breed, and our appliance-fixers are futile when they are not fraudulent. (I know a man with a $7000 new car who took it to the garage four times to be "fixed" for the same thing.)

Giving such people more money is not the answer, for a good chef nowadays can command a salary many a junior executive would envy. It is mainly a matter of social values, of recognizing that a man who can elegantly dovetail the drawers of a cabinet may be a higher specimen than a second-rate signer of papers sitting at a mahogany desk. Computers may soon replace many people who work with their minds; but nothing yet can replace that finest physical tool of all, the human hand.

The only legitimate purpose of haste is to achieve subsequent leisure; but most people who are in haste treat it as an end in itself and not as a means, thus condemning themselves to perpetual breathlessness.

*

We speak of the "solar system" because we can clearly see that it operates as a system; but we are too close to our own world to think in terms of a "world system" — and yet unless we can learn to apply systems analysis to the operation of our globe, all our partial efforts at peaceable survival are doomed to frustration and defeat.

Our Taxation Mythology

IT SAYS SOMETHING for the changing climate of realism in this country that so conservative a magazine as *U.S. News & World Report* recently published an economic survey blasting the whole mythology of taxation.

It has been widely believed, and disseminated by interested parties, that the tax structure in the United States takes it out of the hide of the rich, while favoring the less affluent. Not so, reports the magazine's Economic Unit — it is the poor, as usual, who get the dirty end of the stick.

When *total* taxes — federal, state, city, Social Security, sales, property and all the hidden bites — are taken into consideration, it turns out that poverty-line families making $3000 a year or less pay 34 per cent of their total earnings.

Only slightly better off are the struggling families in the $5000 to $7000 bracket, who pay 33 per cent, or about $1980 a year, out of their meager income.

Best off are the people in the $15,000 to $25,000 bracket, and those over $25,000, who pay only about 28 per cent of their income in total taxes, which still leaves them a goodly sum for other purposes.

Moreover, the more affluent are able to invest their money, to buy tax-deductible municipal bonds, to take advantage of numerous devices for reducing their taxes and augmenting their income — none of which are available to the poor or even the average family.

In the past, there has been a lot of loose and self-serving talk about the poor rich man "in the 91 per cent tax bracket" — which is so much poppycock. Anyone making enough to be in that bracket is also in a position to cut that rate fully in half, through all sorts of fiscal and legal arrangements. Indeed, as we have lately learned, dozens of multimillionaires pay no federal income taxes at all.

Our present tax structure is inequitable toward the poor, not toward the rich, who have flourished in the last two decades as never before, while the average family is barely able to save a few hundred dollars a year, and would be wiped out by one medium-sized emergency.

In this most affluent of all societies, about 30 million Americans are still treading water, barely able to keep above the economic surface. When so staunch a spokesman for the Establishment as *U.S. News & World Report* deplores the heavy tax burden on the poor, we are moving into an atmosphere of intellectual honesty and out of the moral miasma that has suffocated public dialogue for so long in the past.

Discontent is the first step toward progress — and just as often, the last step toward destruction; perhaps the primary task of civilization is to learn to distinguish rationally between its discontents.

*

What we define as "history" is mostly a record written by the winners, whose version of events has become standardized, while the losers' story is buried in the debris of conquest or annihilation.

*

People, and countries, wouldn't have to do so many bad things as a "last resort" if they paid more attention to first resorts.

Crimes Are Created by Our Laws

WE MUST NOT FORGET that "crime" in a society is anything that the society cares to call crime. A community can arrest women for wearing skirts too short or children for staying out too late, if these are defined as offenses.

And much, if not most, of what we call crime in our society is the result of such arbitrary definitions.

Gambling, narcotics and prostitution have been, in the past, the three main sources of income for organized crime in this country. None of them, in my view, should be defined as a crime — for all three are emotional and medical problems we have not even tried to cope with.

Narcotics are responsible for much prostitution and for many robberies. Girls go on the street because they need large sums of money for dope; and they need large sums of money because dope is illegal and therefore expensive to obtain.

And many men commit strong-arm robberies because they need $50 a day or more to satisfy the dope habit. If addiction were defined as a sickness, and we were ready to spend as much for treating and rehabilitating such people as we are for jailing them over and over again, we might beat this problem inside of a decade.

Gambling, of course, would not be classified as a "crime" in a rational society, because (like narcotics and prostitution) it hurts no one except the person who inflicts it upon himself. Moderate gambling is harmless, and immoderate gambling is a form of emotional sickness.

But our hypocritical laws against gambling are what keep the crime syndicate rich and flourishing, making the police corrupt and feeding the kitty for many a political campaign.

"Respectable" society does not care to know about such things. It closes its eyes to the absurdities of legislation and then screams for "crime clean-ups" every four years — even though the very system it supports tends to perpetuate the evils it deplores.

Slum dwellers see all this much more clearly than the bourgeoisie, for they live in the middle of prostitution, addiction, illicit gambling, cops on the take, politicians in the fix, the juice racket and all the rest of that nightmare environment. Asking them to observe "law and order" in the midst of affluent corruption is just a sour joke.

Those who live in the lower depths see the true workings of the social organism, just as those who work in the bowels of a ship know much more than the passengers strolling on the "A" deck. The machinery does its dirty work below, and unless we help get down and refurbish it, it matters not how gleamingly we scrub the deck and polish the brass.

One law that all communities should pass immediately is that every new industrial enterprise must build in anti-pollution facilities at the start, not only as a health measure, but because it is infinitely cheaper to prevent pollution than to rectify the problem in a plant already built and operating without such facilities.

*

Genuine progress is so slow because of psychological impediments more than any other; as Simone Weil succinctly put it: "We are drawn toward a thing because we believe it to be good; we end by being chained to it because it has become a necessity."

An Unjust System of Justice

WHAT do you suppose a man ought to get for breaking a grocery store window and running off with five boxes of cookies? Thirty days? Sixty days? Maybe ninety days?

In Detroit this spring, a twenty-seven-year-old man went on trial on charges of stealing five boxes of cookies. He had been waiting in jail one year since his arrest, in lieu of $10,000 bond.

No matter what the sentence — even if he is freed — he has already spent a full year of his life in confinement for stealing cookies. Justice is already too late for him.

Local officials, when the case was brought to their attention, blamed the delay on overcrowded dockets and undermanned courtrooms. But those were not the real causes; the real cause was the man's poverty. An affluent thief would not have spent a day in detention.

Quite apart from the rank injustice that runs through our whole class system of jurisprudence — and that makes the poor contemptuous of our slogans like "law and order" — there is the practical matter of these "overcrowded dockets." What are they overcrowded with? Moving traffic violations, automobile accident cases, personal injury suits and other such civil matters.

Governor Rockefeller of New York not long ago proposed that most cases involving moving traffic violations be removed from the criminal courts to the state department of motor vehicles.

"By relieving the criminal courts of most traffic cases," he said, "the city courts would be able to provide prompter handling of serious criminal matters in a more judicious atmosphere."

Our courts are clogged with merchants using the judicial system as "collection agencies" for bad credit risks, with landlords seeking to evict tenants, with motorists suing insurance companies and with thousands of trivial torts that postpone criminal cases for months and even years. And, in the old legal saying, "Justice delayed is justice denied."

We desperately need special courts, or quasi-courts, or commissions, to process this vast backlog of civil actions, so that our judges can promptly and fairly hear serious criminal cases, so that no man is kept in detention longer than is necessary or humane, so that no victim of loss or injury must wait years and years to collect a pittance.

It is these inequities, these delays, these disproportions of recompense and retribution that make the law a mockery and destroy the common people's faith in the integrity of our legal system.

A truth we have not yet fully recognized in our drivers' tests was enunciated thirty years ago by Buckminster Fuller, when he observed: "The traffic manners and ethics of people while driving reveal their character as a whole far more readily than would their cultivated mannerisms and behavior while walking or talking."

*

Biochemists are now seriously suggesting that malnutrition in the first year after birth can permanently deprive the brain of some of its thinking capacity — which gives the human race another massive reason for trying to eliminate poverty and starvation throughout the world.

Lawlessness Seeps Down from the Top

WHAT IS lawlessness?

Is it a fourteen-year-old Negro boy stealing a radio through a smashed store window during a riot?

Is it college students marching around a public building to protest the Vietnam war, or blocking a doorway and forcing the police to carry them away?

Is it high public officials in a town on Long Island rezoning land, rigging prices and making illicit fortunes out of crooked real estate deals?

Is it policemen in Chicago stealing and hiding a truckload of tires for resale later, or other policemen in the same city shaking down a poor motorist for $500 because he was driving with a revoked license?

Is it three of the largest pharmaceutical firms in the United States being prosecuted for conspiring to inflate the price of a certain medical drug a thousandfold beyond its cost?

All of these are "lawlessness" — in one way or another, to one degree or another. And does one kind excuse any other kinds? No, of course not.

But — and this is a most important but — one kind *leads* to the other kinds, one kind seems to make the other kinds, if not permissible, at least excusable and understandable.

It is immorality and illegality at the *top levels* of society that filter down their dubious ethic and set the tone for attitude and action in the lower strata of society. It has always been this way, and always will be. What the king does — whoever the king may be — gives the commoners their cue for conduct, both privately and publicly.

When elected officials are flagrantly crooked, when police are venal or responsive to political pressures, when large corporations grossly violate laws against conspiracy or price-fixing, then the general public turns sour and cynical and opportunistic and amoral.

When the worst people seem able to hire the best lawyers, when the voice of the medical profession seems to care more about doctors than patients, when power and profit and prestige (none of them bad in itself) seem to be the *ruling criteria* of worth in a society — then why take it all out on the looters, the demonstrators, the protesters, the frustrated, fearful, angry people who get a shafting whichever way they turn?

Lawlessness? It sinks down from the top, it doesn't seep up from the bottom. Like children, people imitate what they look up to.

Any minority group, discriminated against long enough, will find itself treating its own less-favored members as contemptuously as it is treated by the majority; feelings of inferiority are always made more tolerable by being projected "downward."

*

One of the reasons so many mediocre men enter politics is that its standards are delightfully low: everyone who has not yet gone to jail is considered as honest, and everyone who is not blatantly foolish is considered shrewd.

*

People are stronger in opposition than they are in accord; conditions change, and governments fall, because our motivations against are always more powerful and active than our motivations for.

Polluted Air Will Never Get Any Cleaner

SOME MONTHS AGO, while doing research on the general subject of pollution, I learned how dumb I had been all my life about something as common and familiar — and essential — as air.

In my ignorance, I had always thought that "fresh air" was infinitely available to us. I had imagined that the dirty air around us somehow escaped into the stratosphere, and that new air kept coming in — much as it does when we open a window after a party.

This, of course, is not true, and you would imagine that a grown man with a decent education would know this as a matter of course. What *is* true is that we live in a kind of spaceship called the earth, and only a limited amount of air is *forever* available to us.

The "walls" of our spaceship enclose what is called the "troposphere," which extends about seven miles up. This is all the air that is available to us. We must use it over and over again for infinity, just as if we were in a sealed room for the lifetime of the earth.

No fresh air comes in, and no polluted air escapes. Moreover, no dirt or poisons are ever "destroyed" — they remain in the air, in different forms, or settle on the earth as "particulates." And the more we burn, the more we replace good air with bad.

Once contaminated, this thin layer of air surrounding the earth cannot be cleansed again. We can clean materials, we can even clean water, but we cannot clean the air. There is nowhere else for the dirt and poisons to go — we cannot open a window in the troposphere and clear out the stale and noxious atmosphere we are creating.

Perhaps every child in sixth grade and above knows this; but I doubt that one adult in a hundred is aware of this basic physical fact. Most of us imagine, as I did, that winds sweep away the gases and debris in the air, taking them far out into the solar system and replacing them with new air.

The United States alone is discharging *130 million tons of pollutants a year* into the atmosphere, from factories, heating systems, incinerators, automobiles and airplanes, power plants and public buildings. What is frightening is not so much the death and illness, corrosion and decay they are responsible for — as the fact that this is an *irreversible process.* The air will never be cleaner than it is now.

And this is why *prevention* — immediate, drastic and far-reaching — is our only hope for the future. We cannot undo what we have done. We cannot restore the atmosphere to the purity it had before the Industrial Revolution. But we can, and must, halt the contamination before our spaceship suffocates from its own foul discharges.

The conservative believes that "left to themselves, things will get better"; the liberal believes that "left to themselves, things will get worse"; the sensible person believes that, left to themselves, some things will get better, some will get worse and others will remain the same — it being the task of intelligence to distinguish among them.

*

The paradox of humanity is this: that all men are created unique, but the only way this uniqueness can be preserved is by treating all men as if they were created equal.

A Neglected Type of Police Training

AT A MEETING of police officers in Chicago last month, Chief Fred Ferguson of the small California town of Covina told his colleagues about putting into practice the "empathy approach" I have been recommending to police officials for more than two decades.

In training his forty-four-man police department, Chief Ferguson has them booked in jail as suspects, walking picket lines and living on Skid Row — in order to get a feeling of the way the dispossessed and the dissenters are treated by the law.

In one case, he reported, two "winos" walking along the Los Angeles Skid Row turned into a parking lot and shared a drink from a bottle one had pulled from his pocket. Two uniformed L.A. cops appeared, spread-eagled the winos against a wall and searched them.

One of them, panicking and afraid of the treatment he might receive, blurted out his true identity — a policeman from suburban Covina, assigned as part of his training to play the role of a wino.

I can't imagine a more important aspect of modern police training, especially in the increasingly urbanized areas of the nation. The need for police to "empathize" with the poor, the foreign-speaking, the uneducated, the minority groups of all kinds, has never been more pressing.

It is easy to blame the police or the slum dwellers, or both, for the civil war that rages sporadically in such neighborhoods. But the fact remains that both are the victims of something bigger than themselves — the technology that has eliminated foot-to-foot and face-to-face contact between the police and the inhabitants of such areas.

Policemen used to walk through the worst slum sections of

New York and Boston and other cities without fear of attack or even taunting. They knew everyone on their few blocks, and could easily separate the sheep from the goats.

Nowadays, they confront just a faceless mass, staring back at them balefully, suspiciously and contemptuously — because slum dwellers know they are all considered an equal threat and menace by the police, who have neither the time nor the facilities to distinguish among them.

If it is too late — and I suspect it is — to bring back the cop on the beat, Covina is doing the next best thing in giving its policemen first-hand experience at being on the other side of the shield, the stick and the gun. Strangeness begets fear, and fear begets force. When the police begin to comprehend the needs, the feelings and the responses of the "enemy," they might find they have more friends than foes in that no-man's-land they now patrol so warily.

When falsely attacked, we refute; when falsely praised, we accept; it is not a lie about ourselves we object to, only a damaging lie.

*

By the time a man gets a gold watch from his firm, he doesn't care what time it is anymore.

*

Everyone knows that "absolute power corrupts" — but we fail to grasp the opposite maxim that absolute powerlessness also corrupts in its own way, by making the powerless indifferent to the consequences of their actions, and ready to follow the most irresponsible of demagogues.

Catholic Unrest Typifies All

ALL ONE HAS TO DO is to take a look at the Roman Catholic Church to realize that today's mood of disagreement and dissent and downright defiance of tradition is not, as some say, led by "agitators" and "anarchists" and "communist-inspired" agents.

For here we have the most orthodox, conservative, traditionalist and authoritarian establishment in the Western world torn by conflict on a dozen different fronts — on contraception, on celibacy for priests, on rituals and observances, on civil rights and the participation by the church in affairs "secular" and even "political."

If this can happen in the Catholic Church, with its heavy emphasis on conformism and obedience, little wonder that the same thing has happened in the more fluid world outside. If priests can form unions, and nuns can march in picket lines, then we see clearly that the modern wave of unrest, of questioning and repudiating ancient forms and doctrines, is much more than a matter of left-wing agitation or collegiate rebellion or confrontation between the races.

Change is in the air, and change is always painful while it is taking place — like surgery without anesthesia — even though the end result of the change may be beneficial, and may even have saved the patient's life.

Of course, not *all* change is progress; but in the long pull, it is astonishing (and heartening) that most social change has turned out to be, historically, an advantage even to those who at first opposed it.

The change from absolute to limited monarchy was a blessing that paved the way to self-government; the change from feudalism to capitalism was an improvement, as even Marx himself admitted. And the Church itself has lately confided that the Reformation, which it so implacably fought, was perhaps a good and necessary thing for Christendom at the time.

But change while it is going on has an acrid smell and a bitter taste. Until the smoke clears, it is not easy to see the real issues or to accept the fact that the only way older institutions can survive is by mutating into a form more relevant to new conditions — just as animal species perish unless they adapt to a changing environment.

Then, too, psychologically, most of us find it hard to stand the ambiguity in a period of change. We like clearness, firmness and the black-and-whiteness we have become used to; this is what the call for "law and order" really means — a return to the older injustices we have become accustomed to. Anything seems preferable to change, even repression — but if repression succeeds, it brings its own kind of change, for the worse, and never restores the old order it so wistfully yearns for.

If communities can't conquer boredom among the young, by setting up suitable outlets for their energies and interests, then the young will inevitably disrupt the community merely in order to generate the excitement it lacks.

*

A lady in town tore the decal daisies off her station wagon and replaced them with an American flag decal; she reports that with the daisies on her car she was stopped at least twice a week by police squads; with the flag she hasn't been stopped once in two months.

The Real Harm of Communism

THE WORST THREAT of communism in our time is neither attack from the outside nor subversion from the inside. The greatest harm that communism has done us — and is doing us — is in its role as a bad example.

The existence of communism in our century allows us to use it as a bench mark for our own values, aims and activities. And it thus permits us to be a lot worse than we ought to be, or have any need to be.

It is like a family with one bad boy. No matter what mischief the other kids engage in, they can always point to the bad boy and say (truthfully) that they are better than he is. This is how we use communism in our family of mankind.

Or, to take another analogy, it is like a person with a mild disease comparing himself to a person with a severe disease, and refusing to take measures to cure himself because he's already so much healthier than the very sick person.

If critics point out something that is awry with American capitalism and that needs to be corrected, they are often met with the comment that things are much worse in Russia and we ought to be glad we live here.

But the fact that our next-door neighbor has pneumonia should not allow us to shrug off our own minor illness until it becomes major.

We consistently use communism as a cop-out for our own ills, just as a criminal who hits a lady on the head and steals her purse tries to mitigate his offense by pleading that he didn't rape her — the way the fellow in the next cell did to someone else.

This attitude has done us more national damage than almost anything else in our century. It has given us a "horrible example" to hold up before ourselves, permitting us to preen ourselves on our superiority and to fall into complacency and self-satisfaction about our own defects.

Parents properly tell their children that they should not compare themselves to the worst, but to the best. And the same is true of societies. If we use the grotesque repression of Russia or China as a bench mark for our own social virtue we can do some pretty rotten things and still be better than they are. But what standard is that to live by?

Marx would be revolving in his grave if he could see how the rise of dictatorial communism in the twentieth century has retarded the progress of mankind rather than aiding it — not merely retarded it in the communist countries but in the non-communist ones as well, by providing them with "bad boys" they can feel better than.

We must stop looking out, and start looking in; stop saying we're lucky to have just a cold and not pneumonia — for colds have a way of turning into pneumonia if fed by smugness, negligence and superiority.

Young radicals should read the memoirs of Emma Goldman, one of the earliest anarchists, whose disillusionment with the movement was summed up in this warning: "No revolution can ever succeed as a factor of liberation unless the Means used to further it be identical in spirit and tendency with the Purposes to be achieved."

*

The people with the clearest insights are not necessarily those with the finest minds, but those who were least damaged by their environment while growing up.

The Police and the Girls Next Door

"SOMETIMES I think the police make as much trouble as they prevent," said the lady, "and there's very little we can do about it. Like the girls who moved in next door.

"They seemed quite pleasant, ordinary girls," she went on, some of the friends who visited them were hippies — at ney looked like hippies.

side of their looks, they were no trouble at all. No loud , no unseemly behavior. In fact, they even kept their unlocked when they went to work during the day — tainly they had nothing at all to hide.

"But I guess some of the neighbors were upset because of their hippie friends' visiting them, and must have told the police. Well, you would have thought the police were investigating a major narcotics ring, the way they kept surveillance on that apartment.

"They staked out a car in front for two days running, with a plainclothes detective in it — so obvious that my little children knew what it was. And the detective was a pig — he sat there reading a gun catalog and throwing cigarette packs and candy wrappers onto the sidewalk.

"Police cars were forever cruising by and stopping there. I guess they didn't have a warrant to go in, but they were peering in at the windows and just generally making themselves obnoxious.

"Mind you, these girls had done nothing at all — they weren't even hippies themselves, although there's no crime in that. Just a couple of girls from a small Midwest town, I imagine, who had come to the big city to work and make some new friends of their own choosing.

"Well, this harassment finally got so bad that the owner

of the building, who had rented the basement apartment to the girls, was forced to tell them they had to move at the end of the month — because they were attracting too much attention to the building and the block.

"The owner hated to do it. 'They're the nicest tenants I had in years,' she told me. 'They're clean, pay their rent on time and have no objectionable habits at all. But I can't have the cops here all the time.' The girls are moving out in a few days.

"This is the kind of thing that embitters young people today — the lack of discrimination on the part of adult society, and especially the police, who look on anybody a little different with deep suspicion. This attitude will only drive them further into the camp of the extremists — and maybe next time the cops *will* have something to pull in."

"Law" and *"order,"* though linked verbally, are not at all the same thing and do not necessarily go together: if laws are bad, or unequally enforced, there can be no order; and if the order is not organic, but imposed by force, laws will continue to be violated en masse.

*

Those frightened defenders of the status quo, who urge more jail sentences for more offenders, ought to heed the psychologically acute comment by Judge William Burnett of Colorado, who said that while prison is a tremendous deterrent for middle- and upper-class people, "when you get to the subculture, where being in and out of jail has been accepted as part of family living for generations, it loses its effect. There is no moral stigma. In fact, a jail experience often increases prestige."

4

OF WAR AND PEACE

But Who Speaks Up for All Mankind?

"Humanity" is an abstraction. "Mankind" is a word. It is hard to feel passion or loyalty for words and abstractions. Hard, but necessary.

Everyone gives his loyalty to something larger than himself — the father to his family, the communicant to his church, the citizen to his country, even the juvenile delinquent to his gang.

But who is loyal to humanity? Humanity has no flag, no song, no colors, no troops, no salutes, no rituals, no face nor body. It is a word like "justice" or "peace" — cold, perfect and dead.

Yet all the crises of our time can be rolled up into one crisis — that nobody speaks for mankind, even though mankind today is threatened with annihilation as a whole species.

Watching the UN proceedings early this summer, I thought of how fluently and ardently the partisans of each nation spoke up for their sides. But nobody spoke up for everybody, for that faceless, stateless man called "humanity."

Almost every other species of animal is loyal to its own kind, and not merely to its own pack or flock or den. Only man and the shark mortally attack their own kind, and represent their own worst enemy.

The other species are loyal by instinct; and we must learn to be loyal by intellect. But the time is running out for us to learn that it is not enough to be a good parent, a good communicant, a good citizen. It is time to be a good man.

This means that no loyalty must override the survival of mankind, that in any conflict of interest between this and lesser loyalties, the lesser loyalties must be curtailed or surrendered. If no one speaks for humanity alive, what is there to prevent humanity's death?

Space and time have shrunk with terrifying compression in our age. Ancient boundaries are meaningless, except for political purposes; old divisions of clan and tribe are sentimental remnants of the pre-atomic age; neither creed nor color nor place of origin is relevant to the realities of modern power to utterly seek and destroy.

Yet we walk around as if nothing had changed, mouthing the same old platitudes, waving the same frayed flags, imagining somehow that we are invulnerable to the tremors that are shaking the whole of the earth. It is hard, almost impossible to cherish mankind beyond all else. But nothing less, in our century, will suffice. This crisis in loyalty may well be the watershed of the human race, leading to survival or extinction.

The really shocking state we are in isn't fully grasped until we are ready to accept the difficult fact that nothing less than reaching for Utopia can save us; the most "ideal" — such as the abolition of war — has become the only practical means for assuring the survival of man.

Mark Twain and the Pentagon

AT THE BEGINNING of this year, Secretary of Defense Melvin Laird formally dedicated a small room in the Pentagon as a quiet place for prayer and meditation. "Until now," he said, "this building lacked a place where man's inner spirit could find quiet expression."

The thought of a "prayer room" in the Pentagon reminded me of Mark Twain's bitter diatribe "The War Prayer." It begins Sunday morning in a church, the day before the battalions would leave for the front. The preacher gave the "long" prayer, and none could remember the like of it for passionate pleading and moving and beautiful language.

The burden of its supplication was that an ever-merciful and benign Father of us all would watch over our noble young soldiers, and aid, comfort and encourage them in their patriotic work; bless them and shield them in the day of battle . . .

Then an aged stranger entered, moved down the aisle to the preacher's side, and said: "I come from the Throne — bearing a message from Almighty God! He has heard your prayer and will grant it, if such shall be your desire, after I, His messenger, shall have explained to you its full import — for, like many of the prayers of men, it asks for more than he who utters it is aware of."

The stranger continued: "When you have prayed for victory, you have prayed for many unmentioned results which follow upon victory — *must* follow it, cannot help but follow it. Our Father commandeth me to put the unspoken part of the prayer into words. Listen!

"O Lord our God, help us to tear their soldiers to bloody shreds with our shells; help us to cover their smiling fields with the pale forms of their patriot dead; help us to drown the thunder of the guns with the shrieks of their wounded, writhing in pain; help us to lay waste their humble homes with a hurricane of fire; help us to wring the hearts of their unoffending widows, to turn them out roofless with their little children to wander unfriended the wastes of their desolated land in rags and hunger and thirst . . . broken in spirit, worn with travail, imploring Thee for the refuge of the grave and denied it — for our sakes who adore Thee, Lord, blast their hopes, blight their lives, protract their bitter pilgrimage, make heavy their steps, water their way with their tears . . . We ask it, in the spirit of love, of Him who is the Source of love, and Who is the ever-faithful refuge and friend of all that are sore beset and seek His aid with humble and contrite hearts. Amen."

After a pause, the messenger said, "Ye have prayed it; if ye still desire it, speak! The hearld of the Most High waits . . ."

A jolting statistic to all parents, from a UNESCO bulletin, is that the nations of the world spend on the average of $100 a year to teach a child how to read; and a few years later, $7800 a child to teach him how to shoot.

*

Only if capitalism can demonstrate the ability to sustain prosperity without recurrent wars will it justify itself as a system in the eyes of young people today; for war is a form of "external socialism," by which a false, hectic and temporary prosperity is maintained by immense government spending on nonproductive capital goods.

World Still Living in the Wild West

THE TWENTIETH-CENTURY WORLD, with all its magnificent technology, is very much like a small Western town in the early days of our nation, before sheriffs and judges and courts turned the town into a genuine "community."

Everybody arms himself for what he claims is defense; but the line between "defense" and "aggression" is a thin one, and nobody has the authority to decide which is truly which.

While our scientific and technical achievement staggers the imagination, our civil and political arrangements have not progressed an inch beyond the frontier mentality. There is no common law, no common protection, no peaceable means for adjudicating disputes.

Each nation is its own law, its own sheriff, its own judge. Each has its own arsenal of weapons hidden away, and — out of fear more than out of hostility — each feels it must maintain an "arms superiority" over the others.

The Western towns could not long exist in this fashion, for only the outlaws flourished as long as the law was in private hands. And the country did not grow and prosper until all assented to a common law with enforceable powers.

World law today is in private hands — which means that there is no law, and therefore there is no order. There is only anarchy masquerading as national sovereignty. But there is no sovereignty, either, for nuclear weapons make defense meaningless and victory for any side impossible.

These are the plain facts of the case. They have always been the facts of the case, because all that can ever exist between independent sovereignties is an uneasy truce, never a genuine peace. But the big difference today is that no nation has power to defend itself — it can only retaliate in kind.

War used to be called an "extension of politics," and with some reason. Now, war has become obsolete because, pushed to the ultimate, it can merely end in mutual self-destruction. *Atomic energy has given us so much power that we have lost the power to use it,* as a means of getting our own way by threats or by violence.

The Western town grew too big for anarchy, and the modern world has grown too small for it. We are all locked into the same little cabin, and any shot through the ceiling can depressurize the craft, destroying the destroyer along with his victim. Not to recognize this paramount truth of our time is to betray the act of creation.

Murder one man, you're a villain; murder a dozen, you're a hero; murder a million, you're a World Leader.

*

If we judged the long-term behavior of nations as rigorously as we judge the conduct of individuals, which would escape sentence to a prison or a lunatic asylum? Only a small handful, at the most.

*

Because the world spends annually on armaments a sum 25 times greater than the total spent in all foreign assistance countries, the gap between the per capita incomes of rich nations and poor nations is widening rather than narrowing — thus making certain that sometimes those armaments will have to be used by the haves against the have-nots.

We Don't Need More Treasure

SINCE THE UNITED STATES already owns a vast disproportion of the world's resources and riches, and since the inequity between the rich nations and the poor nations is increasing rather than decreasing, we must obviously find some way to bring the world more into economic balance if we want to avoid widespread rebellion and revolution.

There is one way to do this without sacrificing a single dollar or resource we already possess. It would be a gracious and generous gesture, signifying to the poor and struggling countries of the world that we are not the oppressors and exploiters as depicted in Marxist demonology.

It is agreed by all experts in the various scientific disciplines that the wealth on and under the floor of the oceans is many times greater than our resources on land. The seabeds of the globe — which represent two-thirds of the total area of the world — contain enormous natural riches we are now technologically ready to develop and utilize.

Since the international seas belong to everybody, those nations with the most money and equipment would normally be the first and most successful to take part in this new "gold rush" for underwater minerals and other resources. And the United States would be first of all.

It is my view that we have not only a moral obligation but a practical stake as well in relinquishing all claims to this subaqueous treasure. We should work with the UN's Political Committee of the General Assembly to assure that international regulation will apportion the largest shares to the countries in greatest need.

More than this, rather than giving military and economic aid to nations, which only foments conflict and often keeps corrupt administrations more securely in power, we should offer equipment and technical help (on a loan-and-repayment basis) to the underdeveloped lands for working the sea-beds.

The United States already commands some 60 per cent of the world's renewable and nonrenewable resources. Much more will come in when we cultivate our own coastal waters on the continental shelf. Only shortsighted greed would compel us to engage in a new race of underwater colonialism, and compound the anarchy we have created on land.

Our generosity (which is only a form of common sense) would do more to undercut the Marxist attacks on our hegemony of the world's riches than almost any other step we could take. To say "We want no more, and recognize that poverty must be alleviated if peace is to be maintained," would testify most eloquently to our sincere aim of avoiding a nuclear holocaust in a struggle for oceanic treasure.

If present plans continue, by 1975 the United States will have more than 10,000 nuclear warheads, capable of destroying Russia's 50 largest cities 40 times over — this is called national "defense."

*

The real tragedy implicit in McLuhan's concept of the modern world as a "global village" is that we have indeed been compressed to the small dimensions of a village without at the same time having become neighborly; which is worse for world relations than if we still lived weeks or months apart from each other.

Patton a Most Honest General

I WAS SORRY to miss a preview screening of the film *Patton*, because I wanted to see how this unique general was depicted. Although I did not like Patton, or what he stood for, I respected him as one of the most honest generals of our age.

He was totally free of the cant and self-deception that afflict almost all his military colleagues. He liked fighting, he enjoyed war and he made no sentimental obeisances to peace.

Patton was practically the only military leader I have heard who refrained from the customary gush about "defense" and "security" and "we can't have peace unless we have a strong fighting force."

He enthusiastically accepted the fact that armies are for fighting and for killing, not for keeping the peace. He was restless and unfulfilled out of battle, and felt himself fully alive only in warfare.

This is why men go into the army, and rise in the ranks. They like to command and they can command best in combat. They want victory, honor, decorations, authority, and life-and-death decisions to make. This is their form of self-expression.

Barbarous as we may find this, it is at least a far more honest attitude than the public utterances of most military leaders, who pretend that they find peace preferable to war.

Military men, like politicians, are the same the world over, and have more in common with one another (even though they wear different uniforms) than they do with their own countrymen. A "patriotic" American general would be just as patriotic a Russian general if he had happened to be born there.

The combative temperament, like the political temperament, is a supranational trait; it may take on the coloration of its country, but the aim of the general is to win, just as the aim of the politician is to get and stay in office. In both cases, the ideology is subordinate to the conflict. Patton, I dare say, might have been just as happy fighting with the Nazis as against them, and would have found adequate reaons for justifying his role. Generals are not natural democrats.

Indeed, military men often feel themselves "obstructed" under a democratic form of government, and they thrive much better in nations where civilian control has been weakened or usurped. Our founding fathers understood this quite well when they stipulated that a civilian President should be commander-in-chief of the armed forces.

What is tragic is that the combative virtues of such men as Patton must be enlisted in the service of killing rather than of leading us in conquest of our common enemies — disease, famine, flood and, most menacingly, that pervasive prejudice that may eventually conquer us all.

The greatest harm done by the Industrial Revolution is that, more than ever before in history, knowledge became enslaved to power, and was directed by power to ends inconsistent with wisdom.

*

To pursue at the same time policies of armament and disarmament, as we are doing, is as futile and contradictory as trying to find a common cure for malaria while engaging in separate research to breed new species of malaria-carrying mosquitoes at the same time.

Mankind Should Repudiate War

EVERYBODY is against war. The United States says it is against war. Stalin said he was against war. Even Hitler said he was against war.

What governments usually mean by this statement is that they are against war *as long as they can get their own way by other means*. If the other means fail, they will resort to war.

But to be genuinely and meaningfully against war is to be against *the preconditions that create war and make it inevitable*. These preconditions are: anarchy among nations, the lack of an international court and the absence of an international police force.

Until the nations are willing to give up some of their external authority — just as cities give up some to the states, and the states to the nation — then there is no way to resolve national disputes except by force and violence. It is as simple, and as difficult, as that.

First of all, we must get over the thought that war is a "natural" social phenomenon, when it is in truth a disease of mankind. In earlier eras, it was thought that cannibalism was natural; later, it was believed that slavery was natural. Both these practices have been abandoned in the world, and there is no rational reason that war cannot be repudiated by the mass of mankind.

In my view, it will never voluntarily be repudiated by governments as such. Governments have too much of a stake in ruling ever to relinquish any part of their authority — dubious as that authority is in this age of mass retaliation and mutual destruction.

It is the peoples of the world, acting in concert, who must persuade their governments to adopt "law and order" in the international sphere, just as those governments urge us to follow law and order in the domestic sphere. How absurd for a government to preach a doctrine of nonviolence to its own citizens, and to practice ruthless violence abroad whenever it so desires. What an immoral contradiction!

In my view, also, the student protest movement is the most heartening sign of a moral revolution in this area. The students are not merely objecting to our involvement in Vietnam; they want to stop war altogether, so that other Vietnams do not crop up yearly.

This can be done only by youth calling across the barriers of nations; by students appealing to students in all other countries, by going over the heads of governments and arousing and mobilizing young people everywhere. I don't think that even the Russians or Chinese could control their own youth in the face of a worldwide movement to stamp out the pandemic disease of war that has for too long afflicted the best, the bravest and the youngest of mankind.

Doesn't it seem peculiar that a nation incessantly engaged in the production of hydrogen bombs should have laws banning fireworks?

*

One of the most prevalent and dangerous myths is that recurrent wars are a "natural" necessity because they appreciably reduce the population every few decades; but even this function isn't served by war, for all studies show that its "depopulation" is quickly made up in a few years.

Cantons of the World, Unite — Or Else

I WAS with some friends from Switzerland when the UN was celebrating (if that's the proper word) its twenty-fifth anniversary, and they expressed surprise that the organization has lasted as long as it has.

The Swiss have even less faith in the ability of the United Nations to prevent, or even delay, war than do the other people of Europe. The reason for their pessimism is to be found in the unique structure of their own republic, which was begun in the year 1291, as the first democracy in Europe.

In that year, the three original cantons of Switzerland formed a confederation against Rudolf of Hapsburg, who coveted the beautiful country around Lucerne. The peasants and mountaineers, who tilled the land cooperatively, formed a Pact of Perpetual Alliance which has grown stronger with the centuries.

Soon, other free cities asked to join the confederation, as a protection against foreign aggressors. Although this was a kind of United Nations (or United Cantons) setup, the big difference was that the confederation was given real teeth from the very beginning.

All disputes between cantons must be settled by arbitration. If one canton refuses to accept the decision, the confederates are pledged to assist the other. And no canton has the right to reject the verdict of the arbitrator — this is the cornerstone of the pact.

When nations were granted "veto power" in the UN, the Swiss immediately felt that the UN was doomed as a peacekeeping agency, and that another large-scale war would begin as soon as one nation considered itself strong enough to defy the Security Council.

And, even more than before, the Swiss point to their own confederation as the only workable model for a successful league of peace-loving nations. Theirs has been in existence for almost 700 years, and they are wondering wistfully how long it will be before the rest of Europe — and the world — is ready to try the same.

This pessimism extends even to Switzerland's possible participation in a future war. Hitherto, the mountains have been her blessed protection; no army of invaders could successfully negotiate the passes. But, with the coming of airborne invasion and the H-bomb, Switzerland's rich resources may be grabbed by a hungry aggressor.

No country is "safe" anymore, and even the most powerful are subject to retaliation that could wipe them out or cripple them forever; yet the "cantons" of the world refuse to unite for their own survival.

Those who look for "conspirators" or "outside agitators" as the causes of revolutionary movements should recall the words of Wendell Phillips more than a century ago: "Revolutions are not made; they come. A revolution is as natural a growth as an oak. It comes out of the past. Its foundations are laid far back."

*

Compared with geological time, man is only about one hour old; compared with astronomical time, we were just born a thousandth of a second ago; and yet our predicament is such that our survival depends upon our blossoming into maturity before we have left the playpen.

So We Pour Money into the U.N.?

WHEN I PUBLISHED some figures a few weeks ago on the relatively small amount of foreign aid the United States has given the last few years — in terms of the percentage of our Gross National Product — many readers were incredulous.

The figures checked out. What doesn't check out is the vast discrepancy between reality and our perception of it — most people have highly distorted views of themselves as individuals, and this distortion carries over to our national self-image.

As another example, I attended a dinner last month for the twenty-fifth anniversary of the founding of the United Nations. Many Americans seem to feel that we are carrying a disproportionate share of the costs of running the U.N. But how many actually know what these costs represent?

The total United States contribution to the UN in 1969 was less than

— The New York City Fire Department budget
— Half the New York City Police Department budget
— One-sixth of one per cent of the United States Defense budget
— The cost of the war in Vietnam *for three days.*

What it amounts to in cash is $1.22 per person per year, or 2½ cents a week.

Even if the UN weren't involved, however feebly, in trying to keep countries talking as an alternative to fighting, all the subsidiary activities of the UN alone would be worth that pittance — the support it gives to health, science, education and cultural interchange. These would be desperately needed in our time even if no political organization existed.

Similarly, we have exaggerated notions about what we spend for welfare within the United States, as contrasted with our war spending and our "luxury" spending. We need more hospitals, better mental institutions, effective rehabilitation centers for juvenile offenders and drug addicts, and a host of other social apparatus to cure or alleviate a dozen disorders in the community — and all these areas are hurting for money.

Yet we blithely permit billions to be poured into military experiments of dubious value, without even questioning their necessity or validity — and those few who do are promptly labeled unpatriotic. But genuine patriotism means wanting what is best for one's country, and *demanding sufficient information to be able to make a rational decision.*

As long as we imagine that we are squandering money on foreign aid and subsidizing the UN for huge amounts, we are living in a fantasy world of our own making, while the real squanderers go on their merry way unembarrassed by the candid scrutiny of an informed electorate.

What are we spending for "military research" — and how much for that almost unknown phrase, "peace research"?

*

The greatest and most dangerous fallacy still existing in this world is that unilateral national defense *is in any way feasible as a means of avoiding war, deterring war, or "winning" war; rather, without the reformation and strengthening of some such agency as the UN, the more the international system expands its offensive and defensive capabilities, the more likely the outbreak of an irreversible catastrophe.*

"Merchants of Death" — New Style

WHEN I WAS GROWING UP, between the First and Second World Wars, we knew all about the "merchants of death" — those shadowy and sinister figures like Krupp and Zaharoff, who made and sold arms to any nation that could afford them.

We naïvely thought, at the time, that if such men and their companies could be prevented from turning a profit on weapons of mass destruction, it might help the world along the bumpy road toward disarmament and eventual peace.

Such men and their companies no longer exercise the power and influence they once had; instead, their place has been taken by the nations of the world themselves. All of us today, through our governments on all sides of all curtains, are the Krupps and Zaharoffs of modern conventional warfare.

This is the inescapable conclusion from reading George Thayer's thoroughly documented book, *The War Business*, which shows how governments themselves have taken over the international trade in armaments, and how billions of dollars a year in arms are sold (or even given away) by so-called "peace-loving" countries — with the United States leading the procession.

In some cases, our rationale for this wholesale merchandising of weapons is that we are trying to "stabilize" a situation and help maintain an equilibrium that will prevent war. But this has never worked, and never will; since both sides are provided with weapons, it merely escalates the hostilities, as it did between Israel and the Arab states a few years ago, and as it threatens to do again now.

All major nations are equally guilty of this traffic; some do it for profit, some for mistaken notions of "balance of power," and some for its pure trouble-making potential. While all these nations speak up for "peace" on the floor of the UN, none of them genuinely supports efforts to create international machinery that would limit their traffic in arms.

The War Business is an ugly book to read, in the sense that a suppurating wound is an ugly thing to look at — but turning our eyes away to lovelier prospects will only speed the moment when death comes to the patient; and, of course, the "patient" in this book is the entire human race.

It is not evil and greedy men, but governments themselves, that sustain and replenish the dangerously high level of weaponry all over the world, and by so doing make a mockery of the "law and order" they preach for domestic consumption only.

In order to insure his survival in the past, man had to make a virtue out of necessity; in order to insure our survival in the future, we have to do a much harder thing — namely, make a necessity out of virtue.

*

For a nation that considers itself "peace-loving," the United States has a curious history of engaging in about one major military campaign every sixteen years since our founding.

*

In the unprecedented boom of the last decade, it is disheartening to realize that the two greatest "growth industries" in the United States have been — warfare and welfare.

Power As a Substitute for Love

"MAKE LOVE, NOT WAR" is the best of the graffiti that to-day's youngsters have passed along to us. It is a new phrase representing an old truth — the ancient Greeks coupled the god of war with the goddess of love, to symbolize the strange relationship between the two.

Man is said to be essentially composed of an "erotic" and an "aggressive" drive. I believe it, and I also believe that an excess of the one indicates a deficiency of the other. Undue aggressiveness, in my view, is the result of a lack of the ability to love or be loved.

If there were some way we could examine the private lives of public men — with a sort of psychic x-ray — I think we would discover that the loving faculty in them had been dammed up and diverted into channels that ran toward power and position and conquest.

It was easy enough to see without such a device in the case of a Hitler, who had no personal emotive life, and in whom the excitement of hate evidently gave the same thrill that love gives to normal people. I suspect much the same was true of Napoleon, despite his amorous adventurings; he lacked the gift of intimacy, and while he could "possess" women, it was only as possessions, not as persons.

It is no historical accident that leaders are almost always worse than the people they lead, or that their power to summon their subjects' worst instincts for cruelty is far greater than their power to call upon the people's vast capacity for good will and generosity.

We find the same tendency among children, where good or at least average boys will follow the worst of their number — who appeal to their suppressed and forbidden feelings

— but will rarely follow the best of their number. Virtue seems individual, while vice is collective.

Since political power goes to those who crave it and combat for it, and since those who crave it (in my opinion) are enjoying it as a substitute for the erotic pleasure they cannot achieve, it is hardly surprising that most leaders have plunged their nations into blood baths with dismaying regularity throughout the centuries.

This is doubtless what Socrates meant when he observed that "power should be entrusted only to those who do not want it." A man whose aggressive and erotic drives are in balance will no more abuse his office than he would abuse his love object; but such a man has to be drafted for public life. Those who volunteer to lead us too often want to lead us into making war, and away from making love.

Most tyrannies are the result of frustrations, accidental or otherwise: If Hitler had been a successful painter, there would have been no Putsch; if Napoleon had been accepted by the Russian army in 1799 (which refused to give him the rank of major), there would have been no Austerlitz, and no Waterloo.

*

To become successful too young is a trap for the unstable personality — nothing afterward savors so sweetly, and life becomes an anticlimax; Alexander the Great at thirty was disconsolately looking for new worlds to conquer and dying of a fever while proclaiming his divinity.

We Astronauts Better Stop Fighting

I WAS LISTENING to a lecture by an astronomer last month, and he mentioned the relative size of our world in the universe. He said that the best modern telescope can now see so far into space that if we took the whole United States as our model, the earth would not even appear on it, when looked at with electron microscopes.

This is a hard image to illustrate with words, so let me try again in another way. If that part of the universe we can already see were the size of the United States, the size of the earth in that area would be about as small as a virus compared with the whole country. Is that clearer?

How provincial of us, the astronomer went on, to imagine that our galaxy with 150 million stars as large as our sun, does not have other planets with life on them — especially since there are 150 million other galaxies in the universe, each containing as many millions of stars.

Other stars no doubt have planets. Other planets, somewhere, must have pretty much the same environmental conditions that bred life on earth; and out of this life must have come what we call "intelligent" life on some of these planets — and possibly millions of years before this planet began to cool off. To believe we are unique is the height of anthropocentric arrogance.

If we could steadily see ourselves in this light — as a tiny speck of dust whirling about in one tiny corner of the universe, with the whole time-span of the earth no longer than a twinkling — we might be able to reach a saner perspective on human and social problems.

Buckminster Fuller's old analogy of the earth as a "spaceship" is another useful concept. We are all riding together in a spaceship that is smaller than the one the astronauts went up in, compared with the size of the cosmos. We are locked into this ship together and forever, and we survive or perish together and forever.

The first and absolute imperative in the spaceship of the astronauts is cooperation, and the subordination of individual will to the welfare of the ship as a whole. Only *after that* is there room for idiosyncratic differences. Disharmony among the astronauts means disaster for all.

Man must begin to take the "astronomical" view of himself and his world if he is to survive. It is far too late for any parochial view; too late for politics, too late for race, too late for class distinctions. Our ship is now so highly explosive, so charged with incendiaries, that we have only two options: We stay up, or we blow up. Not to see this, clearly and steadily and primarily, is to perish in the universe as obscurely and ignobly as we have lived.

Not much has changed since Mark Twain wrote Tom Sawyer Abroad *nearly a century ago, and commented: "I asked Tom if countries always apologized when they had done wrong, and he says: 'Yes, the little ones does.'"*

*

The only lesson we can learn from history is that people will behave well when they are filled with hope, and badly when they are filled with fear; this is why democracies flourish on hope, and dictatorships rise only when fear overwhelms the citizenry.

Peace Isn't Just the Absence of War

"ALL MEN," wrote Thomas à Kempis in the fifteenth century, "desire peace, but few desire the conditions that are requisite for peace."

Nothing has changed in the five centuries since he uttered that melancholy truth. Hardly anyone is willing to recognize the fact that "peace" is a word much like "health."

Everybody desires health, but we are more realistic about its preconditions. We know that we cannot engage in bad habits, ignore the needs of the body, neglect our diet or sleep or exercise, and then expect to remain healthy.

But this is exactly what we expect in the realm of social health — which is peace. We permit injustice to fester (so long as we are not its immediate victims); we ignore the needs of the underprivileged; we neglect the machinery of law and justice and amity — and then are shocked when civil or military war breaks out.

Peace, for most of us, is a sentiment, a pious expectation, a vague spiritual condition. We do not regard it as something we have to work for — like a job; or make sacrifices for — like a family. Yet we daily jeopardize both our jobs and our families, as well as our whole society, by our apathy toward "the conditions that are requisite for peace."

Our biggest intellectual and emotional mistake lies in regarding peace as the mere absence of war, as a negative thing. But health is not the mere absence of disease — it is a positive thing, a regimen, a way of life, a discipline that prevents illness as far as possible.

What we loosely call "times of peace" are really uneasy truces, lulls between wars. This is all the world has known for most of mankind's history. The patients recuperate from the damage of one war — and this convalescence is called "peace" — and when they are strong enough they engage in another.

But the end of one war always breeds the germs of the next; and between these two periods no preventive "medicine" is at work to make sure that the disease will not recur. If we took the same attitude toward public health that we do toward war, we would still be having worldwide plagues every thirty years or so.

War must come to be looked upon as an infantile social sickness of mankind, or we cannot survive in the atomic age. The conditions of peace must be widely understood and broadly practiced, as we practice preventive medicine in other areas. For the first time in history, man has the productive, industrial, technical and economic power to relieve the conditions that make for war — but most of this power is still going into the war machine.

Conservative administrations can take steps in foreign relations which, if undertaken by liberal administrations, would promptly be labeled as "soft on communism"; and it might be plausibly argued that while reforms and rapprochments are initiated by liberals, they are effectuated by conservatives.

*

To suggest that war will end only when "human aggression" is subdued is to fail to understand both the nature of man and the nature of war; aggression is biological, but war is social, and new social mechanisms can eliminate war, just as the older mechanisms eliminated cannibalism, slavery and the burning of witches.

Violence Is as American as Mom's Apple Pie

WE TOOK the country by violence, in the days when we were still a colony. With muskets and booze, we wrested and defrauded the land away from the Indians.

We shot our way West. We killed off the animals. We killed off the tribes we could not "pacify." Then we began killing each other off, until federal troops had to be called into many towns.

We took Texas by force in the Mexican War that was so unjust that even Lincoln opposed our brutal actions there.

We refused to let the Confederate States secede, though they had both a legal and a moral right to do so — and we plunged the nation into four years of the bloodiest fratricide ever known to man.

We fabricated the Spanish-American War, won it by sheer weight of arms, and started an empire of sorts.

We dropped the atom bombs on Hiroshima and Nagasaki, even though there was no military justification for doing so, and the war against Japan was already won without this hideous act of violence.

We have been involved in more than 100 wars, aggressions and military actions since we shot our way to independence in 1776.

We have hanged, burned, gassed and electrocuted thousands of our citizens who broke the law — and what is capital punishment but a calculated act of violence by the state?

We have broken all the world's records for every category of homicide from manslaughter to murder in the twentieth century.

There are more homicides in New York City in one month than in *all of Great Britain in an entire year.*

There are more guns privately owned in the United States than in the whole rest of the world put together.

We are, and have been for a long time, the most lawbreaking nation in the world, in almost every category of crime — and especially in crimes of violence, in attacks against persons.

Now we are worried about "crime in the streets." As if it were something new. But the only thing new is that the Negro is following the example of the whites.

We have gained, and kept, what we have by raw power. We have been "peace-loving" when it paid, and violent when it did not. This is the example we have provided, while telling ourselves sanctimonious lies about our sweetness and goodness and essential decency.

Now some of our chickens are coming home to roost. And how will we deal with them? By violence, of course. In the good old tradition.

Everybody is "against" war, verbally; and the most passionate opponents of war are the generals who fight them and the statesmen who declare them — but the war they are against is abstract, while the one they are waging can always be rationalized as a necessary exception.

*

In our four biggest wars (the Civil, the Spanish-American and the two World Wars), we demanded and got "unconditional surrender" — with the eventual result that the South remained intractable, Cuba turned communist and there is more instability in Europe and Asia today than there was before the First World War! So much for military solutions to political problems.

"Vaccinating" Nations Against War

WHEN PEOPLE tell me that the idea of any sort of "international government" is impossible and unrealistic — even though they may admit that war cannot be avoided on the national level — I am fond of pointing out that, as early as the last century, certain aspects of international rule were already set up, to promote the common interests of nations.

First there was the Universal Postal Union. This was followed by the Telegraphic Union, the Metric Union, the International Institute of Agriculture, and many others dealing with public hygiene, transportation, literary and artistic property, the slave trade, legal protection of workers, medical and chemical discoveries and commercial statistics.

A half-century ago, Leonard Woolf pointed out (as the British journal, *New Scientist*, recalled recently) that these organizations constituted a true beginning of international government. The international trade union movement, the Inter-Parliamentary Union and the International Polar Year were further steps to make men in different places parts of one community.

And, since the end of World War II, there have sprung up the Food and Agriculture Organization, the World Health Organization, UNESCO, the World Bank and International Monetary Fund and many others in diverse fields of interest.

As the *New Scientist* goes on to enumerate: "The control of nuclear fuels for peaceful purposes, the regulation of broadcasting standards and frequencies, air safety regulations, vaccination regulations for travelers, machinery for the conclusion of tariff agreements . . . all these and many other practical functions of government have been willingly surrendered to international institutions."

It is quite plain, to any open mind, that the technical requirements of modern society are breaking down the barriers between nations in almost every nonpolitical area of activity, and
eroding "national sovereignty." Business and industry have
likewise found that narrow national interests have less and less
meaning in the modern world.

If international cooperation is necessary and desirable in all
the other facets of human life, then obviously it is even more
imperative in the vital matter of war and peace. If it is important that we vaccinate people against carrying typhus across
borders, how much more essential to "vaccinate" nations
against the danger of carrying the virus of war across borders?
Otherwise, we may find that we have achieved world government in everything except the one area that negates all the
others and turns their cooperation into just a prelude to international suicide.

*In our age, the only practical alternative to war is not some-
thing nebulously called "peace," but prosperity for all nations,
with a sharp reduction in the differences between haves and
have-nots, which is a far greater threat to world stability than
all ideologies put together.*

*

*The ICBM and the nuclear warhead and the "deterrence
system" are not only meaningless but probably fatal, for they
are merely negative aspects of national rivalry, and must be
accompanied (or preceded) by positive steps; otherwise, as
even so dour a technologist as Herman Kahn has observed,
"All we are doing is buying time, and we are doing nothing
with the time that we buy."*

Unused Avenue to Peace

EVERY COUNTRY insists that it wants peace, but what every country really wants is to have its own way. If peace were truly a desideratum, it could be easily accomplished.

There is an International Court of Justice, sitting permanently in The Hague, the Netherlands, which consists of fifteen judges, all from different states, chosen by the General Assembly and the Security Council of the UN.

This court is empowered to decide on the interpretation of treaties, questions of international law and breaches of international obligation. All states that are members of the UN are ipso facto members of the court, and other states are permitted to adhere to its decisions.

An international dispute — such as we have in Vietnam — may be brought before the court by consent of the parties in the particular case, or by virtue of an advance formal declaration to automatically accept the court's jurisdiction.

Some forty states have made such declaration, but the United States is one of those that excludes all matters it chooses to regard as "domestic." This means that if the United States considers the Vietnam war an "internal issue," it refuses the court the right to adjudicate it. With such restrictions, the court spends most of its time deciding matters of little international importance.

If our government sincerely desired peace, it would admit frankly that Vietnam is not a domestic issue — as everyone knows it is not — and ask that the International Court of Justice decide the rights and wrongs of the situation there.

We would put the whole matter before the court, agree to stop the fighting in Vietnam completely and immediately, and ask our opponents in Vietnam to do the same.

This would put the ball squarely in their court, and the brunt of the world's moral opinion would then be on their shoulders, not ours. By referring the conflict to an impartial international agency, and by agreeing to abide by its decision, we would prove that we are as much in favor of "law and order" among nations as we are among citizens within a nation.

One of the bitterly ironic paradoxes of our position today is that the President of the United States speaks out boldly against the "violence" within our borders, while at the same time we engage in bare violence outside our borders, recognizing no law or order higher than our own will. How can we expect young people to respect the law of the land, when the land itself respects no human law outside itself?

The League of Nations failed; the United Nations is failing — and therefore many persons conclude that such federations are forever incapable of preserving the peace; but this is as foolish and premature as saying that because two vaccines have failed to halt a disease, no further and better vaccines are possible; if we were as pessimistic about personal health as we are about social health, we would still be falling victim to typhoid epidemics.

*

Until this age, man had only the power to make history; now we possess the unprecedented power to end history — which is surely a usurpation of the role of God, or whatever name you ascribe to the creative and regenerative force in the cosmos.

The View from the Saucer

ANTHROPOMORPHIC, as any smart high school senior could tell you, means "conceived in the shape or form of man"; and anthropocentric means "believing that all values and standards center around man."

I think of these two jaw-breaking words whenever I see a cartoon purporting to depict inhabitants from other worlds, like the little men who come out of flying saucers. They are invariably "odd" creatures, with antennae for ears, oblate bodies, and looking somewhat like those mechanical wind-up toys.

It rarely occurs to us, if such creatures exist, and if they should actually capture a specimen of mankind, what *their* reaction might be. Yet it might give us a little healthy humility to try to objectify the human organism from the point of view of a Saucerian.

"What sort of deformed and defective and rather loathsome person can this be?" is a likely response. "The creature has two eyes in front, and none in back, which makes no sense. Its skin is vulnerable to the slightest piercing, and cannot sustain any degree of heat or cold without external protection. And parts of it are covered with a rough and ugly substance called 'hair,' which keeps growing to no purpose.

"The apparatus for hearing," the Saucerian investigator might continue, "consists of two projecting flabs of flesh, connected to a canal that is often filled with something called 'wax.' And the apparatus for smelling is equally strange — a double 'nose' that is usually filled with hideous substances that must be 'blown out.' Likewise, the apparatus for eating is filled with billions of tiny bacilli, which regularly infect the whole system."

He goes on relentlessly: "The interior of this creature is a complex and bafflingly inefficient mass of tubes, tissues and organs, all of them teeming with micro-organisms, and highly susceptible to injury, disease and decay. The eliminatory processes are crude and the reproductive process has an embarrassing propinquity to the former. The less said about all this, the better."

With mingled fascination, wonder and disgust, the Saucerian decides to take back with him a "specimen" of this highest form of life on earth — but first encasing it in a thoroughly sterile covering, so that none of the thousand infections and contagions it is prone to would be likely to contaminate his home planet.

"And the most amazing thing," he tells his colleagues, "is that this polluted and odoriferous creature actually fights with others of the same species, out of a sense of 'superiority.' Incredible, eh?"

Antique mythology coupled the goddess of love with the god of war to warn us symbolically that everything we do not learn to love we will eventually destroy — mankind cannot remain indifferent, and is inescapably pulled toward one of these polarities or the other.

*

The fact that less than 10 per cent of recorded history has been entirely without war makes some people feel that war is "inevitable" — but the fact that less than one per cent of the human race is entirely without colds doesn't make us give up our relentless search for a cure for the common cold.

Giving Ourselves to "The Group"

IN HIS RECENT BOOK, *A Very Strange Society*, Allen Drury examines the government, people and problems in South Africa today, with a fairness that bends over backward.

Yet, when he comes to discuss the totalitarian methods of repression used to enforce apartheid in that country, he cannot refrain from crying out: "The individual Afrikaner is not a cruel person; what evil genius forces him to be so cruel as a government?"

But the same might be said of any people, anywhere, at any time in history. The Germans were not a cruel people, but they passively acquiesced (at least) in the deviltry of the Nazi government. The Russians are not a cruel people, but they merely turned their eyes away from Stalin's long reign of butchery and barbarism.

It is not merely when mob hysteria seizes them that people act worse in groups than they do individually. All "causes," all creeds, all ideologies make people behave far worse than they would individually. The most horrible savagery has not been committed for personal, selfish motives, but for church and state and flag, for "loyalty" and "group solidarity" and "common cause."

Of course, most Afrikaners are decent people. Most Mississippians are kindly folk. Most Germans are industrious, law-abiding, warmly sentimental. Most Russians are friendly and outgoing. And the United States troops bombing villages and burning peasants in Vietnam include some of the finest, sweetest boys you would ever hope to meet.

All this is beside the point. The point is that we feel desperately alone and insecure as individuals; we require a sense of *belonging* to some unit larger than ourselves. This unit can be national, racial, religious, ideological or socio-economic, as in slum gangs. And then we transfer our reason, our will and our passions to this larger unit.

What the gang does, no individual boy would do alone. What the South African government does, hardly a single Afrikaner would do. In the bitter centuries-long religious wars between Protestants and Catholics, it was the thought of "pleasing God," not any petty personal advantages, that prompted millions to mutual extermination — most of them people who "wouldn't hurt a fly."

It is not so much our human "selfishness" that is responsible for the great injustices and tyrannies of the world as it is our need to identify, to transcend ourselves, to form part of a solid group. The group insignia gives us emotional license to destroy others.

What is called "international policy" is as stupidly suicidal as that of the motorist who mutters, "If he doesn't dim his lights, I'll give him my brights!"

＊

In deploring the state of the world, perhaps we expect too much of the human race too soon; on dark days, it is worth remembering that the word "civilization" itself was coined by a Frenchman only 200 years ago.

＊

Nothing done to make us angry is as harmful to us as what we do as a result of such anger; and the instinct for revenge has not only ruined individuals, it has toppled whole empires.

The State and "Killer Instinct"

WHAT IF, in the past, the human race had conditioned its children against killing as rigorously as it conditioned them against sex? Until this modern age, the sex inhibition was fairly successful in keeping youngsters out of trouble, whatever other damage it happened to do.

A social prohibition against killing would not do any other damage, and might have inhibited people from slaughtering one another through the generations. "Aggressiveness," of course, will never be bred out of humans, but aggressiveness can stop quite short of killing.

The main reason this has not been done — even though homicidal violence can be shown to be a far greater threat to our species than sexual permissiveness — is that the state has always needed its warriors. If men will not kill, but will instead peacefully try to adjust their differences by reason or by other contests of skill and strength, then the leaders have lost their prime power over the masses.

The commandment "Thou shalt not kill" has been interpreted in all Western countries to tailor Christianity to national goals, rather than to fit the country to the religious model. Private citizens are not allowed to kill for private reasons; but as public soldiers, they are encouraged to kill for "civic" reasons that are often just as evil.

It is extraordinary that copulation, which is a life-giving and joyous activity, has been so hedged with restrictions, inhibitions and taboos; while killing, which goes against all divine, human and rational principles, has always been rewarded with honors, rank, medals and supreme power by the state.

The strength of "incest taboos" over the centuries, for instance, indicates how strongly the past can *imprint* repressions upon the young, if it sincerely believes them and carries them out effectively. A similar "killing taboo" against members of our own species could be equally exercised, were it not that the ruling caste of every social order is unwilling to do this for fear of losing its ultimate authority of force.

The state kills "enemies"; it kills "traitors"; it kills "revolutionaries"; it kills "criminals"; it even kills mere "undesirables." And it is rarely the populace itself that decides who such enemies and traitors and revolutionaries and criminals and undesirables are; it is its leaders, who wish to preserve themselves in power by all means.

If we were really serious about it, our children could be so conditioned from birth that taking another person's life would be an unimaginable horror that only the most demented or perverted could commit. Instead, we breed a race of moral idiots who think it is glorious to do for the state what it is forbidden to do singly.

If it took forty years for so simple and obvious a convenience as the zipper to be accepted, it may take 40,000 before we replace the world's war-making machinery with peace-keeping machinery.

*

Somewhere in the world there must be a secret school that teaches "military theology"; for just as preachers everywhere warn that we are never safe from sin, so generals everywhere warn that we are never safe from attack, no matter how well-armed we seem to be.

For a New Definition of Lunacy

IN DISCLOSING MORE about her family life and background, Stalin's daughter declared that, in her opinion, her father was not "insane" when he ordered the political purges of the 1930s, although he may have become paranoid a decade later.

I think the world of the future — if there is to be one — will require a new definition of the word *insane*. Heretofore, we have looked upon insanity as a mental aberration; it seems to me that there is something called "moral insanity" as well.

There is no doubt that Stalin was out of his mind in his last years, or that Hitler was a psychopath from the moment he entered the Munich beer cellar in the 1920s. But what of the men around them? What of the cool, plausible, efficient functionaries who did their dreadful bidding?

In some ways, indeed, it is easier to forgive a lunatic like Hitler than a Goering, a Goebbels, a Himmler or an Eichmann. He was possessed by a demon burning in his brain; they had no such excuse for their coldly bestial behavior. Likewise, the men around Stalin who helped murder all the Old Bolsheviks were morally insane.

Our current definition of lunacy is too narrow, too clinical, too conventional, to serve as a socially useful yardstick in judging the actions of public figures. True, we are all reservoirs of private wickedness, and it takes no Shadow to know what evil lurks in the hearts of men.

But public wickedness on a mass scale is not just quantitatively larger; it is qualitatively different. To be unjust, to be cruel, even to kill, for personal reasons, seems part of the defect we were born with; to kill thousands, and even millions, of people impersonally, simply because they are kulaks or capitalists or Poles or Jews, is a form of moral insanity.

In his book, *Functionaries*, F. William Howton defines such men as those who "view their work entirely in terms of a job well done — without stopping to consider whether or not the job ought to be done." Eichmann was just doing his job, taking orders, carrying out the function assigned him.

To divorce ends from means, to dehumanize oneself so that a child shipped to a gas chamber means no more than a sausage slipped into a casing, may not be insanity in the medical sense of the term — but if there is a moral norm in human conduct, what else can we call such a diabolic departure from the norm?

Unless a movement succeeds in making the citizenry think *and* feel *differently, it accomplishes nothing to force a change in their institutional arrangements; as Bernard Shaw observed, "Revolutions have never lightened the burden of tyranny; they have only shifted it to other shoulders."*

*

If nonviolent resistance is rewarded with neglect and contempt, what argument is there to oppose the apostles of violent resistance, except counter-violence?

*

The further removed one is from a problem, the more tempting it is to see it in oversimplified, black-and-white terms: for instance, Jews in America are far more fanatical and one-sided about the Mideast conflict than many Israelis are.

War Is Cancer of Mankind

WE SAY THAT THE AIM OF LIFE is self-preservation, if not for
the individual, at least for the species. Granted that every
organism seeks this end, does every organism know what is
best for its self-preservation?

Consider cancer cells and non-cancer cells in the human
body. The normal cells are aimed at reproducing and functioning in a way that is beneficial to the body. Cancer cells, on
the other hand, spread in a way that threatens and ultimately
destroys the whole body.

Normal cells work harmoniously, because they "know," in
a sense, that their preservation depends upon the health of the
body they inhabit. While they are organisms in themselves,
they also act as part of a substructure, directed at the good
of the whole body.

We might say, metaphorically, that cancer cells do not know
enough about self-preservation; they are, biologically, more
ignorant than normal cells. The aim of cancer cells is to
spread throughout the body, to conquer all the normal cells
— and when they reach their aim, the body is dead. *And so
are the cancer cells.*

For cancer cells destroy not only all rival cells, in their
ruthless biological warfare, but also destroy the larger organization — the body itself — signing their own suicide warrant.

The same is true of war, especially in the modern world.
War is the *social cancer* of mankind. It is a pernicious form of
ignorance, for it destroys not only its "enemies," but also the
whole superstructure of which it is a part—and thus eventually it defeats itself.

Nations live in a state of anarchy, not in a state of law. An
like cancer cells, nations do not know that their ultimate se

interest lies in preserving the health and harmony of th
body (that is, the community of man), for if that b
mortally wounded, then no nation can survive and flour

If the aim of life is self-preservation — for the specie
well as for the individual — we must tame or eradicate
cancer cells of war in the social organism. And this can t
done only when nations begin to recognize that what may
seem to be "in the national interest" cannot be opposed to the
common interest of mankind, or both the nation and mankind will die in this "conquest."

The life of every organism depends upon the viability of the
system of which it is a member. The cancer cells cannot exist
without the body to inhabit, and they must be exterminated
if they cannot be re-educated to behave like normal cells.
At present, their very success dooms them to failure — just
as a victorious war in the atomic age would be an unqualified
disaster for the dying winner.

*One of the best critiques of mindless rebellion was made by
Joseph Conrad, when he observed: "The revolutionary spirit
is mighty convenient in this, that it frees one from all scruples
as regards ideas."*

*

*We save our highest regard for the person who thinks more
of others than he does of himself. Why then do we idolatrize
our own countries, which always put their self-interest ahead
of others?*

The Stuff of Which Fascism Is Made

THE WIDESPREAD CONFUSION about the phrase "law and order" is not confined to the general public; it extends into some high and frightening places.

Recently, Retired Air Force Brigadier General Robert Scott (ironically enough, the author of *God Is My Co-Pilot*) told an American Legion meeting in California that a military takeover of the United States "by devious or direct means" may become necessary if politicians cannot control lawlessness.

It is hard to know if Scott is a wicked man or merely an ignorant one; but it is not hard to tell that God is no longer his co-pilot. For the doctrine he preaches is the doctrine of the Devil.

If the military takes over in the name of "law and order," it would be breaking the law as much as if any other unauthorized gang took over. The military has authority only because it is invested with it by the civilian government; and a military putsch would be as much of a revolution — and a gross violation of our Constitution — as a takeover by Black Muslims or White Klansmen or Riders of the Purple Sage.

A military officer, like a police officer, is simply a private citizen who has been temporarily delegated authority by the state. He has no inherent legitimate power, and is subject to all the normal rules and restraints of civilian society.

If the professional politicians cannot keep law and order, we rectify the situation by electing other and better officials — not by mob rule. For the military is just a mob in uniform, once it decides to administer the government on its own terms.

It is a fascinating example of tortured psychology to hear a man deploring "lawlessness" in one breath, and then in the next breath advocating the most dangerous and diabolic lawlessness any nation could ever face — control by a military junta responsible to nothing but itself.

This is the stuff of which fascism is made. Fascism plays on the fears of the middle class — fears of communism, of anarchy, of crime, of any change in the status quo — to impose its own form of dictatorship, which is as dreadful as the disease it purports to cure.

The twisted thinking of the extreme right is as fearsome as the twisted thinking of the extreme left — perhaps even more so in this country, where left-wingers are customarily suspect, but right-wingers assume all the false trappings of respectability and responsibility.

One wonders how many potentially great leaders have died obscure in a nation of mediocrities that was not ready for them, or that sacrificed them in war before their special talents could come to fruition.

*

The basic paradox that creates so much bitterness today is the fact that, in order to survive as a species, we need institutions on a world-wide scale; but in order to enjoy life as individuals we need more and better personal relations on a small scale — and neither of these objectives is being realized: The world is not moving toward the large universality that would eliminate war, or toward the smaller units that would restore a sense of identity, but merely hanging in limbo between the two.

*

Can anything be more absurd than the victors trying the losers for "war crimes," when nobody has ever been tried for the crime of war itself?

5

OF THE MIND
AND PASSIONS

Motivation a Key Part of "Talent"

WHAT MOST PEOPLE — and especially parents — don't want
to recognize is that motivation is an integral part of talent, and
not just a kind of fuel injection that powers it.

Parents are fond of sighing, "He'd be so good at this," or
"She'd make such a wonderful that" — if only he or she
would *apply* himself or herself.

But the talent is incomplete without the applying. It is
nothing, it is only a potentiality, and cannot be brought into
existence if the motivation is lacking.

Who knows how many "mute inglorious Miltons" have
lived and died without the world having been aware of their
latent talents? If the drive to actualize their ability is missing,
nothing outside of themselves can instill it in them. No
threats, no promises, no praise.

A truly talented person is self-propelled. Not only does
he not need to be encouraged (although it helps), he cannot
be suppressed. He will keep on painting or writing or com-
posing or doing whatever he does best, despite all the rejec-
tions and rebuffs in the world. And he is supremely self-
confident, although despair may attack him from time to
time. Despair about his future, not about his gifts.

This is true not only of the artist but of the student. The student who "could really get an A" if he wanted to, cannot really get an A because he really doesn't want to. And the wanting to is an essential part of the achieving, not a separate thing, as parents imagine, that can be injected into him like a shot of adrenalin.

All genuine and meaningful and lasting motivation comes from the inside, not from the outside. The carrot and the stick work — maybe — only as long as the carrot is in front and the stick behind. When they are withdrawn, the motivation ceases. You can get a mule to move this way, but not a person, for very long.

Parents should learn to stop nagging their children about how well they could do "if you only tried more, or cared more." Trying and caring, in specific areas, is built into people; or else it comes to them later, if they mature properly; or it never comes at all. But it is dead certain that no young person was ever motivated by a querulous, disappointed parent more concerned with his own pride than with the child's ultimate self-actualization.

If she shows "a talent for music" and doesn't want to practice, let it go — the only talent worth cultivating is that which is accompanied by patience, persistence and passion. If these are lacking, you might as well try to make a ballerina out of a "talented" paraplegic.

What most people fail to learn until too late, if ever, was tersely expressed by Freya Stark: "There can be no happiness if the things we believe in are different from the things we do."

Bad Drivers Unsure of Virility

As I WAS EDGING out of a parking lot the other day, some Clyde in his Bonneville cut sharply ahead of me, flashed a sour smile of triumph in my direction and scooted away.

He evidently thought he had "won" something, but in my view, he had lost. He thought he was displaying strength and aggressiveness; I thought he was displaying weakness and bad manners.

What the prevailing ethos in modern American life does not seem to understand is that true strength *always* reveals itself in gentleness and courtesy; this was the whole medieval idea of knighthood and chivalry — a knight was chivalrous because he felt strong enough to afford it.

We tend to confuse rudeness with power, and aggressiveness with virility. Many, if not most, of the bad-mannered drivers on the road are slack-jawed youths who privately feel weak and insecure in their personal relations with the world; tooling a ferocious car gives them a vicarious sense of power they do not possess in person.

Genuine strength of character is always accompanied by a feeling of security that allows one to practice civility and courtesy — but, in our perverse culture, civility and courtesy are often regarded as signs of weakness or some lack of "manliness."

And it is largely this perverse evaluation of what constitutes manhood that accounts for so much of the dangerous discourtesy on our nation's highways — somehow, the education of boys here has stressed aggressiveness at the price of gentleness, so that many youths act like boors in order to be thought of as "men."

This is fairly indigenous to our culture; in other countries, a more balanced view is taken of what comprises "manliness," and one of the main criteria of an adult male is his *considerateness* for others. And the poor result of our misconception of manhood can be seen in many failing marriages, where the wives uniformly complain that their husbands are just "little boys who failed to grow up."

There is little doubt in my mind that girls here grow up to be women more easily and successfully than boys grow up to be men; or that most "immaturity" in the marriage relationship is displayed by the husbands. Women have other conjugal faults, but they tend to accept adult obligations with better grace than men do.

No one, to my knowledge, has ever made a study of the social psychology of driving; but I think that such a study would show that the males with the worst manners are the least sure of their masculinity and the most resentful toward the deeper responsibilities of manhood. For true strength always exhibits itself in generosity of spirit.

Much of what we dignify as "motives" is really "impulse"; we may be motivated to shop for groceries, but it is impulse that makes us buy far more than we had intended, and tell ourselves we always meant to.

*

When Thoreau said, "It's healthy to be sick sometimes," he was anticipating the modern psycho-medical knowledge that the person who never lets go is more likely to be felled suddenly, like a tree too stubborn to bend, which is broken in two by a windstorm.

It's the Majority That's a Threat

"I WAS HAVING COFFEE in a restaurant," said the lady, "and because I was in a hurry, I sat at the counter. Four men were sitting across from me — quite ordinary types, conventionally dressed, perhaps salesmen.

"In came two couples and sat down at a booth. The young women were quite unremarkable in every way — just the kind you see every day. The men with them were unexceptional in their attire, but one of them wore his hair a trifle longer than most men do, and the other quite a bit longer.

"The two couples were chatting away quietly and amiably, bothering no one and attracting no attention. Then I saw one of the four men across the way nudge another and look over toward the two couples. Soon all four men were looking at them and whispering.

"The men got up to leave, and two of them went over to the coat rack, which was close by the booth in which the two couples were sitting. They put on their coats slowly and deliberately, standing right in front of the longish-haired men, laughing at them and pointing them out to their two friends across the room. They they shook their heads in obvious disgust, and stomped out.

"You know," she went on, "it really made me feel quite sick. The two couples weren't doing a thing, weren't even hippily dressed, weren't trying to attract attention, as some do. And, in our neighborhood especially, most of the boys in school — up through high school and college — wear their hair longer than the ordinary. Nobody pays any attention to it.

"But there was something so ugly about the calculated reaction of these men, something so mean and provincial and full of hate for no real reason, that it turned my stomach. It was an act of aggression — although not actually physical — without the slightest provocation. And, in a way, it was crueler than a blow struck in anger or passion.

"This is what frightens me in our country today, more than the riots or demonstrations by the underprivileged, by the poor or desperate. What frightens me is the — what shall I call it? — the 'hickishness' of ordinary people, the resentment of differences, the ignorance of other ways of life, the unthinking reaction and resistance to change, no matter how harmless or how necessary.

"Our country can handle its minority problems; it's the majority problem that troubles me — the almost hysterical need to make everybody conform to the pattern of the majority. This is the biggest threat democracy faces. And I saw that naked threat in the eyes of those four men."

How many travelers would bother to take trips if they were bound to a vow of silence about the venture upon their return?

*

Basically, all ideologies aside, there are only two kinds of states: those in which the police are an arm of the government, and those in which the government is an arm of the police.

*

"We hear and apprehend only what we already half know," said Thoreau; *but it is the other half that is more likely to shape our future.*

We Never Let Ignorance Deter Us

ONE IMPORTANT "LAW" that Parkinson neglected to formulate is perhaps the most important in the field of social behavior and reaction. It is this: *The less we know firsthand about a situation, the firmer is our opinion about the way to handle it.*

For example, the people who know least about what is going on in the nation's colleges are the most dogmatic about resolving the problem of student dissent. To them it is clear-cut and simple: punishment for rebels and restoration of the old order.

But the closer one gets to the campus scene, the less black and white the picture becomes. There are many kinds of student revolts, for many reasons, and each must be judged on its own merits and resolved accordingly.

Likewise, the most affluent and isolated segment of the bourgeoisie is the most sure about the way to handle riots and civil disorders in the slums. The fact that they have never spent a day in a slum, and are wholly oblivious to the dynamics of ghetto living, only makes them more cocksure about "getting tough with lawbreakers."

And the same is true for all social problems. The persons closest to them are sensitive to many factors, are aware of the immense complexity and the vast difference between one situation and another. And they have no easy, effortless prescription for solving them — knowing that such prescriptions often make things worse rather than better.

Ignorance does not breed bliss as much as it generates certainty. If you have never had a delinquent child in your family, it is easy to say exactly how he should be handled and what should be done with delinquents. But if you are confronted with the personal reality, your attitude immediately changes.

Knowing a situation first hand makes you think of it in terms of *people* rather than of *problems;* and of *individuals* more than of people in the abstract. It makes you understand how complicated are the causes of human behavior, and how difficult it is to find adequate remedies that will both satisfy the requirements of society and serve the best needs of the individual.

We all agree theoretically that "experience is the best teacher," yet most of us are willing to make bumptious judgments in the areas where we have had no experience at all — the rich tell the poor how to live, the healthy tell the sick, the white tell the black. And all the advice is as fatuous as it is futile.

The more intimately we know a problem, or a person, the less willing are we to make a flat, glib generalization. And the more positive we sound, the more negative we feel — it is the haters who have all the cheap and easy "remedies."

If you shout in an argument, it makes you wrong, even when you are right.

*

Those who protest that the wool was pulled over their eyes have generally done most of the knitting themselves.

*

Ninety per cent of scientific research ends in failure, and we are prepared to accept that proportion in allocating funds for development — but in giving funds for the arts, we demand assurance of success, and feel cheated if some projects turn out badly.

How to Understand What's Going On

How to Begin to Understand What's Happening in the World Today in Ten Not-So-Easy Lessons:

1. Start by taking a long, hard look at yourself, to determine whether you have significantly altered your views or stance in the last twenty years, or even in the last decade.

2. Ask yourself what you have done, personally and practically, to help change what needs to be changed, and to help preserve what needs to be preserved — and on what philosophical or moral basis you distinguish between the two.

3. Look around at your co-workers, friends and neighbors, and assess whether they are engaged in anything but the pursuit of affluence (and if they are enjoying it), and the pursuit of pleasure (and if they are enjoying it).

4. Recall when you last, if ever, had a serious talk with a person under twenty, with a poor person, with a Negro, with a foreigner, with a radical — with anyone whose life-position is sharply different from yours.

5. List and evaluate the kind of things you are reading now that you weren't reading twenty years ago, or a decade ago — are you aware of what's going on in the behavioral sciences, in education, in technology, in psychological research, or are you still reading the familiar and comfortable publications that tell you only what you like to hear or want to hear?

6. Are you reacting to new questions with new insights, or with answers that were beginning to be obsolete a generation ago — and are you able to differentiate between those principles and maxims that have permanent value and those that merely reflect the "received wisdom" of your father's time but are increasingly irrelevant today?

7. Try this imaginative process on yourself: Take a social or political position that is at the opposite pole from your own, and formulate it so that its proponents would be satisfied with the fair way you have stated it — and then, and only then, try to refute it with reason, logic and facts, not with rhetoric, emotion or name-calling.

8. Ask yourself (*a*) what are your proximate goals in life, then (*b*) what are your ultimate goals in life and then (*c*) are your proximate goals leading toward, or away from, your ultimate goals?

9. Consider Bernard Shaw's aphorism: "It is impossible for the smoker and the nonsmoker to be equally free in the same railway car," and reflect on how society can arrange optimum freedom for all.

10. Whenever some act reported in the news particularly outrages you, threatens you, or appalls you, ask yourself under what possible conditions your reaction might be exactly the opposite.

Our touching modern faith in the benefits of formal education ought to be tempered by a reminder of President Theodore Roosevelt's tart observation: "A man who has never gone to school may steal from a freight car; but if he has a university education, he may steal the whole railroad."

*

Laymen imagine that "research" consists mainly in exploring and combining extravagant theories and processes; whereas, in fact, the most fruitful research has sprung from a profound and unsatisfied contemplation of the obvious.

There's Too Little Violence on TV

IT's ODD, as I've remarked before, how we insist on calling things not only by their wrong name but by their opposite name — the "black" problem is really a white one, the "student" problem is really a teacher one, the "war" problem is really a peace one, and so on.

"Violence" is another prime example of such a misnomer. We complain that there is too much "violence" on television, when exactly the opposite is the case — there is no real violence, only a show of it.

Counterfeit violence is what children see on the TV tube. In counterfeit violence, injury and suffering and death are not real. A man is shot, *bang*, he falls down, is dead and the camera moves on. A man is hit on the jaw and tumbles over a cliff and disappears. He is just a dummy, a number, a player in a game who will reappear next week.

Real violence, if it could be shown, would turn the kids off. Real violence is bloody, sickening, frightful, persistent or permanent. It profoundly affects not only the victim but his family, his friends, his whole social group. It tears the fabric of the community, it bereaves women, it orphans children, it fills hospitals and graveyards.

For it is fake violence that makes aggressiveness seem so beguiling and worthy of imitation to young people. They are not shown a close-up of the broken bone jutting out from the skin, or the smashed skull with blood dripping through the ear, or the limp half-man slouched in a wheelchair three years later.

On the screen, violence is merely cosmetic. People die painlessly, or take a brutal beating and a minute later are embracing the heroine; unlike real life, where the kind of fighting depicted on the screen would incapacitate both combatants for the rest of the series, or longer.

What the kids get to see on TV are the dubious benefits of violence, never its dismaying disadvantages. The hero and the villains shoot it out, and the kids know the hero will always win; and since each person is a hero in his own mind, it becomes inconceivable that he could lose. This is the treacherous logic of fantasy adventure.

Artificial violence should be banned, because it is unrealistic, and genuine violence should be shown wherever possible, so that its ugly face will not seem so attractive to impressionable minds. The causes and consequences of violence should be dramatically delineated, not just the surface actions that stir the blood and stun the moral nerve and make us think we can walk away from mortal combat into the sunset of next week's episode.

We mustn't blame the poor for being extragagant any more than we blame the rich for being tight; in both cases, they are seeking to console themselves for having too little or too much.

*

One of the loveliest metaphors describing the aggressive and erotic drives in the human animal was made by J. P. F. Richter, when he wrote: "Anger wishes all mankind had only one neck; love, that it had only one heart."

*

Considering what one has to be before one can become a Senator, it's not surprising that we have so many sleazy characters there, but that there are so many who have been relatively uncontaminated by their upward climb.

Whites Can't See This Ghetto Gap

WHEN I was fifteen years old, I began working as a copyboy on a newspaper, going to school days while working nights. I didn't have to; I just wanted to. But suppose that I had had to — and suppose, further, that I knew I could never rise above the copyboy level.

What incentive would I have had to work hard and well, to take on extra assignments, to study my craft diligently, to prepare myself for eventual promotion? In a dead-end job, I would soon get to a dead end.

I don't think enough people understand this about Negro workers in the past, and still to a large extent today. White people tend to evaluate Negro workers by white standards and expectations, not by the more realistic appraisal Negroes make of their own chances.

Work must have a goal beyond mere subsistence if it is to give the worker any esprit or interest in the job beyond the mere paycheck. The job must promise promotion, or must be essentially interesting, or at the least pay enough so that the worker can anticipate a higher standard of living, for his children if not for himself.

Most jobs available to Negroes in this country, in this century, have been deficient in all three elements. They have been dull and meaningless labor, offering no chance for advancement and paying so little that only day-to-day satisfactions could be fulfilled. The "sense of the future," which keeps most white people going, has not operated, or only dimly, among the mass of Negro workers.

The whites' complaints about the Negroes' indolence and indifference to showing up on time (or at all) ignore the psychological gap between white and black "time sense."

Whites live more for the future, because they *have* a future; blacks for the present, since the future looks too bleak to contemplate.

As Elliott Liebow puts it in his recent study of Negro street-corner men, "The job fails the man and then the man fails the job." If only dull, dirty and dead-end jobs are available to blacks, they lose whatever self-esteem they might have had, and would just as soon loaf or take relief as work — especially when most of the jobs open to them don't even allow them to support a family in a manly, self-respecting and decent fashion.

Asking them to "shape up" is as fatuous and cruel as asking a man to do the broad jump after we have broken both his legs.

This should be a truism, acknowledged by the white community — particularly in a society such as ours, where "incentive" is the key word in our scramble for material advancement. Why the Negro, being a victim rather than a beneficiary of our incentive system, is yet expected to behave the way we do, is a symptom of our own sickness more than of his.

There is no way to "know yourself" except to allow yourself to be known to another, fully and freely; this is why introspection as a means of self-knowledge or self-fulfillment is a dead end.

*

The basic difference between the American and the European approach to life is that the American regards it as a problem to be solved (by more machines and money), while the European regards it as a predicament to be got through.

Politics Attracts the Wrong Men

IT HAS LONG SEEMED quite plain to me that one reason — perhaps the chief reason — that governments of all kinds go bad is that exactly the wrong sort of men are chosen to run them; and it makes little difference which party or principles they adhere to.

The men who get political power are those who want it the most. And with only a few notable exceptions, the temperaments and drives of such men have been responsible for most of the world's woes. It was no accident that the shrewd and ruthless Stalin, rather than the intellectual Trotsky, seized control of the Communist apparatus after Lenin died.

The only man who can be trusted with authority, said Plato, is the man who does not want it; but his opposite is almost always the man who gets it. And he is often willing to push, scheme, shout, bribe or betray his way into positions where his capacity for doing damage is incalculable.

This is not to say that all public men are bounders or bullies, but it is to suggest that men who lust after political power generally get it; and a lustful man is not likely to be cool, moderate or unselfish when his opinion is challenged or his authority is in any way threatened.

Hamilton Fish, the historian, once declared that if, around 1850, a carriage had been filled with the extremist leaders of both North and South and plunged into the river, the nation might have been spared the calamitous Civil War.

And Lecky, that magnificent historian of eighteenth-century England, remarked that "a wise and moderate statesmanship might easily have averted the catastrophe" of the American Revolution, which destroyed the political unity of the English race. The original cause of difference was so small, and so easily capable of mediation, but pride and stubbornness prevented any compromise on the issue.

Indeed, Lecky goes on to generalize, "there has scarcely been a great revolution in the world which might not at some stage have been averted, materially modified or at least greatly postponed, by wise and moderate statesmanship."

That the world has seen so little of this sort of statesmanship may be a flaw built into political institutions; but just as much, I am convinced, it is the fact that public ability is so often coupled with personal aggressiveness — and, in times of crisis, the possessor of such ability cannot distinguish between public and private goals.

"When a man seeks public office," said Jefferson, "a kind of corruption begins to creep into his soul." Perhaps, like the ancient Athenians, we ought to choose our leaders by lottery; could we do much worse?

We like to think that gluttony and obesity are characteristics of our modern culture, as contrasted with the Spartan living of our forebears; but well over 200 years ago, Benjamin Franklin observed: "I saw few die of hunger; of eating, a hundred thousand."

*

The less faith you have in yourself, the more you have in a "cause."

*

One easy way to distinguish a virtue from a vice is that a virtue enjoys seeing itself reflected in others — as generosity appreciates generosity — but a vice resents seeing itself reflected in others — as egotism cannot stand rival egotism.

Find Out If You're a Big City "Hick"

A READER in a small town wants to know exactly what I meant by "hickish" in a recent column in which I referred to those persons who look askance at boys with long hair.

Being "hickish" has little to do with where you live; probably 75 per cent of the residents of a city as big as Chicago are hickish — while I have known plenty of small town and rural residents who were basically unhickish.

If you care to give yourself a "hick test," I have arbitrarily devised a set of questions to ask yourself and to answer as honestly as possible:

1. Do you run to the scene of accidents, or stop your car to gawk at highway disasters, not in any mood of helpfulness, but merely to watch the grim proceedings?

2. Do you loudly point out "celebrities" across the street, or across the room, and make a fuss over the presence of famous people?

3. Do you commonly observe, as a great flash of philosophic insight, that "these days you can hardly tell the boys from the girls"?

4. Do you, if a man, wear pens or pencils sticking out of your suit's handkerchief pocket; and, if a woman, wear curlers to the store?

5. Do you look upon Art Linkletter as a fine performer and a splendid example of an American success story?

6. Do you, if over sixteen years old, carry a transistor radio to the beach or any other public place?

7. Do you have travel stickers pasted to the windows of your car, showing you have visited Mammoth Cave or Tommy Bartlett's Water Ski Show?

8. Do you enjoy what is known as "semi-classical" music?

9. Do you believe that people who don't attend church are less "moral" than those who do?

10. Do you, when traveling abroad, resent it because the "foreigners" don't speak English?

11. Do you think that getting "good marks" in school means that someone is getting a "good education"?

12. Do you believe that marijuana users should be punished (as they now are) by being given jail sentences longer than those meted out to some war criminals?

If you have answered "Yes" to more than two of these questions, you are high on the hickish scale. If you have answered "No" to all 12, it doesn't matter where you live — except that most of your neighbors must find you a little peculiar.

Doctors make the worst patients in a hospital for the same reason that pilots make the worst passengers in a plane — both know exactly how many things go wrong and how fallible their colleagues are.

*

Every discontented person I have ever met has been discontented because, at bottom, he has been trying to be someone he is not; self-acceptance is the indispensable prerequisite of all mental health.

*

The truest test of independent judgment is being able to dislike someone who admires us, and to admire someone who dislikes us.

The Gravest Danger Facing Our Land

YES, I am fearful. Danger is abroad in the land. The ugliness of mass violence is a threat hanging heavy over all our heads.

But the danger does not come from the place most people think it does. It does not come from the Negro rioters or from "crime in the streets."

It comes from "respectable" and "responsible" sources. It comes from smug, affluent and ignorant quarters. It comes from those who are eagerly using "crime in the streets" as an excuse for hate and rage and repression.

This is what frightens me. Not the pathetic and futile Negro summer riots, in which far more blacks than whites were killed and injured. Not the rise in street crime, which a genuine revival of community spirit could reduce in a few swift months.

What frightens me are the faces of the men and women who push into Chicago's Board of Education to oppose busing of students, and of those who picket a public school to which seven Negro children have been transferred.

What frightens me is the standing ovation given to George Wallace's demagogic speech made before an influential executives' club in the same city.

What frightens me are the 10,000 customers who wrote in to cancel their charge accounts when the head of a New York department store put himself on record as favoring open housing and equal opportunity.

What frightens me is a navy captain, speaking as national president of the Reserves Officers Association, telling his group that the United States would be much better off if dissenters against the Vietnam war were "banished" from the country.

What frightens me is the gimlet-eyed sheriff of Cook County in Illinois attempting to recruit a posse to deal with rioters — and his concentration-camp concept of dealing with violators.

These, and many more symptoms, constitute the gravest danger that is abroad in the land. They are horribly reminiscent of the beginnings of fascism in other countries — fascism not in its formal political sense, but in the minds and hearts and passions of ordinary men and women.

We are unwilling to make the vast changes necessary to bring social justice to all the people. We are unwilling to give the money, the energy, the patience, the understanding to solve the very problems we have created. And we are scared to death of the monster we have permitted to grow to maturity in the basement of our national life.

But which is really the monster — the rioter, or his re-presser?

The only true test of a classic work of literature is its ability to survive the stupidity of the people who teach it and the indifference of the pupils who study it.

*

The worst form of disappointment often consists in getting exactly what you wanted.

*

If someone dislikes you, try asking yourself whether the dislike is rooted in something within him or in something within you; if within him, nothing can be done about it; if within you, a lot can be done, if you care to.

Why It Is Different for the Negro

WHENEVER I hear someone say, "Well, my parents (or grandparents) came over to this country without a penny, lived in the slums and worked themselves up out of it — so why can't Negroes do the same?" I recall that "false analogy" is one of the most treacherous contortions of the human mind.

Let me illustrate concretely what is meant by "false analogy." In his splendid book *Personal Knowledge*, Michael Polanyi tells of taking a Hindu to tea in New York. When his tea arrived, the Hindu opened the tea bag and poured the loose tea into his cup.

Polanyi gently explained that he didn't have to do that — the bag was porous and the tea would seep through it into the water. The Hindu politely thanked him, and then promptly dropped a lump of sugar — still wrapped in paper — into his cup of tea.

The Hindu was making a justifiable, but utterly false, analogy: If the tea soaks through its container, then the sugar soaks through its container. But the tea bag was designed to let the tea *out*, and the sugar wrapper was designed to keep the sugar *in*.

To the ignorant or thoughtless, however, paper is paper, and people are people, and it is far easier to lump them than to like or understand them.

The fact that other ethnic groups came over here and worked their way out of the slums would be relevant to the Negro situation only if all other factors were similar; but they were not, as a moment's honest reflection would persuade us.

The ethnic groups who made it in America had a religious background that was deeply rooted in the Old World and effectively transplanted here.

They had a cohesive family pattern, a tradition of the father taking care of the family and the mother working in the home.

They had the opportunity to live where they could afford to, go to school freely with children of other classes and backgrounds and make their way in business or the professions as fast as their talent would allow.

The Negro was kidnaped from his homeland, enslaved, made to do the most menial work, denied an education, humiliated and despised, his family broken up and sold to different slave owners, his old religious ties obliterated and a passive pie-in-the-sky Christianity substituted for it. His incentive was steadily and remorselessly extinguished, and his individualism was ground into a stereotype.

Given these long-term handicaps, how do you imagine your parents or grandparents would have fared in the New World, Mr. Honky?

If all the statisticians in the world were laid end to end, they'd disagree about the significance of the total length.

*

The first, and almost whole, task of a school is to stimulate curiosity; if it cannot do this, it cannot truly educate, it can only train, for an educated person remains curious his life long, while a merely trained one only performs rituals.

*

The most common form of suicide has never been by violent means, but by passivity — by slowly shrinking within oneself so that the functions one performs take control of the personality performing them.

Learning Is a Part of Living

WE LOOK UPON learning as an isolated process that takes place in the mind; but nothing takes place in the mind alone. The total environment in which we learn something is an integral part of that learning.

Everyone who speaks a second language, however poorly, has had the experience of "forgetting" the language when he returns to his homeland. Yet, if he goes back to the country of the second language, he quickly picks it up again — because the environment promotes speedy recall.

The specific environment becomes a "part" of what is learned. For instance, experiments have shown that when the classroom learning of schoolchildren is later examined in a different room, the amount recalled is smaller than when the exam takes place in the original room.

Even having a different teacher in charge of the exam impairs the recall. And, more strikingly, even a minor element such as color is important — when pupils are given nonsense syllables to learn against a colored background, it takes more time to relearn them later when presented against a different color than when the background color remains the same!

What the German psychologists call *gestalt* — the total pattern with all its associations and interrelationships — determines how well we learn and how easily we recall what we have learned. If we learn under unpleasant conditions, the learning tends to be rejected along with the negative environment it took place in.

If we understand this, we can sympathize more fully with the demand for integrated schooling on the part of the underprivileged. It is not so much that the all-white schools have better teachers and more adequate material; it is that the *total environment* of learning promotes retention and recall, and thus results in higher marks for crucial examinations.

An atmosphere that is conducive to learning is fully as important as the actual tools and techniques of education. Most learning is a process of *association* — and if pupils associate the material with bleak conditions, indifferent teachers, inattentive pupils and a prison atmosphere, then the subjects themselves will be repressed and rejected. Mind and the emotions cannot be separated by anyone.

Continuity of background, constant stimulation and adequate motivation are the three most important elements that make for effective learning — and when these are lacking, it is a lot more comfortable to forget than to remember.

Humility, like honesty, disappears at the first trace of consciousness of itself.

*

Whatever studies have been made indicate that there is little or no relationship between grades given in school and subsequent achievement — like the University of Utah study showing that medical school grades bore no relationship to the students' later performances as doctors.

*

There will be no rest, and no release, for the human spirit as long as we stubbornly keep confusing the pursuit of pleasure with the pursuit of happiness.

*

Someone who has offended you never forgives you for it.

How We Make Prophecies Come True

"THE WHITENESS of a man's teeth," observes St. Thomas in the *Summa*, "primarily belongs, not to him, but to them."

If the whiteness of the teeth belongs to the teeth, and not to the man, then the blackness of the skin belongs to the skin, and not to the man. And, thus, all the accidental attributes of the body must not be ascribed to the essence of the individual personality.

This is a lesson mankind has not yet learned. We identify, and stratify, and treat persons largely on the basis of their accidental characteristics, which have no deeper meaning.

Then, because our treatment of such persons makes them sensitive and resentful and angry and out of joint with us, we turn around and blame them for being "different." This is the history of all discrimination and persecution.

Suppose we did this with a child in our family, who had some peculiar physical characteristic, one not shared by the rest of the family. By the time the child was adolescent, the weight of disapproval would have shaped (and misshaped) his whole character and personality. Our thinking him different makes him different; our dislike makes him unlikable.

We can clearly see what would happen in the case of an individual child; but we somehow cannot grasp the analogy to a whole race or section of people who are treated in the same fashion.

What social scientists have lately called "the self-fulfilling prophecy" is hard at work in such cases. Because of our prejudice or fear or ignorance, we *expect* certain groups to behave in a specific negative way; and the very thrust of our expectations tends to drive them in that same direction. Then we feel justified in condemning them, because they have predictably reacted as we thought they would.

In this truly vicious circle, all racial and religious and geographical discrimination is constantly being reinforced — because the objects of our prejudice eventually come to resemble the stereotypes we have cast them in. And our contempt becomes their self-contempt. Even their new-found "pride" is reactive, not spontaneous — black is neither "beautiful" nor "ugly," it is merely pigment.

The vast revolutions awaiting us in the latter third of the twentieth century may take political form, but they will be racial revolutions in substance, using as their tremendous lever the insane delusion of the white race that the blackness of the skin belongs to the man, and not merely to the skin.

Ignorance can't be bliss, or many more people would be happy.

*

The whole art of living nearly consists in knowing which impulses to obey and which must be made to obey.

*

The only way to be meaningfully "successful" is always to compete against yourself, against your previous best, rather than against others; in this way, you win even when you lose, in gaining a knowledge of your proper limits.

*

Nature abhors a mental vacuum, too; when a mind is devoid of ideas, she fills it with prejudices that call themselves convictions.

What's Sexy About Nude Bodies?

THE WORD "OBSCENE" means "tending to cause sexual excitement or lust." I don't know why this should be considered a *bad* thing by society, but even granting that it should, what makes a naked body obscene?

Two University of Wisconsin students last fall were indicted on obscenity charges (later withdrawn when no witnesses could be found) for performing in a nude version of *Peter Pan* at two performances of the musical production.

I didn't see the performance, but I have seen naked bodies, and they are lovely or laughable or pathetic or uninteresting or droll, but none has ever impressed me as obscene, in any sense of the word.

An *act* can be obscene, an *attitude* can be obscene, but a body per se cannot be. It is only a dirty mind that can see dirt in a clean body; to the (unconsciously) impure, all things are impure.

The plain common-sense fact is that a naked body is about as unlustful and unexciting in itself as a plucked chicken. Many years ago, as a reporter, I covered (or uncovered) a nudist convention, which was about the most Puritan convention I had ever attended in my life.

Because the members of this nudist group didn't regard their bodies — at that time, in that place — as provocative or symbolic of sexuality, they were totally unself-conscious; and after an hour or so of reconditioning, I became just as unaware of their nakedness.

Everyone knows that a woman wearing diaphanous garments that tease and promise and conceal as much as they disclose is ten times more "alluring" than a stark-naked woman prancing around. It is her attitude that makes her "obscene" or not; it is not her equipment. And it is the attitude of society, not the fact of nudity itself.

Recently I saw a record album cover of two young singers, totally naked in front-face, as it were. The photograph was amusing because it was so utterly unerotic; they both looked like sad sacks, standing there smiling foolishly at the world, for no particular reason. It was enough to drive a man into a monastery.

Actually, the *more* nakedness, the *less* sexuality; the more we take the body for granted, the less we feel prompted to fumble for forbidden fruit. It is the false aura of mystery that invests the body with a meretricious glamour. Japan, where men and women freely bathe together, has fewer rape cases in a year than the United States has in one day.

The reason that hatred is an inferior emotion to love is not merely moral, but psychological — in that hatred aims at annihilating the object, and thus extinguishes its own reason for being, whereas love aims at augmenting the object, and thus perpetuates its reason for being.

*

All genuine love comes from strength, and is a kind of surplus energy in living; false love comes from weakness, and tries to suck vitality out of its object.

*

Ordinary folk like each other well without knowing each other well; clever people know each other well without liking each other well; and both groups are only dimly aware of what they are missing.

Why Some Are Doers, Others Aren't

BERNARD SHAW said many wise and witty things, along with a good deal of nonsense. But perhaps the most mischievous comment he ever made is one that is parroted by people every day: "He who can, does; he who cannot, teaches."

This was a cheap, smart-alecky and wholly unthinking observation. *Doing* and *teaching* are two wholly different activities; and if the teacher is often not good at doing, the doer is generally much worse at teaching others how to do.

The most obvious example that comes to mind is athletics. The greatest coaches have often been mediocre players; the most astute prize-fighter trainers usually could not last a round against Tiny Tim; and some of the finest music teachers would disgrace a high school orchestra.

In the sport that interests me most, tennis, the outstanding coach for many years was Mercer Beasley, who brought an astonishing number of youngsters to court greatness. Yet Beasley himself was never more than an indifferent tennis player, as he and all his pupils cheerfully admit.

And, likewise, in the theater, some of the best dramatic coaches can barely stagger out on a stage and recite "Gunga Din" before an audience.

They know *how* a performance should go, and can superbly impart this knowledge — but there is no earthly reason why they themselves should be able to play a role professionally.

This snide attitude toward teaching comes from a mistaken view of talent. The talented person generally does not know why he does what he does, and therefore he cannot transmit his knowledge to others. The spring of his creativity resides in the unconscious mind, and when he tries to formulate it into words, he falls into incoherence.

The teacher acts as a necessary middleman between the professional and the novice. He can understand the deeper motivations of the professional and can translate these into a systematized program for the novices.

Even in academic teaching, it is unnecessary for the English teacher to be a master of prose, or for the chemistry teacher to be a marvel with the test tube. They are *interpreters* of an art, and without skilled interpreters the intuitive language of the artist could not be transmitted to future generations.

Let's revise Shaw's foolish saying to "He who can, does; he who can appreciate, teaches."

The idealist ultimately fails because he refuses to accept the limitations in man; the realist ultimately fails because he refuses to accept the possibilities in man; only a creative fusing of these two attitudes can produce the man who works both with what we are and what we could become.

*

Unless you can transcend yourself, you cannot find yourself; "self-knowledge" is not a burrowing-in, but an arching out.

*

The continuing high consumption of cigarettes does not indicate that the public would rather risk earlier death than forgo the pleasure of smoking, but rather that smoking masks hidden tensions and anxieties, and we would rather risk health than directly confront such anxieties.

Too Many Facts Can Ruin the Story

A GREAT DEAL OF ATTENTION has been paid to the neurotic who indulges in fantasy, who cannot keep his facts straight, and indeed does not respect the dividing line between fact and fancy.

Let me suggest, however, that the opposite case is just as neurotic — and more frequently seen. That is, the case of the person who is so obsessed with irrelevant facts that he cannot make his point, if any.

At a recent party, I overheard a lady trying to relate a real-life incident that had happened to her many years ago. Midway in the story, she bogged down because she was unable to recall the name of the doctor who had treated her in 1938.

Now, this doctor's name had no bearing on the story. He could have been Zilch or McGillicuddy or just plain Doctor X — but she fussed and floundered for five minutes in a desperate effort to recollect — and lost her audience in the meantime.

We have all seen countless instances of this kind of behavior. It is something more, I believe, than mere long-windedness or dullness of personality — it is, somehow, a neurotic attempt to cling to facts as if they were the core of a person's existence.

Countless conversations have been ruined by this pathetic addiction to a place, a date or a name — when none of them is essential to the point of the story. Who cares whether it happened in March or April of 1938, or if the town was in Idaho or Iowa, or whether the girl it happened to was a niece or a granddaughter of Dr. Zilch?

These facts may be important to reporters, lawyers and social statisticians, but in the ordinary run of conversation it is the zest, the humor, the pertinence — in short, the spirit — of the anecdote we are interested in, not the literal accuracy.

It is too easy to dismiss those people simply as bores (as, indeed they are), without understanding what motivates their tedious verbal habit. But we learn nothing from merely dismissing or pigeonholing people in this fashion.

A human being is a compound of fact and imagination. One type of neurotic flees from the world of fact because he cannot bear it; another kind seeks in fact a refuge from thinking, from feeling, from the vast reaches of imagination. He is as frightened at one extreme as the fantasizer is at the other. The only difference is that while the fantasizer is sometimes locked up, the factualizer often becomes the official club historian.

To feel and display anger without becoming less, *but becoming* more, *is the surest sign of emotional maturity; for most of us in anger regress to childishness and resort to insult, which diminish the righteousness of our cause rather than support it.*

*

Some men feel so proprietary about their own ideas that if, in a conversation, you simply restate their own argument with minor modifications, they will fiercely disagree with what you say, and contradict their own earlier position. (This irritating habit tends to be truer of self-styled intellectuals than of anybody else.)

We Read with Our Biases

IN A FEW WEEKS, I'll be beginning my twenty-fourth year of writing a daily column. When people ask me if it's "challenging," I feel like telling them that the biggest challenge belongs to them, not to me.

And that is the one challenge thrown out by every serious writer — to be understood in what he says. For most people read not with their minds, but with their emotions and prejudices. They read *into* or read *out* of a piece of writing what they want to. And when they disagree, it is usually not with what a writer says, but with what they *imagine* he said.

A nearly perfect example was a column of mine about a census taker in Galilee, which appeared some weeks ago. It was a mildly ironic piece, purporting to show that the average official or bureaucrat cannot distinguish a saint from a bum, or a prophet from a nut. The official mind is interested only in superficial and external facts.

This census taker was interviewing Jesus, and was answered by Biblical quotations attributed to the Son of Man. As far as he was concerned, these answers were either incomprehensible or evasive, and the bearded man on the donkey was merely an old-time version of the "hippie."

Those readers who approached the subject without an excess of religious bias immediately understood what I was trying to say in this oblique and narrative fashion — that we must be careful about categorizing or condemning people because of the way they look or dress or express themselves; and that the greatest figure the world has known lived and worked among the most "disreputable" elements in his society.

But many other readers wrote in bitterly to accuse me of

calling Jesus a "hippie" — which would be an absurd mis-reading of history and theology on my part — and to attack the parable as "blasphemous," when it was exactly the opposite. Jesus himself rebuked his own countrymen, by sadly commenting that a prophet is without honor in his own country — often mistaken for a crank or a mere troublemaker.

People filter what they read through the fine strainer of their feelings and preconceptions, their prejudices and fears. If they have a stained-glass image of Jesus in their minds, for instance, it disturbs or infuriates them to hear that the living Jesus would most likely be thrown into jail in our contemporary society — and surely would not be allowed into the "better" churches.

"If the triangles could conceive of a god," said Montesquieu, "he would be in the shape of a triangle." Alas, the squares do the same.

The three hardest tasks in the world are neither physical feats nor intellectual achievements, but simply acts of the will: to return love for hate, to include the excluded and to say, "I was wrong."

*

It is doubtless temperamental on both our parts, but a man who talks as much and as fast as Hubert Humphrey always arouses my suspicion that he is trying to overwhelm my thinking process rather than stimulate it.

*

Good Teachers Hard to Come By

IN ALL the clamorous, confused and contradictory talk about education, one simple fact seems to get lost: namely, that children are much better at learning than teachers are at teaching.

Too often, we blame a child for being uncomprehending, when we have simply not presented something in a form and manner that the child can grasp. Almost the whole art of teaching consists in bending down, rather than pulling up.

One of my daughters said to me this summer that she fumbled through a whole semester of Spanish without knowing what a "past participle" was, until a substitute teacher one day made it all come clear with a sentence or two.

And my younger one chimed in that she never learned how to tell time properly through the formal instruction she got in first grade, but learned accidentally when another teacher explained it some other way during recess.

Good teaching is as skillful and as rare as concertizing on the piano; yet we seem to feel that almost anybody can be turned into a teacher with pay that would insult an illiterate construction worker. (Except for a few of the larger cities and more affluent suburbs.)

Educational groups that invite me to "sympose" with them often ask me what I think of "teaching machines"; expecting me, as a humanist, to object to these devices.

Quite the contrary. I think a good teaching machine is a great improvement over a bad teacher, and that the personal presence is of value only when the personality itself has some particular value. We could make do with a half, or even a third, of the teachers we presently recruit, if we used their time effectively and intelligently.

I recently read an amusing example of good teaching that would not occur to most people in the same position, who would argue, harangue or overexplain, which is what unimaginative teachers do.

An old service navigator was flying with a green and cocksure pilot for the first time. "Change direction one degree to port," advised the navigator. "Impossible," said the pilot. "No one can fly this old crate that accurately; give me a decent amount of correction."

The navigator sighed. "Turn starboard four degrees." "Much better," called out the pilot, very pleased with himself. "Fine," replied the navigator drily. "Now turn five degrees to port."

We must recognize that when we are made happy with a little praise, we are then vulnerable to being made morose with a little censure; and it is not worth the price, for generally praise does not please us as long as censure wounds us.

*

Our desire for intimacy is equaled only by our fear of closeness; and much of the love-hate relationship so common between men and women is due to the fact that closeness threatens precisely what intimacy desires.

*

The immature artist tries to "express himself"; the unimaginative artist tries to "reflect the world"; only the good artist is capable of combining the two — that is, refracting the world through his own personality.

What a Naked Body Is, and Isn't

A YOUNG LADY, whom I take to be a student at the University of Wisconsin, writes to me, apropos of a recent paragraph in which I said that the people who present nudity on the stage and the people who object to it are "both victims of the same fallacy, imagining that a naked body is a sexual object . . ."

Her question: "If a naked body is not a sexual object, what is?" I could tell her, but not within the moralistic confines of a family newspaper. Actually, her attitude is exactly the kind of thing I was writing about — the reduction of the body to an *object*, or merchandise.

A naked body can be, and is, many things to many persons: to the doctor, an anatomical or physiological entity to be restored to wholesome functioning; to the artist, a living piece of form and structure to be captured in pen or oil or clay or stone; to the masseur or masseuse, a complicated network of muscles and tissue and nerve-ends to be rejuvenated; to the photographer, a subtle and strikingly lovely study in plane and contour and shadow.

And even to the lover, if the naked body is a mere sexual object, or mostly a sexual object, then the "love" is in the loins and cannot outlast such transitory needs. Love must include sex, but the more exclusive it is of other qualities, the faster it tires and dies.

Indeed, the body in terms of a "sexual object" as such is largely a cultural product and an act of the mind. As Ortega put it: "Nine-tenths of that which is attributed to sexuality is the work of our magnificent ability to imagine, which is no longer an instinct, but exactly the opposite: a creation."

This is why, of course, naked bodies on the stage are not

erotically stimulating, even in our severely repressed society. After the first moment of shock, they are just bodies, laden with no more sexual significance than the naked body of any other species of creature.

For when the cultural taboo is lifted, and the mind can no longer do its imaginative work, then the body ceases to be a mystery (as in most primitive societies) and becomes simply an organism which can be used in many different ways — for protection, for profit or for pleasure.

It has become largely a sexual object for us because, first, it is exploited commercially to an almost pathological degree, and, second, because of our hypocrisy in promoting its desirability while at the same time prohibiting its free functioning.

We have managed, in this way, to obtain the worst of both possible worlds — neither the moral satisfaction of our Puritan forebears nor the innocent engagements of the primitives, but the frustrations of the former and the promiscuity of the latter. This is why I called us "victims."

One of the prime defects in our educational system is that most Americans grow up feeling uncomfortable when general ideas are discussed, and are conversationally at home only when talking about people or things.

*

Hearing a pianist sublimely perform a Beethoven sonata at the age of seventy-four, it is hard not to agree with the Rev. Sydney Smith, who once said: "If I were to begin life again, I would devote much time to music. All musical people seem to me happy; it is the most engrossing pursuit, almost the only innocent and unpunished passion."

We Ought to Cherish Our Cranks

I RARELY GO to meetings of any sort, but I was roped into attending one not long ago. As the proceedings were grinding to a halt, a man in the audience stood up and began haranguing the group on what it should be doing and wasn't.

"Who is that chap?" I whispered to the person next to me. "Oh, he's always doing that," was the reply. "Just a jerk who's always trying to stir up trouble."

I listened carefully to him, and he was undoubtedly a jerk, with a bad case of halitosis of the personality. But he also happened to be right; he was the only person in the room who came to grips with the real problem that all the others were politely evading.

And I thought sadly how characteristic this was of most organizations. The decent, pleasant, attractive people go along with the tide, for a number of reasons, including their reluctance to being abrasive; while only a person supremely unaware of his obnoxious personality was willing to buck the tide and bring up some unpleasant truths.

We have yet to learn that "intolerable" people are often the ones we should tolerate the most; they are usually the only ones blunt or insensitive enough to remind us that the emperor is indeed naked.

"An idea," Don Marquis once said, "isn't responsible for who believes in it." But we equate ideas, or criticism, with the sorts of people who propound or oppose them. If the Communists are for something, we tend to be automatically against it, even if it is a sound idea. But the source of an idea has no relationship to its validity.

Indeed, most of us would be ashamed and embarrassed to get up at a meeting and tell people directly that they are pussyfooting around the problem. It takes a particularly hard-shelled and unself-conscious personality to oppose the general drift of a meeting; the rest of us merely grumble privately after we get home.

Since we voluntarily abdicate our right of candid criticism, we have an obligation to tolerate, and listen attentively to, the jerks who are often doing our dirty work for us — no matter how much motivated they may be by neurotic drives of their own. If they weren't troubled characters, they would be just as passive and acquiescent as we are.

Society desperately needs its troublemakers, its cranks, its eccentrics. For the wrong reasons, they are often righter than we are. We must learn to ignore their reasons without rejecting their arguments out of hand: the pearl, after all, arises from a tumor in the oyster.

Beautiful women are often dissatisfied with their looks, witty people are often discontented with their wit, rich people are often restless and anxious about their money — and, absurd as it seems to those without such attributes, it is certain that nothing we have brings us happiness, but only what we are, what we feel about ourselves, what we believe to be essentially worthwhile in the core of our character.

*

What is most important to know is that the mind is the cause of most of our troubles, not the world; the mind's resistance to change, the mind's unwillingness to release its own potentialities . . . and that, in the line of William Carlos Williams, "a new world is only a new mind."

Truth Is, We Find It Hard to Take

EVERYONE INSISTS that he really "wants the truth," but most of us don't. What we want are fictions that make us feel more comfortable.

I was lunching the other day with a university president, who was telling me about two of his deans. One of them is extremely popular with most of the faculty, while the other is considered cold and stand-offish.

Yet, according to the president, who knows both of the men intimately, the popular dean is a shallow and self-serving opportunist, while the unpopular one is scrupulously fair and generous in his treatment of others.

The first man is "one of the boys," and the second keeps to himself, separating his personal from his professional life, belonging to no clique and keeping the welfare of the university as a whole above the interests of any special group.

But the truth of this situation is obscured by the faculty's need for bonhomie (however hypocritical), and its resentment of a man who holds himself aloof. They are more comfortable with the backslapper — even though he is a backbiter in his less guarded moments — than with the man who is completely honest and even-handed in his dealings with them.

And the same situation obtains in our public life as in our private. While everyone declaims the need for honest and outspoken political candidates, a politician who truly spoke his mind would be shot down before breakfast — and every successful politician knows this.

What people prefer to hear are comfortable and reassuring statements, whether or not they are true, and whether or not the speaker really believes them. This is why, for instance, the avuncular, bumbling bromides of an Eisenhower appealed to the electorate far more than the tart and thoughtful comments of a Stevenson.

Doctors also know this to be a melancholy fact of medical life. The famous bedside manner often conceals ineptitude or faulty diagnosis masked by false heartiness; and the doctor who tells his patients exactly what they ought to know — and don't want to hear — as often as not finds himself replaced by a colleague of large and empty promises.

Perhaps the most persistent and widespread delusion among the human race is that we are seeking for the truth and appreciate it when it is forthcoming. In any contest between candor and comfortable fiction, candor will always limp in a poor second. This is what politicians count on for re-election, and they are rarely disappointed. What most of us want is flattery served up as "fact."

When we repress a thought or feeling, we do not thereby get rid of it; for it inevitably takes its revenge by returning, far stronger, in a form that shocks us with its unexpected intensity.

*

People who see pornography everywhere they turn remind me of the patient being shown a series of pictures by a psychiatrist — a dog, a horse, a barn, a car and geometric figures — and every picture seemed to have a sexual connotation to the patient. "You seem to think a lot about sex," observed the doctor. "Don't blame me," snapped the patient. "You're the one showing me the dirty pictures."

"*Measure of a Man Is from Neck Up*"

A FRONT-PAGE story in my local paper not long ago reported the findings of a personnel director at the University of Pittsburgh, indicating that the starting salary of a job applicant is related to his height — that men over six feet make about 10 per cent more than men under six feet.

"The sad thing about this," he said, "is that we are not talking about laborers . . . but about men recruited by corporations because they are presumably bright, have got a brain, and the brain has been trained."

Social psychologists, however, have long known this to be true in Western civilization; because we are, on the whole, taller than Oriental peoples, we tend (consciously or unconsciously) to consider height as one sign of superiority, whereas it plays no part in Eastern culture.

A few years ago, the *Journal of Social Psychology* reported on a most interesting experiment in the relationship between status and perceived height of a person, made by a teacher at the Australian National University.

He worked with 110 college students, separated into five groups. Each group of 22 was asked to estimate — to the nearest half-inch — the height of the same man, when introduced under a variety of titles.

The estimates grew steadily higher as the academic status ascribed to the model grew more impressive. Introduced as "a student from Cambridge," one group estimated his height as 5-9½; as a demonstrator in psychology from Cambridge, his height was estimated as over 5-10; when introduced as a "lecturer in psychology," he grew another half-inch; a "senior lecturer" title added a further inch; and when made a full professor, he leaped to over 6 feet.

(As a control, when these same student groups estimated the height of their own instructor, there was no such variation.)

We somehow expect "important" men to be larger than they may be in actual fact. People were always surprised at the relatively short stature of such notables as Einstein, Freud and Thomas Mann, invariably saying to them, "You look much taller in your pictures." But, of course, the "pictures" were in the people's minds, not in the photos themselves.

No doubt this irrational preoccupation with height in our culture has made shorter men overreact with the aggressiveness and defensiveness that is so often characteristic of them. When Lloyd George was Britain's prime minister during World War I, a dinner guest tactlessly remarked upon his shortness. "In Wales, where I come from," he retorted, "we measure a man from his neck up; here, you apparently measure him from his neck down!"

The faculty that is most taken for granted by most of us is actually the rarest ability — and that is, to see what we really see.

*

There is only one real success in life — to become who you are, by the freedom to find out what you do best, and the security to do it.

*

When it is generally recognized that only the undersexed and impotent find it "exciting" to read about sexual activities, then pornography will lose the attraction of wickedness and become a source of ridicule.

Elderly Must Retain Drive to Create

WHEN IGOR STRAVINSKY died, at the age of eighty-eight, his was a body worn out before his mind and spirit were ready to leave. Except at his terminal illness, his sense of creativity never left him. Creative people not only tend to live longer than others, they also produce to a later age. Mozart and Schubert are the exceptions, not the rule; they fell victim to diseases induced by poverty and overwork.

At the age of seventy-four, Kant wrote his *Anthropology, The Metaphysic of Ethics* and *Strife of the Faculties*. Tintoretto, at the same age, painted his tremendous *Paradise*, a canvas 75 feet by 30.

Verdi, when nearly seventy-five, composed his most profound opera, *Otello* — and eleven years later wrote *Ave Maria*. At seventy-eight, Lamarck completed his classic work in zoology, *The Natural History of the Invertebrates*, and Oliver Wendell Holmes wrote his *Over the Teacups* when he was seventy-nine.

Richard Strauss lived, and composed, until eighty-five; Sibelius until ninety. While Titian, at a glorious ninety-eight, painted his historic *Battle of Lepanto*. Goethe completed his monumental *Faust*, at eighty-three.

Yet the great bulk of noncreative men retire at sixty-five, and putter around uselessly from then until death takes them.

My own view is that — constitutional differences apart — the productive faculties of men by no means drop off at sixty-five or thereabouts; but the difference lies in the area of interest. In the arts, the area of interest is always expanding; in noncreative fields, the area of interest begins to contract at a certain age.

Stravinsky, again, offers a remarkable example of this. He was an experimenter in music in 1910, and he remained so in 1970. He was never wedded to one form, one mode of expression, but was constantly inventive, forever pushing against the frontier of his own previous work. There was always more to learn, more to try, more to expand.

Few noncreative men understand the therapeutic and life-giving quality of creative expression. Winston Churchill was one of these; his painting was not a "hobby," but a serious and dedicated avocation, which helped keep him going until ninety. He once told an interviewer that painting a thoroughly satisfactory picture is harder than running a country — and, he might have added, more gratifying.

Our population is aging, both absolutely and in percentage. Industry will have little room for older men. Retirement will become increasingly dull and stultifying, unless these men find the creative element (which everyone possesses) and use it to forestall empty death.

Parents who give their children music lessons prematurely kill the artistic instinct more often than they cultivate it; in no other field but music is creativity such a delicate plant that watering it too soon and too often makes it wilt before it is ready to grow.

*

"Nothing is perfect" is what we say when we want to justify our current state of imperfection; the statement is made not because it is true (which it is), but because it offers us a plausible defense against improvement, and thus is more dangerous and misleading than a lie.

Why Simple Solutions Often Fail

WHAT IS THE "CAUSE" of my hay fever, which has begun every year around the same time since I was a boy? The *predisposing* cause is my inherited constitution. The *precipitating* cause is the spread of ragweed pollen in the air around the middle of August. And the *perpetuating* cause is dust, a high wind, and increased sensitivity as the season progresses.

There is, also, I am convinced, a psychological factor: certain types of personalities tend to be more allergic than others. Unless this factor is taken into consideration, the "causes" of an ailment cannot be properly described, understood or treated.

In his splendid book, *For Future Doctors*, which I read and recommended a dozen years ago, Alan Gregg (then Director of Medical Sciences for the Rockefeller Foundation) makes an important point about the word "cause" that should be pondered by every doctor and patient:

"I doubt if I could exaggerate my feelings regarding the stupidity we show in so frequently assuming that one result is due to only one cause," begins Dr. Gregg. "We ought to use the word 'why' in the plural, and ask 'Whys is this patient in coma?' not 'Why is this patient in coma?' "

The next time, he suggests, that you hear someone — including your doctor — say anything that attributes some event to a single cause, ask yourself if he means the *predisposing*, the *precipitating* or the *perpetuating* cause.

"A particular case," he illustrates, "of a fractured jaw in a sailor may be the result of convergent causes — no letters from home, too much alcohol, the loan of a car by a friend, a dark night, an oncoming car on a road covered by ice at a curve, new brake linings, a skid and a telephone pole.

"These constitute the *whys*, not the *why*, of a fractured jaw. Take out any of these whys and the accident would not have occurred. When will we wake up to the importance of multiple causation?"

These passages should be engraved on the walls of every medical school lecture hall — and law school and engineering school, to say nothing of classrooms in history and psychology. For each discipline and specialty tends to reduce a problem to its own dimensions, of seeking its own "why" and ignoring the others, of giving simple answers to complex conditions.

All such single answers are partly right and partly wrong, and what we need in every field is a convergence of views into the composite *whys* that defy any simple and unified solution to most human ills.

Goethe was wrong; there is one thing more terrible than imagination without taste, and that is power without intelligence.

*

Man will comprehend the cosmos before he begins to puzzle out the contradictions in his own spirit; nothing seems as far from us as our inward nature, or as difficult to penetrate with any precision.

*

Righteousness untempered by mercy is a more grievous sin than any it disdains; as La Rochefoucauld put it, "When our hatred is too keen, it puts us beneath those whom we hate."

Wisdom of Ages Is "Relevant"

ALTHOUGH THE WORD RELEVANT has become among the most used, and abused, of slogans today — especially in education — it remains a fact that there is no satisfactory definition of the word.

"Relevant," the dictionaries tell us, is an adjective that means "bearing upon or connected with the matter in hand; to the purpose; pertinent." Some of its synonymns are *applicable, germane, apposite, appropriate, suitable,* and *fitting.*

But relevant has no object of its own. Relevant to what? In modern jargon, education should be relevant to "what's happening now." It should be keyed in to current events, should be helping people solve problems.

But the basic problem of mankind has always been, and remains, twofold: how to think clearly, and how to establish the best relationship between our thoughts and our feelings.

If we think poorly, our good feelings will be subverted by ignorance and muddled logic; and if we are dominated by our feelings, then our intellects will be controlled by our appetites, and we will use our knowledge for selfish purposes.

The students and activists are confused about "proximate" ends and "ultimate" ends. The ultimate end of education — like that of all institutions — is to make a more livable, civilized and humane world for all of us.

But the proximate end — the immediate function of education — is to turn out young men and women who have learned how to use their minds, who have been given access to the best minds of the past and who are disciplined in their thoughts and feelings.

You cannot create a better world if you are ignorant; with all the good will in the world, all you can do is replace current evils with different ones. You cannot work for "justice," "peace," "brotherhood" or any such abstraction, until you understand their philosophical roots, their implications, and their perversions.

The trouble with the schools is that they have dealt with these questions inadequately and have not applied them to our society; this much is true when they are criticized for being "irrelevant." But the way to change this is not to concentrate on the immediate problems but to construct a solid bridge of knowledge leading from the theoretical to the practical, from the usable past to the present and future.

Shakespeare's *Troilus and Cressida* can tell us more about the nature of war and the erotic impulse than anything in the headlines about Vietnam. Relevance means going back as much as going forward.

The surest way to puncture a pleasure at its occurrence is to over-anticipate it; the best things in life are not free, but unexpected.

*

It's only an illusion to imagine that we have a shortage of physicians — what we have is a frightful shortage of psychiatrists, for more than half the patients are taking up their physicians' time with complaints that properly can be attended to only by a psychiatrist.

*

Maturity begins when we're content to feel we're right about something, without feeling the necessity to prove someone else wrong.

Freedom and Security Are Inseparable

ONE OF THE MAIN REASONS people think so poorly (and therefore draw such mistaken conclusions from their thinking) is that they fail to understand the nature of opposites.

Most of us reason something like this: "wet" and "dry" are opposites. Therefore, the more wet you are, the less dry you are, and vice versa. This is impeccable logic, and is also true.

We then proceed from there to abstract qualities, like freedom and security. In one sense, freedom and security are opposites; and so we reason: the more freedom we have, the less security, and the more security, the less freedom.

But this is utterly false. Freedom and security are polarities along the same axis, and not opposites on the same order as wet and dry. They do not deny or cancel out one another, but sustain each other.

Consider what the idea of freedom is rooted in. It is rooted in choice. If you have no choice, you have no freedom. If you are hungry, you must eat what is available, or you will die. If you are hungry, you must satisfy your appetite before anything else; you have no real freedom to choose other or higher goals when your stomach is empty.

If freedom is rooted in choice, and if the man who has no choice has no freedom, then the larger the number of choices, the larger the amount of freedom.

And what gives us the largest number of choices? The amount of security we enjoy. If many kinds of jobs are available, we have the freedom to choose any; if only one, we must choose that. If we live in a society that will not let us starve, we have more freedom than if we live in a society where we must support certain leaders or parties in order to make sure we get enough food.

In the personal, social and political realms, freedom and
security are not opposites like wet and dry, but polarities that
work together to sustain the human person at the maximum of
his abilities. Without freedom, security is slavery; without
security, freedom is an illusion.

Of course, these two may be combined in different measures,
and neither must overwhelm the other — freedom must not
degenerate into anarchy, nor security into servitude. Each
society has the task of finding the just and proper equation for
the best operation of its system.

But the point is that freedom and security are not contraries
that deny each other; rather they are as essential to each other
as the two blades in a pair of scissors. To fail to understand
this is to fail totally in grasping the true needs of the human
animal.

*Actors and entertainers and celebrities of that sort are
judged more leniently for their dereliction of morals than we
judge ordinary people; the reason being that we grant such
figures special privileges in order to have them act out our
private fantasies, so that we might enjoy vicariously what we
lack the resources to experience at first hand.*

*

*Those who are preparing to be happy in the future are
victims of a gigantic self-delusion; for the posture of anticipa-
tion renders a person unfit to seize the moment when it ar-
rives, having trained himself to keep his eyes on a still more
distant future. (This explains, incidentally, why the money-
striver never feels he is really "rich.")*

The Best Argument Against Drugs

THE MOST POWERFUL and persuasive argument against the use of hard drugs is hardly ever made, amidst all the moralizing and the warnings about their physical, social and legal consequences — most of which fall on the deaf ears of youngsters.

What is of utmost importance to stress — and what cannot fail to be convincing to anyone who takes the trouble to verify the fact — is that *hard drugs are a cheat on their own terms.*

If they genuinely gave pleasure, of any real or imaginary sort, to people who must escape the tortures (to them) of reality, then the pleasure factor might be used to overrule all the prohibitions against them. But the absolute fact is that they do not: they cheat the user just as much as they tear the fabric of the family and the community.

I have been looking through a new paperback version of a book I read a half-dozen years ago, *The Fantastic Lodge*, by Janet Clark, which is the autobiography of a sensitive and intelligent addict who finally killed herself.

She learned early in the game what it meant to get "hooked." As she says, "The amount that you have to take is always getting larger, and with it having less and less effect as you go along."

She continues: "In the beginning, the way you get hooked in a lot of ways is because of this tremendous relief that you feel because of all these problems, anxieties and so forth becoming resolved all of a sudden. Here you've been worrying about them your whole life, and they just got resolved, wham, like that."

Then the truth sets in: "As you go along though, that's when you begin to find out that horse is a cheat, a real cheap cheat. Before this, you can have a whole evening or a whole day of wonderful I'm-great-and-the-world-is-all-cool feeling. But after you get hooked, you have to take eight to ten caps to get that feeling and even after you take your ten caps it is just a re-creation of that old relief."

She goes on to point out, in a vivid and personal way that cannot be disbelieved, that pretty soon the user is not taking "H" to get a "high" but simply to escape from the pure misery of doing without. The heroin doesn't afford any positive pleasure, it simply blocks out the terror of doing without it.

But by this time, it is too late. You may know it is a cheat, intellectually, but you are too sick to stop. The dope creates its own appetite for itself, and is actually feeding on itself, with the person only a blind bystander. This is what we must make potential users see.

The maxim most of those worthless "creative writing" classes ought to start with is Bernard Shaw's comment: "In literature, the ambition of the novice is to acquire the literary language; the struggle of the adept is to get rid of it."

*

We might not find the chronic drinker so intolerable when drunk, if we realized how intolerable he finds himself when sober; I have never yet met a lush whose self-esteem was not drenched in self-contempt.

*

The worst kind of selfishness is that which masquerades as self-sacrifice, when the object neither desires nor appreciates it.

The Blessed Sound of Silence

ONE OF THE GROSSEST miscarriages of justice occurred on Christmas Day in an Idaho town, when a woman was fined in court for turning off the radio with a pistol.

The woman told the judge that her husband was playing the radio too loudly on Christmas Eve. When he refused to turn it down, she took the family pistol and fired it, cutting the cord.

Her husband had her arrested on a charge of disorderly conduct, but it seems to me that the judge should have locked up the husband as well — for disturbance of the peace and incitement to riot.

One of the surest indications of a moronic mind and a bestial disposition is the stolid ability to endure (even to enjoy) loud noises, especially when they emanate from a radio or television set.

And each year, as a nation, we are becoming more inured to such noises — until we may eventually reach the point where we cannot dispense with them as background for our intellectual vacuity. Schoolchildren already find it difficult to "study" without a rock group blasting out in stupefying decibels.

More and more restaurants, offices and even building elevators have installed those hideous canned-music programs; airplanes have the same, while waiting for take-off or approaching landing, as if people couldn't stand the "sound of silence" with nothing going on.

I once complained to a restaurant hostess that the canned music was blaring too loudly to conduct a quiet conversation; she stared back at me uncomprehendingly and asked, "What music?" Apparently, after a time, she scarcely heard it at all — but if it were removed, she would feel a deathly silence that might make room for her own thoughts, God forbid.

(Remember the story of the lighthouse keeper, who slept peacefully every night while the machinery hummed away? And one night there was a break in the circuit and the humming stopped; he leapt out of bed and cried, "What was that?")

The ear is a precious and delicate mechanism, naturally attuned to concordant beauties and subtleties of sound. Our commercial cupidity is ruining this sensitive instrument as surely as if we poured hot lye over a magnificent pipe organ.

Acoustics has its own law of diminishing returns. Once accustomed to loudness, we require more and more volume to attract our attention. And the whisper of the mind is obliterated by the cacophony of noise.

Why do the rich continue to work hard at amassing wealth beyond all reasonable needs? For the same reason that the libertine continues to work hard at amassing amorous conquests — he is pursuing not a goal, but an image of himself that he can never quite catch up with.

*

Learning a new language is not merely a matter of "translating," as it were, one's old ideas and concepts from English into another tongue; it is, in a real sense, acquiring an extra facet of personality, and becoming other and larger than you were, in spirit as much as in language.

*

Those persons are happiest who are happy without knowing it; to begin to realize it is already to suffer a diminution of the state.

How We Hypo Our Hypotheses

THERE ARE THOSE who look for truth, and those who look for vindication. Those who seek only evidence to justify or bolster their position, and those who scrupulously search for *all* the evidence, for or against.

I was reading a book the other day, called *Issues in the Economics of Advertising*, by a professor of marketing and economics. This was a 371-page book that took several years to compile and to write.

In concluding his comprehensive survey of the field, the author said: "All this implies that the economic study of advertising is not deserving of great attention except for special problems." Then he added, in a wry parenthesis: "As the reader may realize, this is not a congenial point at which to arrive after spending several years working on the subject."

How rare, how lovely and how utterly honest! Most of us, dedicated for years to such a project, would sinfully tend to find more in it than there was, would puff up our conclusions and pretend that the work had some great positive value — instead of candidly confessing that truth had led us to a dead end. Such negative findings are not without merit, of course, but what a disappointment to the author.

The disinterested search for truth is what gives science its truly "religious" quality — often more so than the religious quest, which too often is concerned with digging out only evidence that buttresses its own dogmas and doctrines. In this sense, the scientist can be closer to the genuinely religious spirit than the zealous theologian.

How many theologians, for instance, would follow the noble and pathetic example of Frege, the mathematician who devised a new symbolic logic at the turn of this century?

Frege began writing a massive two-volume work applying symbolic logic to mathematics. When the first volume appeared, and the second was still in galley proof, young Bertrand Russell pointed out a basic flaw in the very structure of the system, since then known as "Russell's paradox" about sets of classes.

This "colossal and unique intellectual catastrophe," as Isaac Asimov has termed it, forced Frege to add a final paragraph to the second volume of his lifework "admitting that the very foundation of his reasoning was shattered and the books therefore worthless."

Has anyone ever heard of a political or social or religious leader admitting the same, rather than trying bitterly to refute his opponents? The human capacity to process new facts so that they agree with our prior conclusions is almost limitless, and nearly ineradicable.

It is the amount of "dreaming time" rather than "sleeping time" that is important to a person's health and welfare, for the brain "reprograms" itself during dreams; and those who need less sleep than others are peculiarly able to compress the most dreaming into the least amount of time.

*

Giant computers can retard science as much as advancing it; as Dr. Hans Bethe, Nobel prize-winning physicist, recently put it: "Many scientists now think only of how to put the problem on the computer — they no longer think about the problem itself."

Equality Doctrine Still Valid

DOES ANYONE IMAGINE that our Founding Fathers were so stupid that they used the phrase "all men are created equal" without knowing what it meant? In their arrogance, many modern Americans imagine so.

Ignorant or malevolent people are fond of pointing out that, obviously, no two persons are created equal in terms of intelligence, ability, strengths and so forth. Do they think our Founding Fathers were so blind as not to know that simple fact?

Equal does not mean identical. No two persons are identical, just as no two fingerprints are identical. People have different heights, different weights, different color of eyes, different physical characteristics of all sorts. In the same way, we all have different intellectual and emotional traits. Who but a total idiot could deny this?

What is meant by the phrase "all men are created equal" is not that they are identical, but that *everyone at birth is entitled to equal treatment as a person, so that he can realize the maximum of his God-given abilities.*

It means that the state, or the law, cannot arbitrarily treat one person differently from another, as foreign nations (at the time our country was founded) had different laws for the nobility and for the masses.

What is shocking and disappointing, after nearly 200 years of our form of government, is that so many Americans apparently still fail to understand what "equality" means — and perversely interpret it as meaning that everyone has to be "rewarded" identically, no matter how much abilities may differ.

This straw man is too easy to knock down; but the basic

idea of equality under the law is as strong and relevant today as it was in 1776. But, because of ignorant or willful misinterpretations, we are still far from this noble goal of Washington, Jefferson and their allies. Today's Tories are still insisting that because men are not identical, therefore they should not be treated as equals.

In a family, however (and a nation is only a family writ large), we know that our different children have dissimilar talents and abilities. Yet, if we are wise and loving parents, we give them all the same opportunity to rise to whatever level they can; indeed, we often give the duller or less favored an extra lift up to compensate for their weakness or incapacity. The brighter and more fortunate don't need it as much.

This is precisely the way a nation should operate, for its own good and the good of all its members. When do you suppose we will begin?

If you aim deliberately at persuading others that you possess "integrity" you will certainly fail, for the very attempt to give that impression is a mark of doubt, either of yourself or of the essential virtue of "integrity."

*

To remind someone of a favor you have done him is to cancel the favor.

*

A rich man who wouldn't contemplate living off his capital for as much as a month may have been living off his intellectual capital for twenty years without realizing it, until he wakes up one morning and finds that he is totally out of touch with his times.

are so great, so intense, so relentless that not to grow in knowledge is to shrink, and not to learn to enjoy the body and its physical skills is to petrify in our sedentary environment.

But the average sports fan in our society not only snubs knowledge, he also betrays his own body by sitting hunched up in front of a TV set all weekend, watching professionals do his exercise for him. And he betrays his children by making interschool team play so important that intramural sports are slighted, and only a handful of pupils get the benefit of competitive athletics, when all should have it.

The sports nut doesn't even truly respect and understand the virtue of his own interest. If he did, he would dismantle those enormous stadiums for 22 players to compete in, and replace them with fields for thousands to play in, where children might develop into sturdy participants rather than turning into shriveled spectators.

There is as much, if not more, healing power in a Mozart quartet as in a box of aspirins — but people find it easier to swallow than to listen.

*

What the attackers of pickets are too dense to understand was tersely expressed by Paul Valéry, when he said: "To hit someone means to adopt his point of view."

*

The hardness in the saying "the truth shall make ye free" is that we already have to be substantially free in order to want to reach out for the truth.

Balancing Body and Mind

KNOWING my strong feelings about the insane emphasis sports in American society, a friend expressed surprise at se me at a school basketball game with three of my childre dare say he would have been even more surprised to know I urged one of my sons to try to make his school tennis teai his freshman year.

The mistake most of us make lies in assuming that bec: someone is against overemphasis, he is against emphasis. cisely because I am not a locker-room type, I think it impor that my children be exposed to athletics and understand beneficial value; I would be doing them a grave disser otherwise.

What is desperately needed is a sense of appreciation of o modes of life, and of the excellence that goes into every p of doing and becoming. Without this sense we become ri narrow, dull and intolerant of other modes. Then the soci suffers an imbalance which can only injure it — for every k of skill and interest must be fostered in our complex type civilization.

My antagonism to professional and commercial sports cor from a feeling that it pre-empts values and interests that shou be devoted to a wider development of the whole human p sonality.

If I scorned and sneered at sports to my children, I wou be doing them as much of an injustice as the sports-mind father who ignores or rejects the worlds of creativity, of ima ination, of scholarship and thought. I would be an intellect barbarian, just as he is a physical barbarian.

Now, as never before, we need to aim at the whole man - and whole woman, too, of course. Our contemporary deman

Biggest Threat to Us: the "Little Man"

THE GREATEST THREAT facing this country is not from the Military-Industrial Complex. It is not from the Establishment. It is not from the demonstrators, the dissenters, the hippies or even the militant revolutionists. It is from the ordinary "little man," as he calls himself.

It is from the man who is bewildered and frustrated, frightened and angry at social forces he cannot comprehend and does not like. The man who finds his familiar world turned upside down and inside out by the rate of change in modern society.

The truly "alienated" in American life today are not so much the black, the poor, the young or the radical. They are the white, the working- and lower-middle classes, the older and the more conservative. They feel betrayed, unrepresented, manipulated and ignored — and threatened on all sides, by the urban sprawl, automation, racial demands, the cost of living and a war that seems to cut across all of the old shibboleths and slogans they grew up to believe in.

Resentment is their major reaction — resentment of the news media, of the colleges and schools, of intellectuals, of planners, of politicians, of people who push them around against their will and involvement.

It is hard not to sympathize with their bafflement and exasperation. No one has ever bothered to explain to them exactly what is going on in this last third of the twentieth century. Economics is too complex, politics is too confused, philosophy is too abstract, religion is too diffuse — what can a man believe, what can he know, what can he rely upon?

This is the public condition, and the spirit, that makes for Fascism in a country. Fascism is less a political ideology than an emotional response to problems that seem insoluble any other way. It is a gut reaction to ambiguity and frustration; it supplies simple answers to complicated problems, and makes such people feel better about living because it takes out their anxieties on somebody else.

No one has ever taken the time and trouble to educate these people. No one has ever tried to train their feelings. No one has patiently explained to them how modern technology has made the world an utterly new place, and how we must devise new social systems to match our physical systems — or perish in confusion and conflict.

These people are potentially more explosive than any other of the seemingly incendiary elements in our society. They are the ones who carry the big and little Hitlers to power everywhere. Not because they want to, but because we have offered them no options between resentment and reaction.

When we are utterly convinced we are about to do something from the best of motives — then is the time to pause and ask whether we are about to commit some flagrant injustice.

*

The greatness of a man has to do with his "vision," not with the "correctness" of his formulations; much of Newton's mechanics has been revised, much of Darwin's biology has been reformed, much of Freud's psychology has been modified — but they remain great because they saw deeply, not because they were permanently correct.

*

Reform must begin, and practically end, with oneself; as an old African proverb has it: "If you try to cleanse others — like soap, you will waste away in the process."

Don't Rouse the Silent Majority

I THOUGHT about President Nixon's appeal to the "silent majority" as I was going through two new books about Russia — *Message from Moscow*, and *The New Russian Tragedy*, both by qualified Western observers of the current Soviet scene.

It seems that the silent majority is the same in every country, capitalist or communist. It is silent mostly because it is uncaring and self-involved; it speaks up only when its own economic toes are stepped on too sharply.

In Russia, only the intelligentsia oppose the government — only the writers, artists, students, intellectuals and a few professional people. These are the ones who were shocked and shamed by Russia's beastly invasion of Czechoslovakia; shocked by the brutality of the invasion, and shamed because "nobody gives a damn" except themselves.

The few rumbles of dissidence and protest against the Soviet juggernaut have come from men like Solzhenitzyn and Sinyavsky, Belinkov and Merchenko, poets and intellectuals who have given courageous witness to the cold repression of this re-Stalinized era. The main body of citizens — as everywhere — goes along with the government because it is easier and safer and who cares what happens elsewhere?

And this is why the fulminations of the Nixon-Agnew axis against protests and criticism of the government are so dangerous and treacherous. It is not that the protesters are right and the government wrong (though I happen to think that is true); it is that such people are absolutely indispensable if a society is not to degenerate into despotism.

Most people are apathetic, except when someone pinches the nerve of their self-interest. They want to do their job, get along, make no trouble. Only a handful care about abstract issues, about the general welfare, about the rights of people outside their own little sphere. A democratic society must encourage these few, as watchdogs against state repression and tyranny.

In Russia, the masses are silent out of indifference and fear. In the United States there is no fear, but there is just as much indifference, and perhaps even more complacency. It is the young, the powerless, the intellectuals, the artists who act as our national conscience; and their full freedom to speak is what marks us off most sharply from the Soviet system.

Attacking these people — rather than merely answering them — is to make us more like our enemies. Invoking the silent majority against dissidence is to repudiate the whole history of a nation which was conceived in protest and dedicated to self-expression.

The difference between work and a vocation is that, given the proper incentives, a man will work to the limit of his capacities; but without any incentive at all, a man will labor at his vocation beyond the limit of his normal capacities.

*

The man who sees both sides of a question is further along than the man who sees only one, but best of all is the man who sees the hidden third side, too.

*

When a man refuses to do us a favor, his refusal may turn out to have been a favor that neither of us appreciated at the time.

Hostility in Close Quarters

A COUPLE WE KNOW have terrible fights, throwing things at one another, and yet never doing any real damage. They are not mock fights, the couple is angry, and yet the blows are glancing, the dishes miss their aim.

I recalled a book I had read lately, *Self and Others*, by R. D. Laing, a British psychiatrist. He mentioned the report of a policeman who watched a little boy running around a large apartment building.

After the boy had run past him for the twentieth time, the policeman finally asked him what he was doing. The boy said he was running away from home, but his father wouldn't let him cross the road.

Laing then pointed out how this boy's "free space" was curtailed by his "internalization" of this parental injunction. Even at his moment of rebellion, the built-in prohibition against crossing the street still operated to keep the "running away" within limits.

In the same way, the fighting couple unconsciously preserved the inhibition against hurting one another (physically at least) by pulling punches and misaiming the crockery. Real injury in such marital disputes usually occurs only when mutual consumption of alcohol has acted to release the inhibition.

How much "free space" we grow up believing we have tends to determine whether we will actually run away from home or merely circle the block; and whether, in later life, we will strike to hurt or to miss.

Here, the social environment plays an enormous role. It is not true that the mere "poverty" of slum living engenders truancy and violence; for there are as many kinds of poverty as there are kinds of societies.

It is, rather, the restricted amount of "free space" in the slum environment that encourages such actions. It is almost an inverse equation that as physical space becomes more cramped in a neighborhood and in a family, "psychic space" becomes more extended. That is, when the boundaries are too tightly drawn, either flight or fight becomes a prime strategy for survival and self-expression.

If a child can retire to his own room, a wife to her bedchamber, a husband to his den, the sanctuary of this physical space drains off hostilities and allows the recuperative processes to begin. If the family is pressed together — in the house, and also in the ghetto — then running away or striking out remain the only alternatives to tensions. The middle classes are better behaved about such matters because they have room to breathe, to move, to strike out — and to miss.

Fame introduces us to the world; failure introduces us to ourselves; and we cannot successfully cope with the former until we have had at least a taste of the latter.

*

For most people, "getting along with others" means pretending to agree with them even when you don't; but really getting along means being able to disagree without damaging their self-esteem, which is a much harder and more commendable feat.

*

Running water cleanses itself, and so does an active mind; we should distrust as possibly poisonous all those ideas we have held for a decade or more without continually re-examining their source and the degree of their stagnation.

"Former" Can Be a Vicious Label

I'D LIKE TO SHARE with you part of a letter I received from a reader:

"It's disgusting to me," she writes, "to see how often the term 'former mental patient' is used. It's uncanny that labels such as 'former heart patient' or 'former Catholic' or others are seldom used to label people committing crimes.

"Is our society so naïve as to believe that every person who has been in a mental hospital is so-called 'crazy'? Don't they know that there are different types and degrees of mental illness? Do people who have been in mental hospitals have to walk on eggs for the rest of their lives because they have a label?

"There are as many, if not more, emotionally ill people walking the streets as there are in hospitals. It seems to me the ones in hospitals are intelligent enough to recognize their illness and receive proper treatment, or have understanding families who do.

"If one has heart trouble, he seeks professional help, so why do people think emotional illness is any different or in any way shameful? The ignorance and small-mindedness of our society is appalling.

"Will you comment?"

Gladly. I agree with every word you say, and have written about this periodically for more than twenty years. The label "former mental patient" is a stigma that attaches to people forever, when it should be forgotten or at least used as a compliment to their insight and recuperative powers.

Using this phrase — and the newspapers, I am afraid, are as guilty as anybody else in this regard — is usually as meaningless as referring to St. Paul as "a former persecutor of

Christians," or to Gandhi as "a former convict" or to Thomas Jefferson as "a former slave-holder."

Indeed, some of the finest and greatest of men in history have had breakdowns of one sort or another; Lincoln was the victim of severe depression and melancholia, with suicidal tendencies, and might have been treated clinically had there been any mental therapy in his age.

At the same time, while this reader's indictment is just, it must be pointed out that we have come a long way in the last century in our attitude toward, and treatment of, mental illness. Psychological understanding and compassion — triggered mostly by the magnificent breakthrough of Freud and his colleagues — are vastly superior to the fearful and shameful atmosphere of the last century. The tag "former mental patient" may be the last remaining vestige of our primitive recoil; and it, too, may pass, even in our own lifetime.

We can never understand someone until we are able to hear what he is not saying.

*

The paradox of pedagogy is that the subject most worth teaching is character — and this cannot be taught through formal pedagogy.

*

When you run into someone who is disagreeable to others, you may be sure he is uncomfortable with himself; the amount of pain we inflict upon others is directly proportional to the amount we feel within us.

Not Going Too Far, But Too Fast

WE ARE CHANGING our environment faster than we can adjust to it. That's as simply as anyone can state our problem — which has less to do with the *substance* of our affairs than with their form and shape.

This is really what upsets everyone so much, and makes us overreact to political and social and economic events. There is a loss of a sense of continuity, a feeling that we are disoriented, and a desperate psychological need to cling to some permanent landmark, the way a drunk has to wrap himself around a lamppost.

A few weeks ago, I drove past a country house we used to live in every summer for some years. This spring it was struck by lightning and totally demolished. It gave me a weird feeling to drive past this empty lot where only recently we had eaten and slept and played.

In a way, everything we knew has been struck by a kind of lightning in the last few years. The landscape has been radically altered; fields are shopping centers, lanes are highways, lofts are skyscrapers. All the old familiar signposts are gone, or going. There is an uneasy dreamlike aspect to our everyday lives.

A large part of us remains childlike at heart; and we must remember that children above all cherish the familiar, the known, the established. They are dedicated traditionalists: everything must be the same, a story told exactly the same way, a game played in precisely the identical fashion, or they feel lost and cheated.

The acceleration in the rate of change, rather than change itself, is what bothers us to the deepest roots of our psychic constitution. What used to take twenty years now happens in five, or three; and not only to our neighborhoods, our downtowns, our cities, even our villages, but, more importantly, to our moral and social patterns, our modes of relating to one another, our standards of right and wrong, good and bad, guilty and innocent.

Don't even look at the radical left, but at the conservative right — at that bulwark of traditionalism and continuity, the Roman Catholic Church. Who would have imagined a decade ago the cataclysmic changes shaking and altering the ancient and impressive institution? More fissures have appeared in that church in the last ten years than in the preceding 300 years; little wonder that its most devout communicants feel like Chicken Little watching the sky falling down.

Most of the modern change, in my view, is an improvement, in every area. But this doesn't matter. What matters is that we are not able, biologically or psychologically, to deal with so rapid a rate of change — and so we vent our frustration in conflict, in divisiveness, in resistance and resentment that are not amenable to rational argument or logical persuasion.

We are not going too far, as many fear. But we are going too fast. As the body finds it hard to adjust to supersonic speeds, so the mind even more finds it nearly impossible to adjust to the bolts of social lightning striking everywhere around us.

The passion for getting ahead is self-defeating if motivated by the desire to leave oneself behind; only the authentic man can genuinely enjoy his achievements or rest comfortably in his success; the man running away from himself can never stop, no matter how far he goes.

IQ Test Tyranny on Wane

MY LONG-STANDING CAMPAIGN against the so-called "intelligence test" was fortified this summer by an announcement from the British Department of Education and the British Psychological Society.

These groups are readying a new examination that will abolish the old "single score" as in IQ tests; instead, as I have been recommending for more than twenty years, it will measure six different abilities.

These are "reasoning," "verbal ability," "spatial perception," "number ability," "memory," and "ideational fluency" (the last is jargon for general creativity).

We have categorized and stereotyped people (especially pupils) for too long by conventional IQ tests, which are misleading and inaccurate. Even Binet, the inventor of the first such test, when asked pointblank what "intelligence" was, replied with cynical candor, "It is what my test measures." Of course, as he knew, this is a circular and meaningless definition.

In a column more than fifteen years ago, I wrote: "Intelligence is not a single unitary thing, but is rather a composite made of many strands. There are different *kinds* of intelligences, and one is not necessarily better than the others."

There is "social" intelligence, I suggested, which few intellectuals possess — the ability to understand how other people feel and to live and work with them in reasonable peace and tolerance.

There is mechanical intelligence, which I (who score so highly on the verbal part of an IQ test) don't possess an iota of — the ability to manage and manipulate physical objects, to make, to repair, to take apart and put together. My ten-year-old is smarter than I at that.

There is mathematical intelligence — the ability to visualize abstractions in time and space — a rare gift which has often been given to men who are otherwise idiots, or at least mediocre.

And there is a creative, intuitive kind of intelligence that comes close to genius but cannot be measured on any scale; it often displays itself later in life, after a "backward" childhood — St. Thomas, the chief architect of Christian theology, was called the "dumb ox" in school.

I should not be complaining about IQs, because my kind of intelligence does best at them — the highly verbal intelligence. But, knowing how dumb I am in some other important areas of life, it seems clear to me that the "single score" test is profoundly unfair to other, and equally useful, kinds of intelligence. Its abolition can go a long way toward releasing children from the tyranny of a senseless number.

If you imagine that fun is fun and seriousness is seriousness, that only proves you don't really understand either.

*

Aerodynamically, the bumblebee is totally unable to fly; luckily, no theoretician has ever been able to point this out to him.

*

To be ignorant doesn't merely mean not to know; it means not to know what you don't know; being educated means knowing precisely what you don't know.

SST Is an Insult to Our Bodies

My opposition to the supersonic transport planes is not just based on the economics or politics (or even the "sonic boom") of these vehicles; it is based even more on the human factor of adjusting to such speeds.

Even today, on the ordinary jets, a daytime flight between the United States and Europe or any other part of the globe is fatigue-making in a clinical way we still don't fully grasp. Traveling fast through several time zones imposes a severe strain on the body and the mind.

In his recent interesting book, *The Pathology of Leadership*, Dr. Hugh L'Etang, a British physician who for years has studied the medical histories of world leaders, warns that "even the statesman in full possession of his faculties may be exposed to unprecedented hazards as a result of the capacity of modern aircraft to cross oceans and continents in hours instead of days."

Our vital processes, he points out — sleep, brain activity, temperature control, hormone formation, gut activity, mineral metabolism and many others — are geared to a carefully adjusted schedule; and if the body is rapidly transferred to a different time system, "its own carefully synchronized activities will be out of step with the new local time."

The book also quotes Dr. Hubertus Strughold, chief scientist of the American aerospace medical division, as suggesting that these sudden changes "may have some significance in international conferences during the first few days . . . which are not the proper times for important negotiations or vital decisions."

And United States aerospace studies indicate that not only middle-aged businessmen and government officials are affected this way, but also that "actors, chess players, athletes and, last but not least, race horses were not at their intellectual or physical best the first few days after arriving from a region four or more time zones away."

Recent work has confirmed these findings. The results of varying tests after a daylight flight of eighteen hours from Oklahoma City or Tokyo were described as showing "a marked and quite significant deterioration in psychological performance on the first full day in Tokyo as judged by both reaction time and decision time." And, while younger students had a rapid return to normal, in contrast, the older men showed impairment of reaction time and decision making for as long as five days."

It used to be thought that, in traveling at high speeds, the mind could not keep up with the body; now it is known that even the body cannot keep up with the body. Flying beyond the speed of sound, without the "packaged environment" of astronauts, is a flagrant insult to the organism.

If the rest of all the living creatures on earth could take a vote, man would easily win the title of the biggest "pest" in the world. (Our title as the fiercest and most indiscriminate predator is uncontested.)

*

Replying to a student who wants to know the difference between a "hack writer" and an "artist," the best answer I can think of is that a hack writer counts his words, while an artist weighs them.

Treason and "Decline and Fall"

ONE OF THE ODDEST quotes I've read recently came from Lieutenant General Ira C. Eaker, U.S. Air Force (Retired), who said the following in a speech to an Air War College graduating class:

"I believe that when some historian of the future does the job on us which Gibbon did on Rome, he will find that the first certain evidence of our decline was our tolerance of 'treason.' "

In the first place, historically speaking, treason had nothing to do with Gibbon's thesis on the decline of Rome — but whenever a speaker wants to make a show of learning, he cites Gibbon on the decline of Rome as a parallel to our times; one can "prove" anything this way.

More importantly, our nation began in what men like General Eaker would have called "treason." When Patrick Henry stood up in the Virginia House of Burgesses to warn King George the Third that we would not stand for the Stamp Act, the Speaker of the House cried, "Treason!" — and Henry made his famous reply, "If *this* be treason, make the most of it!"

The established authorities call everything "treason" that does not suit their purposes or fit their own particular notion of what is proper. A "traitor" is any dissenter you would like to do away with and cannot find a legal means of shutting up.

This was clearly understood by President James Madison, one of the framers of our constitutional liberties. In the Federalist Papers, which formed our country's political structure, Madison warned of the dangers of "artificial treasons," by which charge each faction seeks to "wreak its alternate malignity on the other."

Because, Madison said, it is so easy and so dangerous for one

faction to accuse the other of being "treasonable," the Constitutional Convention "with great judgment opposed a barrier
to this peculiar danger, by inserting a constitutional definition
of the crime, fixing the proof necessary for the conviction of
it, and restraining the Congress, even in punishing it, from ex-
tending the consequences of guilt beyond the person of its
author."

What General Eaker calls our "tolerance of treason" is
precisely the principle we are founded on. Indeed, anyone
studying the pre-Revolutionary period must be impressed with
the fact that Britain lost her colonies exactly because she called
"treasonable" the attitudes of patriotic men like Henry and
Madison, who simply wanted a larger measure of justice and
representation for the people. Nations decline not when they
tolerate treason, but when they attack legitimate dissent with
what Madison called "the mighty engine of artificial treason."

*There is a sort of "magnetic attraction" between lovers; but,
just as often as not, it is simply the unconscious call of one
neurosis crying for its mate, and time alone can tell if the
attraction is based on real needs or self-punishing drives.*

*

*The trouble with advice is that you don't know whose to
take; and if you know whose to take, you don't need advice.*

*

*The practical function of dreams (beyond their symbolic
content) was probably best defined by Charles Fisher, when
he suggested, "Dreaming permits each and every one of us to
be quietly and safely insane every night of our lives."*

The Insane Are Just Too Logical

LIKE ALL COLUMNISTS, I get quite a few letters from crazy people. They write much more often than sane people, they write much longer letters — and they also write much more *logical* letters.

That last statement might surprise you, but it wouldn't surprise any psychiatrist who has had firsthand experience with the mad. For the essence of insanity is *utterly logical thinking based on a false premise they are incapable of examining or shaking.*

Most of us do not reason logically or precisely; we wander, we skip, we leave larger or smaller gaps in our thinking processes — for the relatively sane mind is loose, flexible and open.

The mad mind is tight, rigid and closed. It operates inexorably from its first premises and has an absolutely airtight explanation for everything that seems to contradict its assumptions. Once you accept its main premise, however, you are relentlessly swept along to its conclusions.

And this is why logic, or reasonable persuasion, is of no use in trying to convince the mad that they are victims of a gigantic mistake. As Dean Swift once said, in a favorite quotation of mine, "It is impossible to reason a man out of something he has not been reasoned into."

There are different levels and degrees of madness, to be sure. But there is one paranoid strain running through most of those people that makes it easy to detect their aberration — they tend to find *one single main cause* for the woes of the world, past and present.

They may blame the "communist conspiracy," or the Catholic Church, or "international Jewry," or the eating of animal flesh, or the gold standard, or miscegenation (which they commonly call "mongrelization"), or the use of spiritous beverages, or anything ranging from the patently cuckoo to the dangerously plausible.

But history is not made this way; human events do not revolve neatly and predictably around a single core, like so many electrons whirling around a nucleus. The real world is diverse, contingent, discrete and, most of all, *over-determined* in its chain of causes and consequences. This means that many convergent factors (some of them accidental) combine to decide what will happen historically.

Orthodox Marxism, if carried far enough, becomes a form of political madness, for it oversimplifies the pattern of society, based on its inflexible (and erroneous) premise of "dialectical materialism." But we ourselves, in blaming the bulk of contemporary problems on some horrendous monolith called "communism," are likewise the victims of the same sort of social insanity.

A thing is "worth" whatever someone can be found to pay for it; and, likewise, a person is "worth" whatever someone can find to love in him, no more and no less. (Whenever I hear that a man is "worth" such-and-such an amount, I cringe inwardly.)

*

When a man lacks expert knowledge in a subject, he makes a virtue of his "common sense" — but common sense is worse than useless (and often dangerous) in dealing with uncommon pursuits.

Sports Only Exercise Our Eyes

BEFORE I PROCEED a line further, let me make it clear that I enjoy physical exercise and sport as much as any man. I like to bat a baseball, dribble a basketball, kick a soccer ball, and, most of all, swat a tennis ball. A man who scorned physical activity would hardly build a tennis court on his summerhouse grounds, or use it every day.

Having made this obeisance, let me now confess that I am puzzled and upset — and have been for many years — by the almost obsessive interest in sports taken by the average adult American male.

Athletics is one strand in life, and even the ancient Greek philosophers recognized its importance. But it is by no means the whole web, as it seems to be in our society. If American men are not talking business, they are talking sports, or they are not talking at all.

This strikes me as an enormously adolescent, not to say retarded, attitude on the part of presumed adults. Especially when most of their passion and enthusiasm center around professional teams which bear no indigenous relation to the city they play for, and consist of mercenaries who will wear any town's insignia if the price is right.

Although I like to play, and sometimes like to watch, I cannot see what possible difference it makes which team beats which. The tactics are sometimes interesting, and certainly the prowess of the players deserves applause — but most men seem to use commercial sports as a kind of narcotic, shutting out reality, rather than heightening it.

There is nothing more boring, in my view, than a prolonged discussion by laymen of yesterday's game. These dreary conversations are a form of social alcoholism, enabling them to achieve a dubious rapport without ever once having to come to grips with a subject worthy of a grown man's concern.

It is easy to see the opiate quality of sports in our society when tens of millions of men will spend a splendid Saturday or Sunday fall afternoon sitting stupefied in front of the TV, watching a "big game," when they might be out exercising their own flaccid muscles and stimulating their lethargic corpuscles.

Ironically, our obsession with professional athletics not only makes us mentally limited and conversationally dull, it also keeps us physically inert — thus violating the very reason men began engaging in athletic competitions. It is tempting to call this national malaise of "spectatoritis" childish — except that children have more sense, and would rather run out and play themselves.

The possession of one particular quality in excess always exercises a stupefying effect upon its possessor: the strong become stupid because they come to rely on power when it is inappropriate; the beautiful become stupid because they utilize appearance in place of reality; and, the most startling paradox, the intelligent become stupid because they put the intellect where the whole personality should be.

*

What pedants never realize (and what makes them such poor teachers) is the basic truth of Galileo's statement that "you cannot teach a man anything; you can only help him to find it within himself."

The "Love It or Leave It" Nonsense

ONE OF THE MOST IGNORANT and hateful statements that a person can make to another is "If you don't like it here, why don't you leave?"

That attitude is the main reason America was founded, in all its hope and energy and goodness. The people who came here, to make a better land than had ever been seen before by the common people, had been rebuffed and rejected by their neighbors in the Old World.

They didn't like conditions where they lived, and wanted to improve them. If they had been allowed and encouraged to, the Old World would have had a happier history, instead of the miserable tribulations that turned the eyes of the people to America as their last, best hope.

Now we find that many Americans — smug and fat and entrenched in their affluent inertia — are saying the same ugly thing to their neighbors: "If you don't like it here, why don't you leave?"

But most people who want to change conditions *do* like it here; they love it here. They love it so much they cannot stand to see it suffer from its imperfections, and want it to live up to its ideals. It is the people who placidly accept the corruptions and perversions and inequities in our society who do not love America — they love only their status and security and special privilege.

Nobody should be faced with the mean choice of accepting conditions as they are or abandoning the place he has grown up in. We not only have a right, we have a responsibility, to make our environment as just and as flourishing as our Founding Fathers declared it must be if it were to live up to its aspiration as "the standard of the world."

Those who want to leave have a right to leave, but those who want to stay and work for what they consider a better society must be protected in that right — for without it, our nation would sink into stagnation, and the process of change would harden into repression by those who benefit by keeping things just as they are.

If all the settlers who came here, with high hopes for a new and finer social order, had been compelled to "go back where they came from," we would have had no United States of America. This country was born out of dissatisfaction with the old scheme of things, and grew on the blood and dedication of men who were not afraid to speak and work for fundamental changes in the whole political and social structure.

Somebody who truly didn't like what America *stands for* ought to be invited to leave; but there is a vast difference between such a person and those who dislike *what we have allowed ourselves to become*, through greed and prejudice and provincial indifference to the great problems we now face. No community can afford to lose these good "agitators."

Most people sleepwalk through their lives — it is the price they are (unconsciously) willing to pay to avoid the pain of confronting reality.

*

Work is emotionally rewarding only when there is a sufficient element of play involved in it; and play is emotionally rewarding only when there is a sufficient element of work involved in it; the two are not opposites, as is commonly thought, but simply obverse sides of the same spiritual coin.

Unmourned Death of the Dirty Joke

A COLLEAGUE in the newsroom sent me a brief interoffice memo not long ago: "The dirty joke has all but disappeared. I seldom hear one. Two years ago, I encountered a couple a week, maybe more. I still meet the same guys with the same frequency. Now, no jokes."

This has been my experience, too, and I am glad. Not because I object to dirty jokes per se, but because not one in a hundred was truly funny — but you felt you had to laugh (at least weakly) to demonstrate your virility and good fellowship.

I think the rapid increase in sexual permissiveness in the United States the last few years has killed off the dirty joke. A dirty joke is basically a "reaction-formation" to sexual repressiveness in a society; it is not a normal outlet for humor.

Many societies have not had any dirty jokes, and would not understand or appreciate them — not because these cultures are puritanical, but quite the opposite, because they are permissive in the area of sex, and find it incomprehensible that we smirk and snigger about a subject that to them is as simple and natural and obvious as breathing.

It is no accident that in Denmark last year, when all censorship of pornographic material was lifted, sales of pornographic literature on newsstands dropped almost to the vanishing point.

In his recent book, *Rationale of the Dirty Joke*, G. Legman points out that "the almost total prohibitiveness of our culture toward the three primary impulses of the newborn and growing child — the oral, anal and genital, in that order — contrasts worse than almost anything else about us with the total permissiveness, in regard to these same impulses in children, in more advanced societies, such as the natives of Okinawa."

It may sound strange to our ears to hear Okinawa cited as a "more advanced" country than ours, but it is part of our national pride and prejudice to believe that because we have attained the highest level of technical and material accomplishment in the world, therefore we are similarly superior in our social, ethical and sexual attitudes.

A joke is generally a form of anxiety release, and sometimes it is a useful and necessary form, as when soldiers jest before battle. But the dirty joke indicates the amount of repressed anxiety about sex in our society; it is a mark of psychic slavery, not of freedom.

Our shifting sexual standards will no doubt drift too far into laxity before they are corrected, but I believe the general tendency is a healthy one, and that out of the chaos and confusion there will come a more realistic and more humane conception of sexuality in our society than we have yet permitted ourselves to imagine — except through the distorted and distorting medium of the dirty joke.

After the novelty wears off, opposites retract.

*

Competition brings out both the best and the worst in us; you can tell more about a man's character by playing poker with him for an hour than you can by living next door to him for a year.

*

"Addiction" to fame can be as fatal as addiction to liquor or narcotics; limelight becomes as habit-forming as cocaine, and when it is withdrawn, the symptoms are equally severe.

"*Upper Class*" *Ignorant on Crime*

OTHER PEOPLE may despair about what they call the "lower classes." But I don't. I despair more about the "upper classes." About the affluent, the educated, the influential — and the basically ignorant.

The magazine *Nation's Business* recently asked its affluent, educated and influential readers: "How can we best get law and order?" And the overwhelming answer came back: "Get tough with the lawbreakers."

This is so basically ignorant that even the most ignorant member of the lower classes would laugh at it. Because it doesn't work. It never has, and it never will.

These magazine readers — who are totally insulated from reality in their little business cells and their snug suburban hideaways — uniformly demand, "Quit coddling the lawbreaker" and "Reverse the recent findings of the Supreme Court" and "Get more judges with the guts to serve a penalty" and "More discipline for our youth" and so on in the same vein.

Why have the laws, and the handling of criminals, become more lenient over the years and over the centuries? Simply because harshness turned out to be the wrong way to handle the problem. When they used to hang people for stealing handkerchiefs, it didn't lower the rate of stealing handkerchiefs — it just upped the rate of murdering the man you stole it from.

What these affluent, educated, influential and dumb citizens don't seem to grasp — or don't want to grasp — is that the *quality of justice* in a state determines the rate of criminality, and not "law and order."

People are fond of pointing to England's orderly system,

and they mistakenly believe that the crime rate there is low because of the severity of sentence. *Actually, the average sentence in England is shorter than in the United States.*

But in England the judicial system is wholly divorced from politics. Defendants are given a speedy hearing. The police behave properly and do not treat a poor man any differently from a rich man. The quality of justice is swift, evenhanded, uncorruptible and based on the fact that if the police don't use undue force, the criminals won't. And they don't.

It is, however, expensive and laborious to reform our whole police-political-judicial system in the United States — a system that makes the so-called lower classes contemptuous and cynical about the law. Moreover, it is perfectly plain in our society that the more you have and the more you steal, the more likely you are to get away with it.

This is the canker in our body politic. It has nothing to do with "coddling" or the Supreme Court or permissive parents. It has everything to do with public corruption, private hypocrisy and gross inequities in the law. Until we know this, we ourselves are criminally ignorant.

The people who love themselves too much don't create nearly as much mischief or misery in the world as those who hate themselves — for all aggression beyond normal limits is a manifestation of intense and unconscious self-hate.

*

People with affections are not vain, but suffer from a haunting sense of inferiority; an affection is a confession that you do not consider your natural self to be good enough to be displayed in public.

We're Not Fit to Colonize Space

A FEW DAYS after our successful orbiting of the moon, a friend expressed the hope that this venture would teach people humility in the face of the universe.

"If this helps us realize how vast outer space is, and how small our globe is," he said, "then it might make us all feel more united as inhabitants of this tiny speck of dust whirling in space."

This would be a commendable lesson to learn, I agree, but I doubt that we would draw so philosophical an inference from the moon project. Rather, I suggested bleakly, it might lead us in the opposite direction.

Instead of regarding space exploration as a common effort binding mankind together, it is far more likely that we will simply extend our competitiveness from inner to outer space, and look upon the solar system as competing nations once regarded explorations on earth — as places to plant flags, to colonize, to use as economic resources and military outposts.

Unless we make some unexpected quantum jump in our thinking and feeling, we will simply extrapolate to other worlds the same greed and vanity, the same lust for possession and domination, the same conflict over boundaries and priorities throughout the solar system.

What is even more dire, we might also export the contamination of our planet, not merely in terms of wars and prejudices and injustices, but quite physically, in terms of bacteria and viruses and all the assorted pollutions of earth, air and water that are rapidly making our own globe nearly uninhabitable.

Nothing in our history, early or recent, indicates that we are not prepared to despoil other planets as carelessly and contemptuously as we have turned ours from green to gray, from fair to foul, from sweet to sour, in the countryside as well as in the cities — so that even sunny, snowy Switzerland has shown a 90 per cent increase in smoke content and turbidity of the air in the last two decades.

We are no more morally or spiritually equipped to colonize other parts of the solar system — given our past level of behavior on earth — than a hog is fit to march in an Easter parade. Our technical genius so far outstrips our ethical and emotional idiocy that we are no more to be trusted to deal lovingly and creatively with another planet than a rhesus monkey can be allowed to run free in a nuclear power plant.

The astronauts are bold men, and the scientists who sent them up are bright men, but they are not the ones who will decide what is done once we get there. The same old schemers will be running the show.

Tea, coffee, tobacco and whiskey were utterly unknown in the ancient world — what did the doctors forbid their patients to take?

*

Egotism is most dangerous precisely when it takes over the role of philanthropist; to give for the wrong reasons is eventually to manipulate the recipients of one's benevolence.

*

There are "lucky" and "unlucky" personalities in life; the unlucky being those whose conscious or unconscious expectations of failure influence the kind of luck they have, regardless of their other talents, abilities or intelligence.

Why Good Executives Are Rare

A FRIEND OF MINE, who is head of a large industrial firm, apologized for being late to dinner. "I just couldn't get away from the office," he said. "It seems I never can get away from the office very long."

I asked him what was so important and compelling there — a merger, a new product development, some technical foul-up along the line? He scowled, and then grinned. "It's people," he said. "Ninety per cent of it is people."

"I thought you had some good people," I said. "They've certainly made a fine record the last few years."

"Of course, they're good people," he answered. "They're good in their jobs. But the problems don't relate to the jobs as such — they relate to the emotional life of the people, to their fears and their angers, their stubbornness and their childishness.

"That's why," he went on, "good executives and subordinates are so hard to find. Most of them are excellent technicians — they know their fields inside out — but their emotional growth is about one-tenth of their intellectual growth."

"Why should this be so?" I asked.

"In my opinion," he said, "because it takes a certain kind of neurosis to succeed in most fields, and business is no exception. The well-balanced man tends to stay where he is, content with his lot — while the driven man climbs up the ladder, and stands quivering anxiously on every rung.

"My toughest job," he went on, "has little to do with our products or our sales. It has to do with a dozen or so men who often behave like children in a sandpile — envious of one another, grasping their pails to their chests, reaching for someone else's toy and dead set in their own ways. And some are frightfully self-destructive.

"Many of them are fearful and insecure, no matter how much success they've already had. You have to keep letting them know you love them and admire them and respect them. Their status is terribly important, all the symbols of corporate eminence are invested with an almost religious meaning to them, and so are the rituals of the business — once they've done something right, they want to keep repeating the same process, whether or not it's relevant to what's happening now.

"That's why I'm late for dinner," he sighed. "Not because I'm a big business tycoon — but because I'm a cross between a nanny and a Viennese psychiatrist, with a little bit of top sergeant thrown in!"

Language is the great repository of male chauvinism. When we mention animals, we refer to the dog, the horse, the lion, not to the bitch, the mare, or the lioness — which is especially ludicrous in the latter case, since the lioness actively supports the family, doing most of the hunting for food, except when nursing her young.

*

The world's store of facts has just about doubled in the last ten years; and most of us, psychically, are in the mood of the old farmer who said he didn't want to learn any more things "because I already know more than I can understand."

*

A fool who is smart enough to be aware of his limitations can get along far better in the world than a wise man who is too obtuse to be aware of his.

6

OF WORDS AND PHRASES

We Waste Our Gift of Expression

IN THE BEGINNING, we are told, was the Word; but it is
no more. The word is no longer honored, respected or believed; not even the Logos of God, which has too often been
perverted by men for selfish ends.

One of the most salient characteristics of young people today, not only in the United States but all over the world, is the
rejection of the word. The young person will not communicate because he distrusts words; he prefers listening to music to
reading books because music is incapable of lying.

We have devalued the currency of communication. The
monetary inflation we so worry about is as nothing in the
grand scheme of things compared with the verbal inflation
we have inflicted on the world. We have taken the most singular gift of man — expression — and forced it to serve our own
proud, profit-seeking or petty purposes.

This is what young people resent most of all. Like all innocent youth, they began by trusting the word, by taking it at
face value. Slowly and painfully, they learned that society
does not say what it means, or mean what it says. Idealism
quickly corrodes into cynicism, and the sullen silence of the

young in the presence of their elders is a deep repudiation of the whole medium of verbal expression.

The task before us — if any real reconciliation is at all possible — is far more than a political or social or economic one. It is a task that goes to the very roots of human existence: that of restoring the word to its pristine purity and its human authenticity.

Communication — and therefore communion — can survive only when there is a genuine "meeting" between persons, when truth encounters truth, clasps it and returns it. But no genuine meeting is possible when we use words as bludgeons, as blackmail, as screens to hide our bad faith or as brilliant lures to hook the fish we are preying upon.

Even without bad faith — even when our intentions, so far as we know them, are the best — we still manipulate the word to defend our weaknesses, conceal our vulnerability, justify our self-centeredness and erect a "philosophy of life" out of fear, prejudice and ignorance.

We are told that "the letter killeth, but the spirit giveth life," and the letter has all but killed the spirit. Man's most precious gift has been perverted from the beginning, but only in this age of "mass communication" has the letter been able to extend its hegemony over the total range of men's relationships. If there is one resolution worth making, it is the resolve to treat the word as a holy thing, not a dark device for attacking, defending or disguising.

We should learn to distinguish more clearly among "work," "labor," and "toil" in our language — work is good and necessary for man, labor may be necessary but is not necessarily good, while toil is always bad.

Even English Is Greek to Americans

I HATE TO MEET young people from foreign countries. They make me feel so inferior — and they make me blush for our own young people in America.

Dining with us last evening was a German boy of nineteen, who arrived on these shores a week ago to attend a college in Ohio. His grasp of English was superb, and I asked him how often he had been to America.

"Oh, never before," he said. "This is my first trip here. But, from my reading, I feel as if I know America very well."

"How did you learn to speak English so well?" I asked.

"I had six years of English in school," he said, "starting when I was ten. But English is simple compared to Greek and Latin. I had to study those languages for ten years."

This boy, mind you, while bright, is no exceptional scholar, no intellectual — just an ordinary, educated European youth. He took it for granted that nobody with a decent education would speak only one language.

I was ashamed to tell him not only that most American students cannot converse in any foreign language, but that most of them are not able to express themselves gracefully in English speech or writing.

The language courses in most American schools are a farcical waste of time and money, for many reasons. First of all, youngsters start too late — by the time they reach high school and begin to take a foreign language, they are too old, too busy and too indifferent to learn it.

It would be better to cut out languages entirely than to persist in this foolish course of teaching them for only a year or two in high school. Not one student in a thousand can conduct a mature conversation in a foreign tongue after he leaves school.

But the root of the trouble lies deeper than this. English itself is not understood by the mass of students. And when one does not understand the structure of one's own language, it is virtually impossible to learn a second, except by living abroad and hearing it every day.

The whole body of language teaching — including English — in American schools needs a radical revision. And not merely for the sake of English (important as it is), but because ignorance in speaking and writing becomes a crippling handicap in all other subjects.

If we cannot communicate coherently, we cannot really achieve a mastery in any field. America is full of tongue-tied technicians, who cannot transmit their knowledge, even to their own countrymen.

One of the most incisive and useful comments on the subject I've ever heard is Paul Valéry's: "The purpose of psychology is to give us an entirely different idea of the things we know best."

*

To say "that's good in theory, but it won't work in practice," is a contradictory statement: if the theory is good it must work in practice, and if it doesn't work in practice, it's a bad theory.

*

Interesting how our "earth language" carries over to outer space: we speak of sending "geological" expeditions to the moon, but of course these scientists will be doing not "geology," but "selenology."

Study of Latin Is No Waste of Time

A HIGH SCHOOL STUDENT in West Virginia has written to ask me if I think he should continue with his Latin studies. "Has Latin done you any good?" he inquires, "and is it useful in your work?"

The answer is "yes" to both these questions. Nobody can speak, write, or understand English properly unless he has some rudimentary knowledge of Latin. For English is a *hybrid* language — fewer than half our words are native, and the rest borrowed from foreign tongues, mostly Latin.

In no other language, for instance, do we find so many native nouns taking Latin adjectives. The adjective for *mouth* is not *mouthy* but *oral* which is straight from the Latin.

Likewise, *nose* gives us *nasal,* *eye* gives us *ocular, mind* gives us *mental, son* gives us *filial, house* gives us *domestic, sun* and *moon* give us *solar* and *lunar.* There are hundreds of similar cases.

We don't even have native English adjectives for the four seasons: fall is *autumnal,* winter is *hibernal,* spring is *vernal,* and summer is *estival.* The first words a child learns, *mama* and *daddy,* take Latin adjectives — *maternal* and *paternal.*

English is primarily a "loan language." If you want to know how much, read any of the books by Otto Jespersen, the great Danish philologist, and you may be surprised at the enormous debt we owe not only to Latin and Greek but also to the Scandinavian languages, to French and even to the Germanic influences upon Old English.

A foreigner learning English would find it insuperably difficult if he did not have a solid base in Latin.

This explains why educated foreigners are able to pick up our tongue so rapidly, and why some uneducated foreigners can live here thirty years without really grasping the language.

As an important parenthesis, I found my own Latin (shaky as it is) of great use while traveling through Europe. I was able to get along handily in Italian after only six weeks of living in Florence, and my French is at least passable, using the glue of Latin to stick together French and English words.

Studying the classic languages is neither a waste of time nor a form of intellectual snobbishness; it is, rather, the quickest and most permanent way to master one's own tongue and to become a genuine citizen in the community of man, past and present.

I have never understood the phrase "self-made man," for everybody is self-made, or he is not made at all.

*

I have never understood why "a heart of gold" should mean anything but a heart that is hard, cold, dead and totally unresponsive.

*

When I hear an orator use the phrase "all right-thinking men," or "all clear-thinking men," it seems obvious that he is really saying, "All men who think as straight and as clearly as I imagine I do."

*

It's surprising we haven't adopted the British term "smarmy" to fill a descriptive void in American usage — meaning excessively or unctuously flattering, ingratiating, servile and falsely sentimental.

The Lingual Laxity of the Laity

WE PURISTS may protest at the perversions of language, but language goes its merry way, ignoring us. We put up sandbags against the rising river of vulgarisms and neologisms, but our efforts are generally as futile as those of King Canute commanding the tides.

Words change willy-nilly, regardless of sense, logic or grammar. This is part of the life force of a vital language, and while its guardians may try to prune the excesses, it is impossible to keep the hedges trim or prevent yesterday's weed from becoming today's flower.

Media is the perfect example right now of a word in transition. It is a popular word, meaning the avenues of general communication, such as newspapers, magazines, radio, television. It is a plural word, the singular being *medium*.

But what has begun to happen is that *media* is now being treated as a singular noun, and *medias* is turning into the plural. This strikes dismay in the heart of all Latinists and pedagogues, but sense and tradition will not prevail — *medias* is well on its way toward acceptance, if not legitimacy. And *medium* is on its way out as the singular form.

Nobody knows why these mutations occur, or what deep folk-feeling lies behind these nearly irresistible changes. We have already lost in English the "compound possessive," the "double genitive," and the "subjunctive preterit" — and much more is still to go.

When did English-speaking people stop saying *some one's else* and begin saying *some one else's?* I have known only one person in my life who said *some one's else*, which is correct but sounds artificial and is totally dead beyond all hope of revival.

When did the passive form, "the house is being built," come into popular usage, as against the old "the house is building"? Grammarians may scream about this bastardized use of the present participle "being" with the past participle "built," but it is of no avail.

And, of course, the split infinitive and the sentence ending with a preposition remain "sins" only in the eyes of the vestal virgins in the temple of language. "It's me," "who did you see?", "than whom," "very pleased," "try and go," "the best of the two" — these are not even glimpsed as solecisms anymore, so familiar is their usage.

One tries, of course, to maintain a happy medium between the rigid primness of the grammarians and the shocking laxity of the uncaring laity — but no one doubts that the medias are the message, and the message is "anything goes."

Few words are more misused in the modern lexicon than "myth" — for a myth can mean either an imagery that displaces truth, or a metaphor that illuminates the inner nature of truth; and genuine philosophy consists in separating the two, so far as is possible.

*

A high school student wants to know whether the word "dickens," as in "Where the dickens did I put that hat?" comes from the name of the author, Charles Dickens; and the answer is no — "dickens" is one of the many euphemisms for "devil," and is to be found as far back as Shakespeare. ("I cannot tell what the dickens his name is.")

We Don't Even Know the Problems

IT CAN HARDLY be a verbal accident that most of our major "problems" are called by exactly their opposite names.

We have the so-called youth problem — which is not a problem of youth at all, but a problem of older age: they are asking us to become, and quickly, more rational, more flexible and more humane. For there is little youth can do about the world until we change.

The same is largely true of the "Negro" problem — which, as every open-minded person knows, is a "white" problem. All it takes to solve it is a 90-degree turn in the attitude of most white people. If that could happen, 90 per cent of racial conflict would disappear overnight.

The "poverty" problem falls in the same category. It is not a problem of the poor, for most of them did not willingly put themselves there and cannot do much about their plight. It is a problem of the more affluent finding room in our society for the less fortunate who are virtually powerless to help themselves.

Then we have the universal "war" problem, which is really a "peace" problem. As Hannah Arendt said recently, large-scale war has now become inconceivable, because it can no longer effect political change.

But nations have not found — because they have not looked for — any genuine substitute for force in international affairs, and so the concept (and the threat) of war persists in the world, hanging over us like a cloud that can deluge the entire globe, devastating "victors" and "victims" equally.

We call diseases by their symptoms. Youth rebellion is a symptom of adult apathy. Black militancy is a symptom of white bigotry. Poverty is a symptom of maldistribution of income and opportunities. War is a symptom of power-driven anarchy among nations. And many people merely want to suppress the symptoms, falsely imagining that thereby they are getting rid of the disease, when they are only making it worse.

Confucius said that the good state must begin with the right use of words — because if we call things by the wrong word, then we are blinded by our verbal delusions and cannot take realistic steps to correct the evils in society. Justice must end in deeds, but it must start with the proper use of words.

And even the word "problem" is not the right one to describe the troubles in each of these areas — they are "deficiencies," like the deficiency diseases, and must be nourished by our loving concern, or any systematic "solution" is bound to fail.

It's worth remembering Whitehead's axiom for scientific inquiry: "Everything should be made as simple as possible — but no more so."

*

Definition of birth control: avoiding the issue.

*

Frustration is the difference between what you are and what you know you ought to be; at this level, everyone is frustrated.

*

Hard to believe, isn't it, that when the word "politic" first appeared in English, its original meaning was "wise" and "prudent"?

Facts Alone Don't Communicate

DOES A MERE DIFFERENCE in a word make a difference in a thing, in an attitude, in a relationship? Of course it does. If we use the wrong word for the right one, then we imagine we are saying something when we are saying something else.

Take the two popular words today, "information" and "communication." They are often used interchangeably, but they signify quite different things. Information is *giving out;* communciation is *getting through.*

This is the basic trouble with so-called communication within and between large groups. In most cases, it is simply information that is being given out, not communication that is getting through.

Many large companies, for instance, privately deplore the lack of "communication" they may have with their employees. But what they fondly imagine is communication is really not — it is just information, and only the kind of information the company wants the employees to have.

Communication is at least the beginning of a dialogue; information is a monologue. Communication is alert for a response; information shuts off the switch when the message is ended. Most of all, information *tells what;* communication *explains why.*

Business and industry, among other institutions, expend tens of millions yearly under the mistaken notion that they are communicating with their various publics; when, in nine cases out of ten, they are only processing information in a way that is palatable to their self-image. These publics, being no fools, quite properly refuse to believe official communiqués, house organs, publicity handouts and all the rest.

Strictly speaking, genuine communication can exist only

between persons in what Buber has called the I-Thou relationship; anything else is an I-It relationship, where we are not speaking to another person, in the fullness of his uniquely created humanity, but to an "object," a "mass," indeed, a "public."

But, even allowing for this basic difficulty, there is no question but that institutions, organizations, corporate bodies, can move from the information end of the spectrum closer to the communication end. They can do this, however, only by sacrificing some false pride and acting like persons who are fallible, uncertain, sometimes wrong and willing to learn from mistakes.

When we inform, we lead from strength; when we communicate, we lead from weakness — and it is precisely this confession of mortality that engages the ears, heads and hearts of those we want to enlist as allies in a common cause.

What the "realist" sees is that without logic there can be no reasonable action, and he is right; what he does not see is that the application of logic alone (to situations that call for feelings) can lead to madness.

*

A hypochondriac is someone who believes that a pound of prevention is worth an ounce of cure.

*

Whenever someone mentions his "sincerity," I recall Henri Peyre's fine observation that "The primary condition for being sincere is the same as for being humble: not to boast of it, and probably not even to be aware of it."

Don't Talk Down, Just Talk Sense

"IF YOU WANT to appeal to the young people, you've got to talk in their style," said a friend recently. "Otherwise, you can't make the scene with them."

I don't believe it. What young people are looking for — and what they appreciate — is *content*, not style. They want it told the way it is, but you don't have to tell it in their barbaric jargon.

For a middle-aged person to express himself in hip-talk, or in hip-writing, would be ludicrous, affected and patronizing. It would be, in effect, talking down — which young people properly despise.

In nearly thirty years of writing a daily column, I have never talked down to anyone, and will not begin now. I have heard too many speakers at schools try it, and fail miserably. Young people would much rather you made them reach for you a little, if they feel the message is honest and worthwhile.

Besides, it is cheap and demeaning for a writer to scatter current slang phrases in his prose, like corn to attract the birds. He must first of all be honest to his own personality and his own mode of expression before he can communicate meaningfully with anyone.

Many television ads today, for instance, try to beguile young people by using a kind of mod language that is supposed faithfully to represent the way kids talk. Almost all of it is stilted and unbelievable — and most of the phrases are usually passé by the time they have been recognized by the Establishment.

The whole point of youthful slang is that it is a private language for a select society; by the time it becomes public, the leaders of the society have already discarded it, and only the little kids are using it. Most ads addressed to sixteen-year-olds are received warmly only by six-year-olds.

Everyone knows that the father who tries to be a "pal" to his son is really abdicating his true role as a parent; the son doesn't want a "pal" thirty years older than he is. In the same way, adults who seek to ingratiate themselves with the young by mimicking their language defeat their own purpose and sound even "squarer" than ever.

The only way to appeal to young people is to put it on the line, in your own terms, in your own way, with the full force of your own background, your experience, your sensitivity and your authentic voice. If these can't carry conviction, there's something wrong with your music, not with your words.

An old man complaining that "things aren't the way they used to be" rarely includes himself in that appraisal.

*

Words like "permissiveness" and "strictness" are almost meaningless in talking about the way children are, or should be, brought up; it is the dynamics behind these parental attitudes that are important, not the attitudes themselves, and the dynamics determine how the child will turn out, not the surface rules or regulations.

*

It is impossible to know only your own subject thoroughly and still be an "expert" in it; for a genuine expert is one who knows how his subject relates to allied subjects, and grasps both the hierarchy and the interdependence of disciplines in a broad continuum of understanding.

Yes, Harris Hasn't Changed a Bit

WHEN I PLEAD, as I often do, for greater precision in our use of words, perhaps it is because I am so prone to confusion. I remember as a little boy reading the signs on some highways and bridges: HEAVY TRAFFIC NOT PERMITTED.

It puzzled me for a long time how the individual motorist was going to decide whether the traffic was too heavy for him to continue on the road or over the bridge. It was a year or more before I realized that the sign meant: HEAVY VEHICLES NOT PERMITTED.

And I may have been more stupid than most, but when I heard in fourth grade that a special class was being formed for "backward readers," I silently wondered how many of my classmates possessed that marvelous gift of being able to read backward.

A friend recently told me of an incident in a veterans' hospital. The physician in charge of the mental ward had a sign on his door: DOCTOR'S OFFICE. PLEASE KNOCK. He was driven to distraction by an obedient patient who carefully knocked every time he passed the door.

Youngsters, and people out of their right minds, are likely to take words more literally than they are meant. Unless we say exactly what we mean, youngsters will read another meaning into it.

Even idiomatic phrases are not without their danger to the growing mind. James Thurber confesses, in one of his delightful books of reminiscences, that whenever his mother would say at dinner, "Dad is tied up at the office," he had a mental picture of the old man struggling to free himself from the bonds that were lashing him to his chair.

Another of my own childhood perplexities was the sign:

IN CASE OF FIRE, BREAK GLASS. I couldn't figure out how breaking the glass was going to help put out the fire, and it's a good thing I was never called upon to turn in an alarm.

I am not suggesting that everything should be spelled out in a-b-c fashion, thus reducing us all to the condition of children or savages. But words should be *accurate* and *explicit;* except for poetry, they should say no more and no less than they actually mean.

As Mark Twain remarked, "The difference between the right word and the almost right word is the difference between lightning and the lightning bug."

A lovely example I ran across in California last summer was a sign in a public park: PEOPLE WITHOUT DOGS ON A LEASH NOT PERMITTED. I wonder if the good aldermen realized that this banned everyone not owning a dog from entering the park? As you see, I haven't changed much since the fourth grade.

To suggest that something called "science" is conquering something called "disease" is more illusion than fact. What has happened is that the diseases of deprivation have been replaced by the diseases of affluence; especially our biggest killer of men in their best years, coronary thrombosis, which is hardly known in more primitive societies.

*

One of my favorite aphorists is the anonymous Scotsman who defined a "tip" as a small sum of money you give to somebody because you're afraid he won't like not being paid for something you didn't ask him to do.

Watch That Word

IF YOU'RE GOING to use these words, please remember:

— That "nicety" has nothing to do with the usual meaning of "nice."

— That "noisome" has nothing to do with "noise."

— That "fulsome" has nothing to do with "full."

— That "sacrilegious" has nothing to do with the usual meaning of "religion," and should not be spelled like it.

— That "cohort" means a large group, band or company of people, and cannot be applied to an individual, in the sense of "colleague."

— That a "compendium" is not an all-embracing complication, but an abridgment or brief abstract.

— That "climatic" refers to climate, and "climactic" to climax.

— That people "immigrate" *to*, and "emigrate" *from*.

— That a "cause" is not "due to" something, but is itself the cause.

— That a "podium" is not what a speaker speaks from, but what an orchestra conductor conducts from; a speaker speaks from a "lectern."

— That "ravel" means what most people think "unravel" means, and there is, therefore, no need to use "unravel."

— That "enormity" is not the noun for the adjective "enormous," for an "enormity" is a large wickedness, or an outrageous act or offense; the proper noun is "enormousness."

— That "insignia" is the plural of "insigne," and cannot be used as a singular to denote one particular badge or emblem. (Even more common, and more appalling, is the use of "strata" as a singular, instead of as the plural of "stratum.")

— That a "jurist" is not necessarily a judge, but anyone

versed in the law; all judges should be jurists, but not all jurists are judges.

— That "kudos" (a hideous word), if used at all, should be used as a singular and not as a plural; there is no such thing as "a kudo."

— That "masterful" means "domineering," while "masterly" means "skillful."

— That "partially" means "showing favor," and should not be used when "partly" would do as well, or better.

— That "notorious no longer means merely "noted" or "notable," but carries a connotation of ill-fame, and is never a simple synonym for "celebrated" or "famous."

Why don't people ever tell you anything nice "for your own good"?

*

People who live rigidly by the "rule of reason" eventually drive themselves into a fanatical excess of reasonableness, failing to recall Santayana's gentle reminder that "reason is only a harmony among irrational impulses."

*

Both those who respect tradition and those who reject it have little idea of the proper lesson to be drawn from a study of the past; the former are all roots and no branches, while the latter are all branches and no roots.

Casualties Never Die — They Can't

WHEN YOU USE various expressions, do you know that

— "To the nth degree" doesn't mean to the farthest, or largest, or infinite number?

— "a shambles" is not just any kind of mess, but one that involves bloodiness?

— "a dilemma" is not a mere difficulty or problem, but a set of two choices, each of which is equally unsatisfactory?

— "to enhance" means to make or become larger, and thus it is absurd to write an ad about "a girdle that enhances your figure"?

— a French "gendarme" is not the equivalent of a London bobby or a New York cop, but one of a corps of military police?

— a "blueprint" is not just a plan or scheme, but (in the engineering industries, which it comes from) it is the *final stage* of paper design?

— a "bottleneck" is something that impedes the flow because it is too small; thus, to speak of "a bigger bottleneck" is a contradiction in terms?

— a "casualty" is an accident, and not the person to whom it happens, even though the military prefer to ignore this fact?

— "the optimum" is not the highest, or the fastest, or the most anything, but it is the best product of conflicting forces; as the *optimum speed* of a car is not the fastest it can go, but its most satisfactory speed in traffic, which will result in the least gas consumption and least wear and tear, and yet arriving as quickly as possible?

— "the protagonist" is not the opposite of the antagonist, with the one being for and the other being against; a protagonist is a leading character, either hero or villain?

— "begging the question" does not mean evading a straight answer; it is, rather, a precise term in logic, which means assuming the very proposition which is in need of proof?

— "a leading question" is not one framed to trap or embarrass the person questioned; instead, it is one designed to help him give the answer wanted by the questioner — which is why a lawyer is not allowed to ask such a question of his own witness?

— "the devil's advocate" is not a tempter of the good, or a whitewasher of the bad, but a prosecutor who is assigned to find evidence against the canonization of a candidate for sainthood?

— "coming to fruition" does not mean becoming fruitful or maturing, but the enjoyment that comes from attainment or possession of a goal?

"Obfuscate" is one word that sounds exactly like what it means.

*

A *"juicy rumor"* is what makes a man say, *"Who would have thought it?"* and makes a woman say, *"I suspected it all along."*

*

The phrase *"in his (or her) own right"* is pointless in almost every case it is used; its original meaning applied to a title or a state one is born to, rather than acquired; but to say, for instance, that the wife of a senator *"is a poetess in her own right"* is a foolish and needless extension of the phrase.

Is That Man a Patriot or an Agitator?

ANTICS WITH SEMANTICS:

I AM taking "medication"; you are on "pills"; he takes "dope."

I vote on "principles"; you vote on "ideology"; he votes on "dogmas."

Spying by our side is "military intelligence"; spying by their side is "espionage."

When demonstrators make an unprovoked attack, it is a "riot"; when police make an unprovoked attack, it is a "defense of law and order."

An interesting example of reverse semantic logic is the fact that since so many prostitutes officially list their profession as "model," any woman who lists her profession as model may be suspected of being a part-time prostitute.

And, speaking of this subject, the semantics of sex are so primly twisted around in our culture that the phrase "sleeping with" actually means "not sleeping with."

Our overweight child has a "glandular problem," but yours is "fat as a pig."

If a used car can be advertised as "owner-tested," why can't used shoes be sold as "pedestrian-tested"?

When I look at a nude film of colored people ("natives") it is, of course, "ethnography"; when I look at a nude film of white people, it is "pornography."

Educational euphemisms are the most absurdly amusing in modern semantics — such as "underachiever," "disadvantaged," and so on. In his book, *Translations from the English*, Robert Paul Smith aptly translates the jargon, "The child seems to have developed late in large-muscle control," as "He falls on his head frequently."

One of the earliest warnings on the vicious way we twist words was given by George Orwell (long before Vietnam), when he wrote: "Defenceless villages are bombarded from the air, the inhabitants driven out into the countryside, the cattle machine-gunned, the huts set on fire with incendiary bullets; this is called *pacification*."

In the same sense, Mayor Daley was correct when he suggested there were no "slums" in Chicago — only "substandard dwellings."

A "patriot" is an "agitator" whose side long ago gained control of the government.

And remember, finally, if you agree with most of the above items, I am a "courageous" and "challenging" columnist; if you disagree, I am "slanderous" and "irresponsible."

"I'll think it over and let you know" means *"Please wait until I find a mutually acceptable way of refusing."*

*

If the age of permissiveness keeps on this way, we shall soon have to invent some new swear words to take the place of those that no longer carry the thrill of being prohibited.

*

No aphorist in the past half-century has improved upon Ambrose Bierce's definition of a "lawsuit" as "a machine which you go into as a pig and come out of as a sausage."

*

Harold Pinter, the playwright, gave one of the best definitions of fiction, when he called it "fact that is distorted by art into truth."

When the Wench Was a Man

To MANY PEOPLE, the study of words seems a remote and academic pastime, bearing little relation to the real world. Actually, however, it is in words and their changing use that we find important clues to the social and psychological drifts of the society.

For instance, what do all the following words have in common: *bawd, concubine, coquette, courtesan, hag, harlot, hoyden, shrew, termagant, wench* and *witch?*

Of course, they are all demeaning words for women, and today are used only in reference to women. But the really interesting thing about them — and many more — is that originally they were used to denote *either sex.*

Over the last few centuries, however, these words became pejorative and were used only for women — which indicates how male chauvinism in the real world translated itself into the verbal downgrading of the opposite sex.

Bawds, concubines, coquettes, courtesans and harlots initially referred to both men and women of loose sexual practices. Chaucer, Wycliffe, Beaumont and Fletcher, Shakespeare and countless other writers use these terms interchangeably for either sex. Then they suddenly die out as words applying to men, and become "feminine" only.

Why should a "hag" be only an unattractive old woman, when there is no correlative term for such a man? Why should a "termagant" become only a female who rants and rails, when just as many men are nags? Why should a "shrew" be only a woman, when masculine shrews abound everywhere? And a "witch" was at first of either sex; that is why so much Elizabethan literature referred to a "she-witch" when such was intended.

Only 200 years ago, the word "hoyden" was more often applied to a clownish, ill-bred man than to a girl; now it is exclusively used to designate a certain type of female. We really have no masculine equivalent — even such Victorian terms as "cad" and "bounder" were quickly dropped from the language of epithet.

Our speech accurately reflects the prejudices of the ruling group. Since the rulers and the rich and the educated (who directed language) generally lived in cities, we developed such words as "villain," which meant a rustic; "heathen" and "pagan," which also indicated those who dwelt in the country; "boor," which meant a farmer; and many other such words which downgraded rural inhabitants.

The use of a word wrongly understood can affect great events. Some believe that Darwin's *The Descent of Man* evoked such a storm because "descent" seems to indicate a dropping down from the apes; when he really meant it in the sense in which we speak of "descending from royalty."

The most misunderstood phrase in all Christendom consists of only five words: "Love thy neighbor as thyself" — for the generality of people misinterpret the meaning of "love," don't know who their "neighbor" is, and fail to grasp the reflexive nature of "thyself."

*

"Dogmatic" is a word we apply to those who have firmer beliefs on a particular subject than we have; our firm beliefs are called "principles."

*

Has anyone ever been indicted for "low" treason?

When to Use "Dirty Words"

I HAVE no personal objections to "dirty words" in a book, but I don't think they ought to be defended on the grounds of "realism." A book dotted with dirty words may be faithful to the *substance* of low speech, but not to its spirit.

What I mean is that the people who use dirty words in their ordinary conversation do not employ them in an obscene sense, but rather as a form of punctuation, of emphasis, of verbal counters that are nearly meaningless in themselves.

Barracks talk, for instance, is replete with dirty words, but they have no meaning in and of themselves. They are a boyish way of displaying virility, or establishing camaraderie, or simply an unconscious habit of men with poverty of language. Most of the time they are unaware of what they are saying, and would be astonished at a playback of their conversation.

Now, if this speech is taken literally and reproduced on the written page, it assumes much greater content and importance than the speakers mean it to have. Its written impact — because, unlike the spoken word, each written word has the same beat — puts too much stress on the obscenity, which is usually only conversational stuffing.

Although I detest the prudery behind the old literary habit of using dashes as a substitute for dirty words, it is in a certain sense more "realistic" than spelling out the words — for the constant and inveterate use of four-letter words soon becomes no more meaningful than "blankety-blank," or the absurd "#$%&!" of the comic strips.

Dirtiness is an attitude of mind more than a form of expression. It is a sort of spiritual greasiness that films all physical transactions and turns them from experiences into commodities. It is basically unhealthy, because it reduces a multilevel activity to a single and narrow form; just as miserliness is unhealthy because it reduces the joys of money to the mere collection of coinage.

But the way people speak has little to do with their attitude of mind, and people in certain milieus habitually use dirty words as naturally and unconsciously as others avoid them. In most cases, these words have nothing to do with sex at all, and have been drained of all emotional content, the same way the face of a coin is rubbed off by constant usage.

Some of the most sniggeringly obscene books I have read have not contained a single dirty word; while others, chockfull of expletives, have been highly moral tracts. The only "realistic" way to handle four-letter words is to put them in only when they mean what they say.

"Voluptuous" is one of the few words that sound exactly like what they mean.

*

A man who utters truths we find palatable is "philosophizing," but a man who makes statements we find objectionable is merely "pontificating."

*

"Obscenity" is not a disease of the lewd mind, but merely a symptom of society's suppression and distortion of natural sexuality; when we grow up to our sexuality, in all its manifestations, then obscenity will disappear as a social phenomenon, and will lurk only in a few immature and pitiable personalities.

Tiny Words That Reveal Our Values

THE ARTICLES "a," "an," and "the" are among the tiniest and least noticed words in the language; we use them in every sentence, without even realizing their presence. Yet, to an observer of language, even the use of these tiny particles tells much about our attitudes toward things in the real world.

For instance, this morning, a friend visiting from Europe telephoned me at the office, and said, "Let's meet somewhere and have a coffee."

Now, no American would have said "a coffee." And it was not that the European imperfectly understood our language — for "a coffee" is what he says in his own tongue, too.

In the United States, coffee is the accepted national hot beverage. We go down for "coffee," not for "a coffee." In Europe, it is one beverage among many (as we would say here, "Let's go down for a drink"), but in our country its dominance is verbally indicated by dropping the indefinite article.

In much the same way, the British will say, "We have a telly in the house," while the American says, "We have television." This difference in mode of speaking reveals a sharp difference in thinking.

To the American, television has become almost a way of life, while to the Briton it is still only one form of entertainment in the home. Television, moreover, is far more pervasive and influential than broadcasting ever was — as we can tell from the way we speak about it.

During the reign of broadcasting, people would have said "we have a radio" — never "we have radio." In other words, it was the receiving set they had, in a limited and specific way.

But "we have television" — which is the universal expression with us — indicates a far different attitude toward this new medium. It means that we are plugged in, that our home is part of the whole TV environment, that it *is* the medium more than the message that involves us.

The greater importance of the automobile to the newer generation than to the old can be heard in the slang question one teen-ager will ask another: "Do you have wheels?" Old people would ask, "Do you have a car?" but by dropping the indefinite article, young people indicate how primary "wheels" have become in their way of life.

Words, and the ways we use them, or drop them, tell as much about our changing modes of living as our clothes or our customs. It's hardly an accident that "in show business" refers to the only business that has given up the "the."

The idiotic and insoluble controversy about the relative importance of "heredity" and "environment" in determining individual intelligence was put down most neatly by D. O. Hebb, when he remarked: "To ask how much heredity contributes to intelligence is like asking how much the width of a field contributes to its area."

*

A bovine person will call himself "serene," and a nervous one will call himself "energetic"; but true serenity is as far from the bovine as true energy is from the merely nervous.

*

The best and briefest reason for a good education is that the more effort you expend in sharpening the ax, the less effort you have to expend in chopping the wood.

Fads and Fashions in Surnames

UNTIL THE MIDDLE AGES, as we know, people did not commonly have last names. Most surnames come from occupations, or localities, or personal characteristics — like Brewer, Dale or Small.

What interests me in the latter connection is that certain personal characteristics have been perpetuated in names, while others have been ignored. There must be some good social or psychological reason for this.

There are many Littles and Shorts and Smalls — but virtually no Bigs or Talls or Larges. There are no Fats or Thins, but there are Lowes and Highs. (In Russian, however, Tolstoi means "fat.")

Color names are odd, too — why should there be Browns and Whites and Blacks and Greens, and even a few Blues, but no Reds or Yellows? Especially since many families are red-headed, and we even have a given name, "Rufus," which means "reddish."

In ancient times, scores of names came from personal characteristics — even from deformities. Oedipus Rex means "Swellfoot the Tyrant," because his foot was deformed in infancy; while Plato means "broad-shouldered" and Cicero is a nickname that stuck, meaning "chickpea," from a wart on the nose.

(Actually, even a number of given names have unflattering origins and were probably nicknames to begin with, such as Calvin, meaning "bald," Claude, meaning "lame," Priscilla, meaning "rather old," Barbara, meaning "foreigner," Mary, meaning "rebellious," and many more.)

We have Longfellows and Crookshanks, which are self-explanatory, but the first Campbell must have had a crooked mouth, the first Leonard a shaggy mane, and one of the first purchasers of land in Pennsylvania was still named Richard Glutton, evidently proud of his patronymic.

As Gary Jennings points out in his diverting little book, *Personalities of Language*, personal names have been affected by passing fads and fashions. For example, "in an earlier and less delicate society, bluntly descriptive names were considered no great horror. William the Conqueror, in one of his first proclamations to his new English subjects, announced himself as 'I, William, surnamed the Bastard . . .' "

We have long forgotten that Ursula once meant a "she-bear," that Vachel was a "little cow" or that Wilbur was a "wild boar." After all, John is Hebrew for "God is gracious" — which has somehow become twisted into the most popular slang name for the lavatory. What will future philologists do with that, I wonder?

A "middle-of-the-roader" is someone whose interests don't happen to be threatened at this particular time.

*

The worst mistakes of judgment are made by those who believe that "reason" and "passion" are opposites; reason does not exist to oppose the passions, but to mediate among them; and the man who uses reason to repress his emotions will soon be as mad as the man who permits his emotions to override his reason.

*

The "well-rounded" person can be useless unless he also has a cutting edge.

The Mills of Man Grind Faster

IF OLDER PEOPLE want to grasp for a moment the new world their children are living in, it can be done very simply and dramatically just by thinking about all the words that are common currency today — words that did not exist, or had a sharply different meaning, in the past.

Television, of course, is the most pervasive, not only as a word, but as a way of viewing the world. Then there are *isotope, antibiotic, neutron, cyclotron, chromosome, transistor, reactor, decontaminator, radar* and dozens of other scientific terms our children have grown up with.

And these are not even slang words, like *hippie* and *black market* and *LP* and *brunch* and *motel* and *smog* and *prefab* and *pin-up* and *turboprop* and scores of similar new terms.

The language a child grows up with is like the climate he grows up in — it so suffuses him that he is not aware of it. He can hardly imagine a world without *baby sitters* and *miniskirts* and *automation* and *overkill* and *gimmicks* and such recent acronyms as "DNA" and "UNESCO" and "VIP" and "UFO."

Just a generation ago, there was no such phrase as *teenager*, no such noun as *know-how*, no such verb as *contact*, no such adjective as *feather-bed*.

Of course, there has always been linguistic change, but never so fast and never reflecting such speedy changes in the objective world. Most of these are not new terms for old concepts, but new words for new objects, processes and attitudes. The language explosion is keeping pace with the knowledge explosion, where more knowledge accumulates in a decade now than was amassed in the previous two centuries.

The older generation has a built-in sense of time that distorts the past at the expense of the present. For instance, the morality that we preach was not part of a long, unbroken tradition handed down from Biblical times, but a specific set of attitudes in a Victorian social order that lasted only some 80 years; before then, Puritanism was only one strand in the moral and behavioral code of Christianity.

But what took almost a century to change then — and changing so slowly it could hardly be perceived — now takes a decade or less, and we see it happening before our eyes, at a dizzy and dismaying rate. Modern children, used to this speed, think of it as natural; for the rate of cultural acceleration is as normal to them as jet-plane speeds.

We would find it hard to speak consecutively for five minutes without using some phrase or concept that didn't exist in our childhood — and recognizing this truth is one way to reach across the gap of mutual misunderstanding, recrimination and resentment.

When we use the word "replica" to mean simply a copy or an imitation of an original work, we are losing an important and unique sense of this word — which properly means the reproduction of a work by the original producer.

*

Why are some kinds of foods called "roughage," while their opposites aren't called "smoothage"?

*

If English were a logical language, the opposite of "health" would be "illth," and the opposite of "warmth" would be "coolth."

Hear We Go Splitting Some Hares

A HOMOPHONE is a word that is pronounced the same as another, but differs in spelling or meaning, like "pair" and "pear" and "pare." There are many of these in the English language, and in most cases the wrong word is written for the right one.

Even so literate a journal as the *New York Review of Books*, in a large headline offering special holiday subscriptions, wrote "Christmas doesn't phase me," when the word it meant was "faze." It is a common error; most people think "phase" is proper in this usage, and "faze" is only a slang variant, but they are totally different words.

The *New York Times*, which also should know better, not long ago reported in a story that a person was "hailed into court." The homophone that should have been used is "haled," which means "drawn by force." To be "hailed" into court is to be shouted for, which was not meant. Yet "hailed" has almost driven out "haled" in this kind of context.

Recently I read a story in which one character was described as being "hairbrained." This is a common homophonic mistake for "harebrained," which means giddy or nutty behavior, such as is associated with the March hare and other rabbits that seem to go wild in some seasons. The notion of "hair" has nothing whatever to do with the case.

Every language has such problems. Cinderella's famous glass slipper is the result of a homophonic mistake in French. The original title of Perrault's *Cinderella* was *La Petite Pantoufle de Vair*, or "The Little *Fur* Slipper," but the sound of "vair" was confused with "verre," meaning glass, and the mistake is now ineradicable.

But English is especially burdened with this problem. Some 50 years ago, Robert Bridges, the poet and scholar, wrote an essay on English homophones with a list of 835 entries involving nearly 1800 words. These words are troublesome and self-destructive; also, because we are careless in speech and smudge the vowels, words originally different begin to sound alike, and we lose important distinctions.

Almost everyone calls it "Welsh rarebit," when it should be "Welsh rabbit"; all children refer to "cole slaw" as "cold slaw," and I have seen it printed as such on some menus; "buttonhold" long ago lost out to "buttonhole"; "sweetheart" has nothing to do with the heart, but is a corruption of "sweetard," like "dotard" and "coward."

If I recall my *Alice* correctly, it was the Gryphon who remarked that school hours in the sea grew shorter every day. "That's why they're called 'lessons,' you know," he said to Alice, "because they lessen each day." Alice knew there was something wrong with this explanation, but a seven-year-old girl can hardly handle a homophone.

Of the tripartite French slogan, "Liberty, Equality, Fraternity," what the modern world has yet to learn is that the most important of the three is Fraternity — for without it, Liberty is bound to trample the idea of Equality, or Equality will inevitably repress Liberty.

*

I don't consider anyone a really proficient speller unless he can spell "diarrhea" without looking it up. (I looked it up.)

*

The word "mansion" originally meant "a tent pitched in the desert." How the word, and the world, have changed!

It Can't Be Said in English

A HUNGARIAN FRIEND of mine once walked into a drugstore and asked the clerk for "a pack of feeble cigarettes." He finally managed to convey that he wanted a very mild brand — he had looked up "feeble" in the dictionary and learned that it meant "lacking in strength."

There are few adjectives that are truly synonyms in any language. And when we try to translate words literally from one language to another, we can run a whole gamut of errors from the tragic to the ludicrous. Wars have been set off by a mistranslated phrase.

Someone operating a translating machine at the UN has explained how easily such mistakes occur. The machine, one day, was asked to put a common English phrase into Chinese, and then out of Chinese into French.

The English phrase chosen was "out of sight, out of mind." It ended up as "invisible, insane." Of course, out of sight does mean invisible, and out of mind does mean insane. But not in the adage.

Mario Pei, the linguist, tells of an American businessman in Russia who received a cable from home about his daughter: "Harriet hung for juvenile crimes."

The cable had been translated into Russian, then retranslated into English; the original version read: "Harriet suspended for minor offenses." Certainly, suspended is hung, and a juvenile is a minor.

Pei also points out that when the UN was in formation, it was found that French has no equivalent for *trusteeship*, that Chinese has no way of expressing *steering committee*, and that Spanish does not distinguish between *chairman* and *president* — so a new UN dictionary had to be devised.

Russia, strangely enough, has no word for *efficiency*. In French, and other Romance languages, it is not possible to distinguish *house* from *home*. English has no synonym for the French *savoir-faire*, or for the German *Gemutlichkeit*. And no one has yet been able to find an exact and succinct Italian equivalent of our *wishful thinking*.

You may remember that old chestnut about the three French language teachers trying to recall the English word for a woman who is sterile. "Unbearable?" ventured the first. "Inconceivable?" volunteered the second. "You're both wrong," said the third. "She is impregnable!" They consulted their dean. "Ah, I have it!" he exclaimed. "Such a woman is insurmountable!"

Why are children so inordinately fond of riddles? Because it is the only form of interrogation to which they know the answers, and their parents do not; a riddle is a child's way of getting back at the condescension of adults.

*

Most people confuse "efficiency" with agitation and fail to understand Thoreau's remark that "the really efficient laborer will be found not to crowd his day with work, but will saunter to his task surrounded by a wide halo of ease and leisure."

*

"Civilization at the crossroads" is such an outmoded phrase, since those frustrating cloverleafs have been devised; it's now not a question of which road we take, but of where and how to get off before it's too late.

How Clichés Reinforce Our Biases

A FRIEND of mine who has gone to work as administrative aide to the governor of Ohio, John Gilligan, sent me a note the other day for inclusion in my "Vagaries of Language" file. I thought it was too good to keep.

It seems that a black state legislator was called in to ask if he would be available for acting as a liaison man between the governor and the various minority groups in the state.

He expressed enthusiasm about the job, and complimented the new administration by saying: "You know, until now, we blacks and Mexicans and Puerto Ricans and so on, haven't had a Chinaman's chance here!"

It's interesting that he was wholly unaware of what he was saying. He just used the cliché about "a Chinaman's chance" as a familiar figure of speech, and it bore no ethnic overtones to him. But if some white man had happened to mention "a nigger in the woodpile," it would have been a sticky wicket.

We become the slaves of our symbols, and language hardens and perpetuates old stereotypes until we are as little aware of our captivity to them as a fundamentalist preacher is to fire and brimstone. In fact, to "jew down" somebody has even achieved the dubious distinction of a lower-case entry in the dictionary (labeled, however, "offensive").

And, of course, "to welsh" on an obligation has long been a part of English speech, even though it is immensely insulting to the Welsh people. Likewise, we have long maligned the splendid Hollanders by our use of "Dutch treat" and "Dutch courage," which we express unconsciously.

For a long time, male contraceptives were known in England and America as "French letters," for no legitimate reason at all, but simply reflecting the Anglo-Saxon delusion that the French are a wildly erotic people, when in truth no nation is less romantic and more prudent or practical than the French.

They, in turn, have wrought their linguistic revenge by calling syphilis the "English disease" and buggery "the English habit." In France and Italy, what we call a "confidence game" is known as an "American swindle." And, in a stick-up, the crook who waits in the car with the motor running is known as "l'Américain."

Every national, racial or ethnic society attributes "bad things" to some outside group — usually the outside group nearest them — and suggests that most of the evil in the community has been imported by foreigners. The Japanese call the bedbug "Nanking insect," ascribing its fictional origin to the people without a Chinaman's chance there.

Hospital superintendents ought to prohibit nurses from archly addressing patients in the first person plural, viz: "And how are we this morning?" On my next trip, I hope to gather up enough courage to reply, "I don't know how you are — but I feel terrible."

*

The trouble with words like "peace" or "crime" in general discussion is that we use them "univocally" — as though they have only one fixed meaning — whereas there are at least four distinctly different kinds of "peace," and just as many forms of "crime," which we fail to distinguish from one another, turning communication into confusion and controversy by our intellectual laziness and ignorance.

That Curious Word "Discrimination"

DURING A RECENT SNOWSTORM, I recalled having read somewhere that the Eskimos have about 200 different words describing and defining different kinds of snow. To us, all snow
seems pretty much alike; to those who live with it all the
time, it is as strikingly different as leaves to a botanist or
stones to a geologist.

The less we know something, the more ignorant we are,
the more we tend to lump it in indiscriminate categories. The
painter's eye can distinguish 20 shades or tones where the layman can see only a few; the musician's ear can hear a pattern
of melody that sounds only like cacophony to the rest of us.

What is true in these matters is true in the field of personal
relations as well. The less knowledge, the less intelligence,
the less training, the less we are able to distinguish persons as
individuals, and the more likely to lump them in convenient
categories.

Some months ago, I spent a half-day in a large factory, min-
gling with the men. What struck me most about their talk
was their way of referring to co-workers; they seemed
hooked on national origin as a means of identifying and label-
ing one another, especially newcomers.

There were the Greek and the Dutchman and the Scanda-
hoofian and the Dago and the Mick and the Hunkie and many
more. These men were defined and delineated by their an-
cestry or national origin, sometimes in derogation and sometimes in good humor, but always in terms of their background
rather than their individual identity.

This is the way visitors behave in a foreign country that is
very unlike their own: the residents are all "natives," indistin-
guishable from one another. But if one comes to live there a

few months or longer, suddenly the idea of natives is dissolved into its component individuals, and the difference between one native and another is seen to be as great as that between one American and another.

"Discrimination" is a curious word, because it means two opposite things: discriminating *against*, and discriminating *between*. At a low level of intelligence, we lump people into categories and discriminate *against*; at a higher level, we perceive the individual characteristics of snow, or leaves, or stones, or people, and discriminate *between*.

What did Einstein have in common with George Jessel, or Enrico Fermi with a Mafia captain, or Albert Schweitzer with Adolf Hitler, or James Joyce with Pat O'Brien? Until we recognize that the differences among persons belonging to the same group are far greater than between one group and another, we are socially and intellectually snow-blind.

The reason that so much pretentious gobbledygook is spoken and written was succinctly explained by John Locke three centuries ago: "Untruth being unacceptable to the mind of man, there is no defense left for absurdity but obscurity." This explains why Secretaries of State and other foreign ministers so often sound like pompous fools — since so much of their task consists of habitual lying to other countries and to their own constituents, the only way to avoid the imputation of "untruth" is by using words to conceal their meanings rather than to express them.

*

A "primitive" country is one in which the natives have no need for locks on the doors.

Slurs Regardless of Color

A READER who works for a "human relations commission" is upset by a recent paragraph of mine about "white lies." I wrote that "a white lie, used often enough, becomes gray and dirty, and finally black from usage."

He calls this "racism in language" because of the positive connotation of the word "white," and the negative connotation of the word "black." He absolves me of any conscious prejudice, admitting that our language is structured that way, but thinks I ought to be more careful in my usage.

I find that ridiculous and somewhat paranoid. It is true that "black" has many negative connotations in our language — *black ball, black-hearted, black list, blackmail, black sheep* and so forth — but "white" is far from being universally positive in English usage.

Raising the white flag is surrendering; *showing the white feather* is a mark of cowardice; *white-livered* is also cowardly or mean; to *whitewash* a person or an inquiry is to conceal or condone bad behavior; a *whited sepulcher* in the Bible is a pious hypocrite; a *white elephant* is an unwanted and expensive possession; *white trash* is a common derogatory expression used by Caucasians.

To imagine that white lies have anything to do with the color of the person uttering them is to imagine that mostly Indians are guilty of having *red tape*, or being *in the red*, or being caught *red-handed*, or living in *red-light districts*, or drawing a *red herring* across the path, or drinking *red eye*.

We call a coward "yellow" with no reference to any possible Oriental origin. And a *yellow dog contract*, a phrase echoed by the United States Supreme Court, is simply an illegal contract forbidding employees to join a union. The *yellow press* did not refer to Oriental publications, but to wholly white and American newspapers of a sensational nature.

The French call a mystery a "black" novel, while the Italians call it a "yellow" novel. What we term the "cold war" is a "white war" to the French. Our "red" cabbage is "blue" to the Germans, and "black" to the Italians. In medieval Italy the warring Guelphs and Ghibellines were known as "Whites" and "Blacks."

In Germany, one is "yellow" with envy, not "green" with it; in France, to be "blue" is to be amazed, not sad; and our "white lie" is called a "pious lie" there. To find racial slurs in the color-imagery of language is to suggest that the old barrelhouse tune, "I'm Blue Turning Gray over You," was written by an aging Druid.

It's hard to believe that the words "candid" and "candidate" come from the same Latin root.

*

Freedom, said Camus, "is nothing else but a chance to be better," but most of us use the word to justify our desire to be worse without penalty.

*

Why is every circle always "vicious" — aren't there virtuous and benevolent circles as well?

*

Why do we "upbraid" people when we reprove them, instead of "downbraiding" them, which sounds more appropriate?

An "Old Saw" with Teeth in It

I DISLIKE MOST PROVERBS, because they are a cheap and easy source of folk wisdom that takes the place of thinking about individual cases; besides, most proverbs are contradicted by another, like "He who hesitates is lost" and "Look before you leap."

The only one I've ever found of any practical use is the old British saying, "For want of a nail." Most looming crises, when they come, have had their origin "for want of a nail."

You remember how it goes: "For want of a nail, a shoe was lost; for want of a shoe, a horse was lost; for want of a horse, a message was lost; for want of a message, a battle was lost; for want of a battle, a war was lost; for want of a war, a kingdom was lost; and all for the loss of a nail."

Corny as that sounds, the fact of the matter is that history does hang on such little things as much as on any grand design. So do most large tragedies, which have their origins in tiny flaws unperceived at the time. What we call a "catastrophe" usually starts with a nail.

A crack so tiny it could not be seen was responsible for the collapse of the Silver Bridge over the Ohio River a few years ago, killing 46 persons. The crack led to the breaking of a crucial steel eyebar, which plunged the 1700-foot suspension bridge into the river.

Not long afterward, investigating a plane crash in which almost 100 were killed, the CAB found that the mechanical difficulty leading to the crash originated in a small metal part it would have cost a dime to replace. But nobody had bothered to check it out.

These examples could be multiplied scores of times. It is hardly ever that some gross malfunction is responsible for a disaster — for gross malfunctions can usually be caught before they do much damage. It is almost invariably some little defect that passes hasty or negligent inspection. Think of this the next time you are sitting in a plane, at the ramp, waiting to take off, and silently cursing the mechanics for being so tediously thorough.

But, everything human being contingent, there is no way to eliminate error entirely. Around 1760, a number of the professors in Edinburgh University attempted to publish a work that would be a perfect specimen of typographical accuracy. Six experienced proofreaders were employed, who devoted hours to the reading of each page.

After it was thought to be perfect, it was pasted up in the hall of the university, and a reward of 50 pounds offered to anyone who could detect an error in it. Each page remained hanging for two weeks. When the work was issued, it was discovered that several errors had been committed — one of which was in the first line on the first page!

Perhaps one of the most expressive words in the English language is "flabbergasted," which, oddly enough, originally meant "to frighten with a fly-swatter."

*

Passions don't change; just names do; the charge of "communism" will lose a million votes for a man, by people who can't even define the word; the same was true two centuries ago, as Defoe wrote: "A cry of 'Popery' will bring a hundred thousand men to horse, not knowing whether the Pope is a man or a dog."

Questions Key to Polling

RECENTLY, I received a letter from George Gallup, head of the American Institute of Public Opinion, advising that he is at work on a book "which will try to describe and explain polling methods." He asked me to write down any questions I might have about any aspect of polling.

Well, whenever I hear the results of some public opinion poll, I am always more interested in how the questions were framed than in how the answers turned out. Any question can be framed — consciously or unconsciously — to elicit the kind of answer it wants or expects.

I could easily devise two political polls of five questions each, one designed to elicit the answer that the country is drifting rightward, and the other to elicit an equally leftward drift. No trouble at all.

At a college, not long ago, a professor of logic submitted a list of ten questions to his classes; a large majority answered affirmatively to eight of them — which happened to be the ten propositions in Marx's *Communist Manifesto*. Then he rephrased the questions, and just as many opposed them. Both times, they were responding to *words* more than to *ideas*.

Two words may *denote* the same thing, but *connote* different things. Most people do not mind categorizing themselves as average, but they bristle at being categorized as mediocre — which means the same thing.

A recent Gallup poll asked Americans, of all ages and classes, if they were "very happy," "moderately happy" or "unhappy." Apart from the fact that happiness is virtually impossible to define (Aristotle's rigorous definition would not be accepted by any nonphilosopher), people lie to themselves about the way they feel more than about anything else.

If they lie to themselves, they cannot help lying to pollsters.

A psychiatrist knows that one has to phrase such a question far more subtly to get an accurate answer. You may recall the old story about two priests arguing whether it was proper to smoke and pray at the same time. One said it was, and the other said it wasn't. To settle the matter, they agreed that both should write to the pope for his opinion.

A few weeks later they met and compared notes. Each claimed that the pope had supported his view, and suspected the other of falsifying the reply he got from the Holy Office.

Finally, one asked, "How did you phrase your question?" The other replied: "I asked whether it was proper to smoke while one is praying, and the pope answered, 'Certainly not, praying is serious business and permits of no distractions.' And how did you phrase your question?"

"Well," said the other, "I asked if it was proper to pray while smoking, and the pope said, 'Certainly, prayer is always in order.'"

The "liberty" that most men clamor for is merely the right to remain enslaved to the prejudices they have grown comfortable with; genuine liberty — to become who you are — is more feared than coveted.

*

We all accept the truism that "no news is good news" — then why can't those who complain about the prevalence of misfortune in the public prints understand that the reverse is also true: "Good news is no news"?

Guess Who This Rebel Is

What communist said this? — "These capitalists generally act harmoniously and in concert, to fleece the people."

What liquor baron said this? — "If we take habitual drunkards as a class, their heads and their hearts will bear an advantageous comparison with those of any other class."

What revolutionary extremist said this? — "Any people anywhere being inclined and having the power, have the right to rise up and shake off the existing government, and form a new one that suits them better."

What advocate of "black power" said this? — "If by the mere force of numbers a majority should deprive a minority of any clearly written constitutional right, it might, in a moral point of view, justify revolution — certainly would if such a right were a vital one."

What left-wing union leader said this? — "Labor is prior to and independent of capital. Capital is only the fruit of labor, and could never have existed if labor had not first existed. Labor is the superior of capital, and man deserves much the higher consideration."

What unpatriotic internationalist said this? — "The strongest bond of human sympathy outside the family relation should be one uniting all working people of all nations and tongues and kindreds."

What un-Christian and anti-Biblical man said this? — "My earlier views of the unsoundness of the Christian scheme of salvation and the human origin of the scriptures, have become clearer and stronger with advancing years and I see no reason for thinking I shall ever change them."

What cynic about "self-regulation" said this? — "Moral principle is a looser bond than pecuniary interest."

What fatalist and determinist said this? — "I claim not to have controlled events, but confess plainly that events have controlled me."

What hippie-type said this? — "The dogmas of the quiet past are inadequate to the stormy present. The occasion is piled with difficulty, and we must rise to the occasion. As our case is new, so we must think anew and act anew."

What subversive opponent of "loyalty oaths" said this? — "I have found that men who have not even been suspected of disloyalty are very averse to taking an oath of any sort as a condition to exercising an ordinary right of citizenship."

All the preceding statements were made by the sixteenth President of the United States, Abraham Lincoln.

Men may be divided almost any way we please, but I have found the most useful distinction to be made between those who devote their lives to conjugating the verb "to be" and those who spend their lives conjugating the verb "to have."

*

The "culture of poverty" perpetuates itself not so much by economic conditions as by sociological barriers; indeed, it would be more than a mere play on words to suggest that the culture of poverty is largely determined by the poverty of culture.

*

In navigating through life, hope is an essential ballast, but a terrible compass.

Funeral p3
Christmas p3.